T0085901

KALĪLAH AND DIMNAH
Fables of Virtue and Vice

LIBRARY OF ARABIC LITERATURE

GENERAL EDITOR
Philip F. Kennedy, New York University

EXECUTIVE EDITORS
James E. Montgomery, University of Cambridge
Shawkat M. Toorawa, Yale University

EDITORIAL DIRECTOR
Chip Rossetti

ASSOCIATE EDITOR
Lucie Taylor

EDITORS
Sean Anthony, The Ohio State University
Huda Fakhreddine, University of Pennsylvania
Lara Harb, Princeton University
Maya Kesrouany, New York University Abu Dhabi
Enass Khansa, American University of Beirut
Bilal Orfali, American University of Beirut
Maurice Pomerantz, New York University Abu Dhabi
Mohammed Rustom, Carleton University

CONSULTING EDITORS
Julia Bray · Michael Cooperson · Joseph E. Lowry
Tahera Qutbuddin · Devin J. Stewart

DIGITAL PRODUCTION MANAGER
Stuart Brown

PAPERBACK DESIGNER
Nicole Hayward

FELLOWSHIP PROGRAM COORDINATOR
Amani Al-Zoubi

LETTER FROM THE GENERAL EDITOR

The Library of Arabic Literature makes avail-
able Arabic editions and English translations
of significant works of Arabic literature, with
an emphasis on the seventh to nineteenth cen-
turies. The Library of Arabic Literature thus
includes texts from the pre-Islamic era to the

LIBRARY OF
المكتــبة
ARABIC
العربيـة
LITERATURE

cusp of the modern period, and encompasses a wide range of genres,
including poetry, poetics, fiction, religion, philosophy, law, science, travel
writing, history, and historiography.

Books in the series are edited and translated by internationally recog-
nized scholars. They are published in parallel-text and English-only editions
in both print and electronic formats. PDFs of Arabic editions are available
for free download. The Library of Arabic Literature also publishes distinct
scholarly editions with critical apparatus.

The Library encourages scholars to produce authoritative Arabic edi-
tions, accompanied by modern, lucid English translations, with the ultimate
goal of introducing Arabic's rich literary heritage to a general audience of
readers as well as to scholars and students.

The publications of the Library of Arabic Literature are generously sup-
ported by Tamkeen under the NYU Abu Dhabi Research Institute Award
G1003 and are published by NYU Press.

Philip F. Kennedy
General Editor, Library of Arabic Literature

About this Paperback

This paperback edition differs in a few respects from its dual-language hardcover predecessor. Because of the compact trim size the pagination has changed. Material that referred to the Arabic edition has been updated to reflect the English-only format, and other material has been corrected and updated where appropriate. For information about the Arabic edition on which this English translation is based and about how the LAL Arabic text was established, readers are referred to the hardcover.

KALĪLAH AND DIMNAH

Fables of Virtue and Vice

BY

IBN AL-MUQAFFAʿ

TRANSLATED BY
MICHAEL FISHBEIN AND
JAMES E. MONTGOMERY

FOREWORD BY
MARINA WARNER

VOLUME EDITORS
BEATRICE GRUENDLER
JAMES E. MONTGOMERY

NEW YORK UNIVERSITY PRESS
New York

NEW YORK UNIVERSITY PRESS
New York

Copyright © 2023 by New York University
All rights reserved

Library of Congress Cataloging-in-Publication Data

Names: Ibn al-Muqaffaʻ, –approximately 760, translator. | Fishbein,
 Michael, translator. | Montgomery, James E. (James Edward), 1962–
 translator, editor. | Gruendler, Beatrice, 1964– editor.
Title: Kalīlah and Dimnah : fables of virtues and vice / Ibn al-Muqaffaʻ ;
 translated by Michael Fishbein and James E. Montgomery ; volume editors,
 Beatrice Greundler, James E. Montgomery.
Other titles: Kalīlah wa-Dimnah. English.
Description: New York : New York University Press, 2023. | Series: Library
 of Arabic literature | Includes bibliographical references and index. |
 Summary: "A collection of stories designed for the moral instruction and
 entertainment of readers"— Provided by publisher.
Identifiers: LCCN 2022050252 | ISBN 9781479825776 (paperback) |
 ISBN 9781479825783 (ebook) | ISBN 9781479825790 (ebook)
Subjects: LCSH: Didactic literature, Arabic—Translations into English.
Classification: LCC PJ7741.B5 E5 2023 | DDC 892.7/334—dc23/eng/20221109
LC record available at https://lccn.loc.gov/2022050252

Series design and composition by Nicole Hayward
Typeset in Adobe Text

Manufactured in the United States of America

10 9 8 7 6 5 4 3 2 1

To Charles Wendell (1919–1982)

CONTENTS

Foreword

MARINA WARNER

The stories in this collection are travelling tales, and they have been travelling for a while; their long, rich history spans India to Baghdad and Basra and Rome and beyond, appearing in numerous variations over centuries, moving across borders of language, culture, and religion, carrying the sparkling hope and mordant cynicism, the canniness and the wit of a form of wisdom literature that originated in Sanskrit, in the *Panchatantra* ("Five Discourses"), sometime in the second century BC, and then migrated far and wide. The tales retained features of their prototypes but kept changing inventively as they wandered, shedding elements and gaining others, shapeshifting into various media, including the border of the Bayeux tapestry, a formal garden in the seventeenth century called *Le Labyrinthe de Versailles* complete with statues and arbors illustrating the tales; and children's entertainment, in which they are ubiquitous. The stories grew out of that mysterious entity, common knowledge, and survived: the writer Radwa Ashour, for example, recalls in her memoir, *Spectres*, how when she was a child, a beloved relative called Zakiyya Umm Duqduq would come to visit and tell her fables—wisdom stories featuring clever monkeys and talking date palms, playful and witty but carrying an undertow of world-weariness.

Kalīlah and Dimnah, the title characters, are two jackals, both wily and ambitious, but one virtuous and the other less so: the first cycle of fables, "The Lion and the Ox," tracks Dimnah as he schemes to destroy the Ox once he has become a favorite in the Lion's court;

Dimnah's trial ensues, where he offers a dazzling pyrotechnical self-defense, but he fails to persuade his judges. Animal fables are woven into Dimnah's rhetoric, as parables, exempla, jokes, proverbs, homilies, and curious anecdotes, as they continue to be in the rest of the collection after his clever voice is silenced.

The fables strike many echoes with texts perhaps more familiar to European and American ears—Aesop's fables, the brilliantly turned suave verses of La Fontaine, the animal tales included in full recensions of the *Thousand and One Nights*, and the tricks and calamities in the stories of Boccaccio and Chaucer. But they are not identical; the resemblance is a family one, not imitation. For the Arabic *Kalīlah and Dimnah*, the translator-compiler Ibn al-Muqaffa' worked from a Persian text and introduced his own material, with many fresh twists and effects.

Ibn al-Muqaffa' (d. 139/757) was a polymathic scholar and a fascinating figure in himself, as Michael Fishbein describes in his illuminating introduction. His name means "Son of the man with a shrivelled limb," and the writer was so called because his father had been tortured and left maimed. This feature interestingly picks up on the biography of the legendary Greek storyteller, Aesop, who, according to the second-century *Romance of Aesop*, and reprised by the Byzantine historian Planudes in his popular biography of the fabulist, was also "misshapen."

Fables have long been an instrument of the powerless speaking truth to power, and according to Aesop's legend and parts of Ibn al-Muqaffa''s history, the fabulists themselves also appear to be situated as disadvantaged. This marker of outsider difference mirrors the condition of the stories' dramatis personae, who mostly take the shape of overlooked and marginalized creatures—scavengers, vermin, and beasts of burden (jackals, crows, wolves, asses, mongooses, rats, and mice). They are the heroes of the tales, and are often portrayed as shrewd and valiant, cooperative, and quick-witted. They aren't fabulous beasts like the Phoenix or the Simurgh, and in *Kalīlah and Dimnah* we don't meet jinn or fairies. Instead,

by choosing ordinary creatures, the writers naturalize the stories in this world close to hand and achieve a potent reality effect, which helps give voice to opinions that would otherwise be gagged.

These ancient stories are supremely aware of the dangers of public life, whether the participants are speaking up honestly or setting out to deceive in their own interests. It is sobering that Ibn al-Muqaffaʿ himself fell afoul of his patron and rulers, and for something he had written to protect one of them, was horribly put to death.

Kalīlah and Dimnah opens with Ibn al-Muqaffaʿ's account of the making of the book: according to this putative history, a doctor, Barzawayh, was sent by the Sasanian ruler Anusharwan to India to gain the country's knowledge, enshrined in its famous tales; the book in which they were preserved was, however, secret, its contents forbidden to outsiders—the wisdom it contained was extremely valuable, a treasure to be guarded closely. Guile was therefore needed, guile and friendship. And a friendship that mattered more than loyalty to authority (one is reminded of E.M. Forster's now infamous dictum, "If I had to choose between betraying my country and betraying my friend, I hope I should have the guts to betray my country"). Through exploiting the loyalty of one of his new Indian friends, Barzawayh manages to obtain the book, copy its contents, and transmit them to the volume that we have in our hands. The text has been scrupulously established and translated by Michael Fishbein with James Montgomery; the results fulfill the elegant and readable literary standards we have come to expect from the Library of Arabic Literature.

As in the *Thousand and One Nights*, the complex and exciting frame story sets up the themes in many of the tales that follow, which are dominated by acts of friendship and treachery, selflessness and malice, cunning, deceit, and double-dealing. Imagine a stepped pyramid inverted: *Kalīlah and Dimnah* proceeds down from tier to tier in five main sections, remembering its foundation in the *Panchatantra*. The building blocks aren't, however, dressed stone but stories, scores of stories laid end to end along one tier and

then leading down to another tier where the same abundance occurs to support a new theme. Ibn al-Muqaffaʿ's own story is echoed by Barzawayh's, and on the next tier down, by an inset narrative of the king and the philosopher exchanging thoughts in the manuscript Barzawayh has obtained. Sixty-odd pages in, the jackals Kalīlah and Dimnah appear, scheming and disputing, as they unfold "The Tale of the Ox and the Lion"; these enchained fables are followed by the mutual generosity of "The Ring Dove," the mordant debates of "The Crows and the Owls," and finally, the tales of the Turtle and many other characters who are outwitted and outmaneuvered. Tricksiness is the chief defense of the oppressed; allies are important, but craftiness is stronger, though not dependable. The last fable, "The Raven Who Tried to Learn to Walk like a Partridge," relates how in the attempt, he forgets how to walk like himself: one of many cautionary tales against overreaching.

This publication of *Kalīlah and Dimnah* is the first scholarly edition in English and Arabic—most collections of the tales strip away all the framing devices and historical settings and plunge straight into the stories—for example, the Lebanese storyteller Wafaʾ Tarnowska has written a series of the tales for children, *Arabian Fables*, in which she brings out very deftly their fun and mischief and emphasizes their ethical wisdom. By wrapping the tales in their elaborate historical contexts, this edition reminds us how the book was intended to serve as a mirror for princes in a time of absolute rule, and how it contains much insight into the brokerage of influence and power today. As a moral handbook, though, *Kalīlah and Dimnah* is too slippery and double-tongued and sheerly literary: the book is not a work for the pulpit, but is secular, hardnosed, and entertaining, more for private, conspiratorial delectation. It follows a central literary stratagem, that it shakes the reader's moral compass, and splits our sympathies between the vice and virtue of the English translation's subtitle. Dimnah is a villain, but as a storybook character, he steals the show.

The protagonists are animals, but they don't share many characteristics with the creatures in real life. For one thing they talk

and talk. But their imaginary qualities far exceed this aspect; they make powerful alliances across dividing lines of species, such as rats with doves. The protagonists are mischievous and entertaining figments, human types wittily metamorphosed into a sage and kindly ox, a scheming crow, a savvy old monkey. They are types, cartoon characters from antiquity, yet they still convey vivid lessons about humanity and power for our times. Jonathan Swift in *Gulliver's Travels*, Mikhail Bulgakov in *The Master and Margarita*, Franz Kafka in several of his fables ("The Metamorphosis," "Red Peter," "Address to the Academy," and most explicitly, "Jackals and Arabs"), and George Orwell in *Animal Farm* all turned to this tradition of animal transformations, to startle readers into paying attention to the writers' views, their disaffection, their intense dissidence. More recently, the French novelist Marie Darrieussecq produced a searing indictment of consumer dreams with *Truismes* (1996, from *truie*, French for sow, translated as *Pig Tales*), a dazzling satire in which the covetous heroine grows gradually and contentedly into a pig. Far more lighthearted, Rudyard Kipling, who was brought up in India, returned to the form with *The Jungle Books*. Even more successfully, Walt Disney consciously adapted the conventions of the animal fable, especially in his earliest creations of Mickey Mouse, Donald Duck, and Pluto; his animations mark a defining shift in categorization, the point when ancient, fantastic literary conceits came to be deemed appropriate only for children.

The reasons for allocating animal fables, along with fairy tales, to the playroom are various, but one of them grows from the uses of the genre for encrypting messages that might endanger a plain speaker. Joseph Addison wrote in *The Spectator* in 1712, "There is a Fairy Way of writing...wherein the Poet quite loses sight of Nature, and entertains his Reader's Imagination with the Characters and Actions of such Persons as have many of them no Existence, but what he bestows on them." But in many ways the fabulists were too successful: the power of their hidden lessons was eclipsed by the surface hijinks.

Kalīlah and Dimnah is full of very sharp political observation, insider knowledge about human folly, false friendship, faithless wives (it is not untinged by misogyny). Its rude common sense is often summed up in a pithy proverbial saying ("a strong wind doesn't uproot grass; it uproots mighty trees" [§4.25]). Although the tales show their subcontinental provenance (elephants, snakes, and mongooses), their roots lie in a practical working community that's far broader. The topsy-turvy dynamic of comedy, of comeuppance, or the biter bit, the *beffatore beffato*, as in Boccaccio's *Decameron*, governs the action. The dove asks the crow, "How can there be friendship between us when I'm the dinner and you're the diner?" (§6.7). The setting is feudal, justice arbitrary, the poor downtrodden, and kings exalted for their wisdom (perhaps out of wariness on the part of the writers?), yet the tales' lessons and warnings have not become dated: the conflict between the Crows and the Owls recalls current wars, and the crows' debate over strategy permutates possible lines of resistance, until I felt I was eavesdropping on a war council in Ukraine; the many instances of power hunger and jealousy leading to destruction ring true, especially in the present political situation in England, where I am writing this, and in several other democracies today.

Is there something we can learn from these ancient wisdom tales at a time when public discourse is often vituperative and political rhetoric blunt, brutal, and ugly? Could the oblique approach of the fabulist help us find ways through the current conflicts? Could the public sphere be enriched by more engagement with the traditions of fable and parable? In an epoch when citizens are pounded with statistics and blizzarded with empty promises, I would welcome a return to these vivid ways of passing on knowledge. At the very least the actions of the two jackals and their companions in this book open our eyes to the duplicity and lies that thrive in the courts of power.

Marina Warner
Kentish Town, London

Acknowledgments

I owe an immense debt of gratitude to the late Charles Wendell (1919–82) of the University of California, Santa Barbara, who first drew my attention to the significance and beauty of *Kalīlah and Dimnah*, at a time when I was beginning my study of Arabic. Professor Wendell was in the process of preparing a translation of the work, based on ʿAzzām's text, at the time of his untimely death; sadly, his translation, left incomplete, never saw the light of day. Next, I wish to thank my teachers and colleagues at the University of California, Los Angeles (UCLA), and at the American University in Cairo. In particular, I'd like to thank Claude Audebert, who enthusiastically imparted to her students at UCLA the skills necessary to appreciate the beauty of Arabic literature. Anyone working today on the text of *Kalīlah and Dimnah* owes a tremendous debt of gratitude to Beatrice Gruendler of the Freie Universität Berlin, the director of the project AnonymClassic, devoted to collecting and studying all the surviving texts of *Kalīlah and Dimnah*. Professor Gruendler and her associates have been constantly helpful in giving me access to the results of their research and in guiding the present edition and translation. James Montgomery of Cambridge University has been so constant a help with stylistic matters in English and with difficulties in the Arabic that I have asked him to accept the honor of being listed as co-translator. The staff of the Library of Arabic Literature, headed by editorial director Chip Rossetti, assistant editor Lucie M. Taylor, and digital production manager Stuart Brown, have shown constant understanding in tolerating my frequent requests for more

time. Copious thanks are due to all those in the production staff of the Library of Arabic Literature, who worked so hard to make this volume a pleasure to read.

Michael Fishbein
Los Angeles, California

James Montgomery would like to thank Michael Fishbein for so generously acknowledging his contribution to the translation; Beatrice Gruendler for her vital interventions in the genesis of the project; the anonymous reviewer for many improvements to the book, especially the felicity of the English; Keith Miller for his copyediting panache; Stuart Brown for producing yet another glorious book; and Chip Rossetti and Lucie Taylor, without whose skill and dedication the Library of Arabic Literature could not function.

James E. Montgomery
Cambridge

Introduction

Ibn al-Muqaffa': His Life and Works

Ibn al-Muqaffa', who lived from about 102/720 to 139/757, was an author and translator of exceptional ability and broad interests who played a crucial role in mediating between the civilization of Sasanian Iran (AD 224–662) and the Islamic world of his day.[1] He was born in the Iranian province of Fārs into a wealthy Iranian family that had adapted to Arab and Muslim rule. Originally named Rōzbih, he took the name 'Abdallāh upon his conversion to Islam, which must have occurred sometime after the Abbasid revolution in 132/749, his twenty-ninth year. He received a thorough education in the languages of two cultures: Persian and Arabic. The names of his Arabic teachers have been preserved, along with the fact that one was of Bedouin origin—the Bedouins were considered to speak the purest and most eloquent Arabic. The many translations from Middle Persian (Pahlavi) attributed to him testify to his mastery of the Iranian historical and literary tradition; his surviving Arabic works testify to his mastery of the Arabic language and to his broad intellectual interests, which included history, religion, political theory, law, philosophy, and literature.

His father, Dādūyah, a tax collector under the late Umayyads, acquired the surname al-Muqaffa' ("having a shriveled limb; cripple") as the result of being subjected to torture for misappropriation; hence 'Abdallāh's surname, Ibn al-Muqaffa' ("Son of the

Cripple"). Ibn al-Muqaffaʿ at first followed in his father's footsteps and served the Umayyad governors of Fārs and Kirmān provinces. After the overthrow of the Umayyads—the first Abbasid caliph, Abū l-ʿAbbās (surnamed al-Saffāḥ), came to power in 132/749—Ibn al-Muqaffaʿ attached himself to the service of the new caliph's uncle, ʿĪsā ibn ʿAlī ibn ʿAbdallāh ibn ʿAbbās, whom he served as *kātib*, or private secretary. It was a powerful political connection. One of ʿĪsā's brothers, ʿAbdallāh ibn ʿAlī, was the commander responsible for the defeat of the last Umayyad caliph, Marwān II, and for the elimination of much of the Umayyad family. Another of ʿĪsā's brothers, Sulaymān ibn ʿAlī, became governor of Basra, and it was there that Ibn al-Muqaffaʿ spent most of his life, in what was a center of intellectual ferment in the Arab-Islamic world until the founding of Baghdad in 145/762.

Few of Ibn al-Muqaffaʿ's works have survived. Some have been lost completely; others have survived only as excerpted or adapted by later authors.[2] The latter is the case with his translations from Pahlavi: works such as *The Book of Kings* (*Khwadāynāmag*), a royal chronicle; *The Book of Rules* (*Āyīnnāmah*), a picture of the customs of the Sasanian court; and *The Book of the Crown* (*Kitāb al-Tāj*), about the lives of the rulers of Iran, Anūsharwān in particular.[3] These works indicate that his translation of the collection of stories we know as *Kalīlah and Dimnah* was part of a larger interest in the cultural and historical heritage of Iran, not an isolated fascination with a single literary work.

Beyond its significance as a monument of Persian literary culture, *Kalīlah and Dimnah* may have been of interest to Ibn al-Muqaffaʿ for more specific reasons. One of his other surviving works, *The Great Book of Conduct* (*Kitāb al-Adab al-kabīr*),[4] resembles *Kalīlah and Dimnah* in purpose, if not in method: a section addressed to a prince offers advice about the skills, moral qualities, and conduct required in a successful ruler; a subsequent section describes the skills, moral qualities, and conduct appropriate to a ruler's minister or adviser; the final section deals with the value of friendship

and proper relations between friends. Another surviving work, the *Epistle on the Caliph's Entourage* (*Risālah fī l-Ṣaḥābah*), gives practical advice to a ruler—apparently the second Abbasid caliph, al-Manṣūr (r. 136–58/754–75)—about the proper management of a variety of issues. The work also discusses more theoretical questions, particularly the nature and limits of caliphal authority in the context of the developing system of Islamic law.[5]

The relation between these two didactic works and *Kalīlah and Dimnah* is evident. Although the stories of *Kalīlah and Dimnah* are, on the surface, entertaining narratives, their underlying purpose, as Ibn al-Muqaffaʿ emphasizes in his Preface (Chapter 2 in this edition), is didactic: to inculcate certain skills and virtues, and warn against certain vices. The original Indian collection from which the Middle Persian book was assembled was explicitly addressed to the sons of a king, to teach them the skills needed for the proper governance of the state. The stories display the benefits of judiciousness (*ḥilm*) and careful examination of the facts (*tathabbut*) before acting; they warn against rash action. They stress the role of the good counselor, warn against incompetent or malicious counselors, and highlight the danger of rivalries among courtiers. Many of the animals who populate the book are, in effect, ministers giving advice to rulers, friends giving advice to friends, or wives giving advice to husbands. The book contains many set pieces in which successive advisers debate policy by giving competing advice to a ruler: the speeches offered by the advisers in Chapter 7 ("The Crows and the Owls") serve as an example. Other stories illustrate the importance of alliances for a common goal, even between former enemies, along with the limitations of such ad hoc alliances (for example, Chapter 10, "The Cat and the Rat").

Other aspects of the work that might have attracted Ibn al-Muqaffaʿ's interest were personal, religious, and philosophical. We have already mentioned his relatively late conversion from Zoroastrianism to Islam. Many readers of *Kalīlah and Dimnah* have interpreted the biography of Barzawayh,[6] the physician

who procured and translated the text of *Kalīlah and Dimnah* for Anūsharwān (his autobiography appears here as Chapter 3, "The Chapter of Barzawayh the Physician"), as having been "enriched" by Ibn al-Muqaffaʿ to give a hint of his own religious development, particularly as regards a certain skepticism about all religious traditions, thus making the Persian physician a kind of alter ego for Ibn al-Muqaffaʿ. But given the disappearance of the Middle Persian text, such speculation, however attractive, cannot be proven.

The anecdotes transmitted in the works of Arabic historians and biographers focus on Ibn al-Muqaffaʿ's mastery of the Arabic language, including correcting others' mistakes, his generosity, his elegant lifestyle, his meticulousness in matters of food and cleanliness, and his wit. The latter, unfortunately, may have hastened his demise, as he is said to have ridiculed in scurrilous verses the very man who by an ironic turn of fate subsequently replaced his patron's brother, Sulaymān ibn ʿAlī, as governor of Basra and carried out Ibn al-Muqaffaʿ's execution.

One might have thought that Ibn al-Muqaffaʿ's close connection to the caliphal family would have protected him. The opposite turned out to be the case. Ibn al-Muqaffaʿ fell victim to a conflict within the ruling family. Upon the death of the first Abbasid caliph, al-Saffāḥ, in 136/754, ʿAbdallāh ibn ʿAlī, the brother of Ibn al-Muqaffaʿ's patron, refused to acknowledge the succession of his nephew al-Manṣūr and claimed the caliphate for himself. ʿAbdallāh ibn ʿAlī was defeated in 137/754 and fled to Basra, hoping to be protected by his brothers from the wrath of the new caliph. The situation was precarious: although al-Manṣūr seemed reluctant to take action against his rebellious uncle, in the absence of a formal safe-conduct (an *amān*) there was danger that al-Manṣūr might change his mind at any moment. ʿAbdallāh's brothers, ʿĪsā (who was Ibn al-Muqaffaʿ's patron) and Sulaymān, decided to obtain a formal promise of safety for their brother from al-Manṣūr, and commissioned Ibn al-Muqaffaʿ to draft it. Ibn al-Muqaffaʿ, who could hardly refuse, performed the task only too well. To ensure ʿAbdallāh's

safety, he included a warning that if al-Manṣūr should in any way harm his uncle:

> Everything that he owns in the way of slaves, clothes, goods, vessels, beasts of burden, and [his] landed property . . . will be [taken as] alms for the poor Each slave or concubine that he owns . . . will be freed Each of his wives will be divorced three times, irrevocably Muslims as a generality will . . . be completely freed from the oath of allegiance incumbent upon them to him, and relieved of the oaths regarding it.[7]

The caliph was to sign the document with his own hand. Al-Manṣūr was enraged. He secretly ordered the newly appointed governor of Basra to do away with the writer who had caused him such offense. Despite the pleas of his brothers, this was done. Ibn al-Muqaffaʿ was invited into the new governor's palace. He never emerged. According to one account, his limbs were severed one by one and thrown into an oven, and what remained of his body was incinerated.[8] Such was the untimely end of the translator–adapter of *Kalīlah and Dimnah* and, although the transmission of the text has been so faulty that we cannot recover with certainty the exact words of Ibn al-Muqaffaʿ, his achievement deserves full recognition.

THE ODYSSEY OF *KALĪLAH AND DIMNAH*

As Ibn al-Muqaffaʿ explains in his Preface to *Kalīlah and Dimnah*:

> This book is a work of parables and stories composed by the people of India, who sought to incorporate into it the most eloquent speech they could find in the style they preferred. In order to make their intentions comprehensible, scholars of every nation and tongue have employed a variety of devices and means when presenting their arguments. One device was to put eloquent and elegant language into the mouths of animals and birds. This enabled them to accomplish a number of things: they found a way to

speak indirectly and to communicate through implication. Because such a book combined entertainment with wisdom, the wise would study it for its wisdom, and the simple for its value as entertainment. (§2.1)

Many of the stories derived from a collection of fables composed originally in Sanskrit, sometime between the second century BC and the third century AD. Because the collection was organized into five books, each focusing on a particular theme, it was entitled *Five Discourses,* or *Panchatantra.*

In the middle of the sixth century AD, the work came to the attention of the ruler of Sasanian Iran, Khusraw I Anūsharwān (r. AD 531–79), or of figures at his court who were interested in Indian learning, and it was adapted into Middle Persian (Pahlavi). The process by which the book made its way from India to Persia is narrated in the first chapter of the present volume: "How Anūsharwān Sent Barzawayh to India." In Sasanian Iran, additional Indian stories translated from the *Mahābhārata* and elsewhere were added, and the composite work came to be known as *Kalīlah and Dimnah*, after the main characters who appear in its opening chapter. This Middle Persian work of translation and adaptation has not survived in its original language.

Sometime before the Islamic conquest of Iran, the Middle Persian *Kalīlah and Dimnah* was translated into Syriac, one of the languages of the Christians residing in the Persian Empire, and that translation survived in a single manuscript; it was edited and published in the nineteenth century, but is now lost. In the second/eighth century, the Middle Persian text came to the attention of Ibn al-Muqaffaʿ, who translated it into Arabic prose. This version became popular, inspiring many adaptations into both Arabic verse and prose, new Persian adaptations and versifications, and a later Syriac translation (from the Arabic this time, not from the Persian). Eventually the book made its way westward: in Islamic Spain it was translated into Old Castilian; other translations were

made into Hebrew (from which it was translated into Latin) and Middle Greek. Each of these translations was made independently from different forms of the text. Later, the work was translated into German (from Latin), Ottoman Turkish (from Persian), and other languages. Regrettably, Ibn al-Muqaffa''s translation has not come down to us intact. Of the many surviving manuscripts of the Arabic *Kalīlah and Dimnah*, most are relatively late in date. They present a great diversity of versions.

The first printed edition of *Kalīlah and Dimnah* was published by Sylvestre de Sacy in Paris in 1819. He assembled a composite Arabic text based on a relatively late manuscript in the Royal Library in Paris, supplemented by additions and emendations based on other manuscripts available to him.[9] Earlier manuscripts have since become available. In 1905, Louis Cheikho published a critical edition of the work, based on a manuscript from Dayr al-Shīr, Lebanon, dated 739/1339. Later, 'Abd al-Wahhāb 'Azzām used the earliest known dated manuscript—an Aya Sofya manuscript dated 618/1221—as the basis of his 1941 Cairo edition. Early though this manuscript may be, it dates from more than four and a half centuries after the author's death. Another early manuscript, its text as yet unpublished, is located in the Royal Library in Rabat, Morocco, and can be dated on the basis of its illustrations to the second part of the thirteenth century (between 663/1265 and 679/1280).[10]

The discrepancies between these texts demonstrate that by the time of the earliest surviving manuscripts, *Kalīlah and Dimnah* had ceased to have a single authoritative text.[11] Even earlier evidence can be gleaned from quotations from *Kalīlah and Dimnah* in older Arabic works, such as *'Uyūn al-akhbār* by Ibn Qutaybah (d. 276/889) and an entire work composed by a certain Muḥammad ibn Ḥusayn al-Yamanī (d. 400/1009) purporting to show that anything of value in Ibn al-Muqaffa''s translation was anticipated by Arabic authors.[12] Yet even these early citations differ among themselves.

Surviving manuscripts of *Kalīlah and Dimnah* diverge so widely that it is impossible to recover the text as it issued from the pen of

Ibn al-Muqaffaʻ. It is not simply a problem of the usual copyists' mistakes, omissions, and misunderstandings; such things can be identified and corrected. The surviving manuscripts, even the earliest, differ so significantly in wording and content that one must conclude that the text has come down to us in differing recensions. Even worse, all of these recensions, or "continua," show clear evidence of adaptation and cross-copying.[13]

The connoisseurs of Arabic literature who oversaw the copying of *Kalīlah and Dimnah* for their own or their patrons' libraries, or for general circulation, felt free to adapt the text to their own interests and literary tastes or to those of their patrons and audiences. Passages were sometimes omitted, sometimes expanded; the flexibility of Arabic syntax was exploited to rephrase a given passage in a variety of ways. Sometimes the literary register of the language was highlighted by using learned vocabulary and complex syntax, and sometimes the vocabulary and syntax were simplified or bent toward a more colloquial register. Certain philosophical or religious ideas were emphasized or downplayed, and the role of certain characters was changed.[14]

Several factors contributed to the freedom with which the text was handled. First, *Kalīlah and Dimnah* is a work of secular literature. Unlike the primary religious texts of Islam, such as the Qurʼan and the Hadith (the sayings of the Prophet), which had to be copied verbatim or transmitted orally according to strict scholarly standards because of their theological and legal importance, literary works did not necessarily benefit from the same meticulousness. Books that formed part of the scholarly curriculum in Islamic schools were typically studied by students under the supervision of a professor, who ensured that the students' copies of the text were accurate—but *Kalīlah and Dimnah* never formed part of the scholarly curriculum. Collections of poetry were protected from change by their meter: changes would destroy the rhythm and would be obvious. The ornate style of rhyming prose known as *sajʻ* also enjoyed a certain degree of protection due to its complex,

intentionally inimitable style; works in relatively straightforward prose, such as *Kalīlah and Dimnah*, were not so protected. Finally, a work known to be a translation from a foreign language did not enjoy the prestige of original Arabic works.[15]

THE INDIAN SOURCES OF *KALĪLAH AND DIMNAH*

The ultimate source of most, but not all, of the book Ibn al-Muqaffaʿ introduced to Arabic readers was a collection of Sanskrit fables known as the *Panchatantra*, or *Five Discourses*, as it was organized into five books.[16] The collection was intended to be a kind of "mirror for princes," teaching worldly wisdom to rulers. Each of the five books contained a main narrative illustrating a unifying theme, and each enclosed many related subordinate stories or parables. The actors in most of the stories, especially in the first three sections of the collection, are anthropomorphized animals, who combine aspects of their animal nature with human abilities of speech and reasoning, human virtues and vices, and human resourcefulness and cleverness in dealing with life's vicissitudes.

There is an ingenious weaving of stories within stories within stories: animals cite fables to each other in order to promote or discourage a course of action and, more generally, to illustrate instances of wise behavior and to warn each other against unwise behavior. Although the stories were narrated in Sanskrit prose, the wise sayings cited by their characters were in verse, a feature not preserved in the Arabic versions.

The frame story of the *Panchatantra* presents the entire work as narrated by a Brahmin sage commissioned by a king to teach his three unwise sons the principles of good conduct in this world: conduct that would lead to the princes' personal welfare and to the good order of the state. This frame story does not survive intact in the Arabic; it is replaced by a conversation between a king and a philosopher, with no elaboration of the motive for the conversation. In the Arabic edition presented here, teachings about the wise conduct of life in this world are set against a larger framework of

Islamic ethics connecting conduct in this world with reward or punishment in the hereafter. The behavior of many of the characters may be, as Franklin Edgerton described it, "Machiavellian," but the overall world of the Arabic *Kalīlah and Dimnah* is moral and Islamic in coloring.

Each of the five major chapters of the *Panchatantra*, with their corresponding chapters in *Kalīlah and Dimnah*, illustrates the application of cleverness, resourcefulness, or foresight to a particular situation. The following are the five main *Panchatantra* stories (the translations are Edgerton's) and the corresponding stories in this edition:

1. "The Separation of Friends, or, The Lion and the Bull," corresponding to "The Lion and the Ox" (Chapter 4).
2. "The Winning of Friends, or, The Dove, Crow, Mouse, Tortoise, and Deer," corresponding to "The Ring Dove" (Chapter 6).
3. "War and Peace, or, The Crows and the Owls," corresponding to "The Crows and the Owls" (Chapter 7).
4. "The Loss of One's Gettings, or, The Ape and the Crocodile," corresponding to "The Turtle and the Monkey" (Chapter 8).
5. "Hasty Action, or, The Brahmin and the Mongoose," corresponding to "The Holy Man and the Mongoose" (Chapter 9).

THE MIDDLE PERSIAN VERSION

Because the Middle Persian text from which Ibn al-Muqaffaʿ translated has not survived, we have only indirect evidence about the changes to the original Sanskrit collection that took place before Ibn al-Muqaffaʿ translated the text into Arabic. The prefatory material explaining the circumstances under which the Indian work made its way to Sasanian Iran, along with the autobiography of the physician who brought the work to Iran (Chapters 1 and 3 of the present edition), almost certainly derive from Middle Persian

materials, but it is not clear whether these prefatory chapters formed part of the Middle Persian *Kalīlah and Dimnah* or were attached to the book by Ibn al-Muqaffaʿ from other Middle Persian sources. There are two versions of the first preface, a longer and a shorter. Manuscript London Or. 4044 presents only the longer version. It relates how the physician Barzawayh, on orders from the ruler Anūsharwān, journeyed to India; how, through the good offices of an Indian scholar whom he befriended (the theme of friendship thus forms an important element even in this introduction), he surreptitiously obtained a copy of a book kept under lock and key in the royal library; and how he transcribed it, translated it into Persian, and brought it back to Anūsharwān. Anūsharwān is said to have rewarded Barzawayh by commanding that his biography (Chapter 3 of the present translation) be attached to the book.[17] (These introductory chapters do not form part of the Old Syriac translation, but no conclusion can be drawn from their absence, as the sole manuscript of the Old Syriac translation has lost its initial pages.)

A further departure from the *Panchatantra* in Ibn al-Muqaffaʿ's translation is the addition of stories from other Indian sources. Eight chapters of the present book can be so identified. Three of them (Chapters 10, 11, and 12 of the present text) came from Book 12 of the *Mahābhārata*, a section in which the sage Bhīṣma uses parables to instruct King Yudhiṣṭhira in the proper behavior (*dharma*) of a wise king; the remaining five (Chapters 13, 14, 15, 16, and 17) are of unknown provenance. In this case, the Old Syriac translation, made from Middle Persian sometime before Ibn al-Muqaffaʿ's Arabic translation, provides evidence that some of these additional stories were already part of the Middle Persian book.[18] Chapters 10, 11, 12, and 13 do occur in the Old Syriac, indicating that they were part of the Middle Persian *Kalīlah and Dimnah*. That leaves four chapters (14–17). The Syriac translator may have omitted them, or the surviving text of the Old Syriac may have lost its concluding chapters, or Ibn al-Muqaffaʿ may have taken them from other Persian translations from Sanskrit and added them himself to the Arabic *Kalīlah*

and Dimnah. There is evidence from Ibn al-Muqaffaʿ's treatment of Middle Persian historical materials that he regularly combined material from several sources.[19] A reasonable hypothesis is that Ibn al-Muqaffaʿ supplemented his translation of an existing Middle Persian text with other Indian materials that he judged appropriate.

The added stories differ in construction from the *Panchatantra*-derived chapters: Although Chapters 10, 11, 12, and 16 have animals as their protagonists, they contain few embedded stories, and those that do occur (two in Chapter 13 and one in Chapter 17) are short and narrated by human beings, unlike the embedded stories in the *Panchatantra*-derived chapters, which are narrated by animals to animals. Chapters 13, 14, 15, and 17 have human protagonists. Even where there are animal actors, as in "The Mendicant and the Goldsmith" (Chapter 14), they carry out their roles in the human world. Thus, it is something of a misnomer to call *Kalīlah and Dimnah* as a whole a book of animal fables.

IBN AL-MUQAFFAʿ'S ADDITIONS

Two chapters can be attributed to Ibn al-Muqaffaʿ with confidence. Chapter 2 is a preface explicitly addressed to the Arabic reader. It presents the book as a serious work, stressing the benefits to be derived by a careful reading and warning against treating the book as mere entertainment. Another addition, Chapter 5, "The Investigation of Dimnah," records the subsequent trial and punishment of the crafty jackal Dimnah for his treachery; no such denouement exists in the *Panchatantra*, and it appears to have been absent from the Middle Persian as well, as the Old Syriac shows no trace of it. In Chapter 4, "The Lion and the Ox," Dimnah has tricked his master, the lion, into murdering Dimnah's rival, the ox Shanzabah, and, at the end of the chapter, apparently has succeeded to the ox's position at court. The story in the *Panchatantra* ends at this point. In the chapter added by Ibn al-Muqaffaʿ, Dimnah's treachery is uncovered, the lion's mother persuades her son to order a trial, and Dimnah is convicted and executed, despite his

eloquent orations in his own defense. The chapter gives a sense of closure absent from the Sanskrit and presumably from the Middle Persian, where Dimnah, far from being punished for his duplicity, succeeds to his unfortunate rival's position and, we imagine, lives happily ever after. Although Cheikho postulated a Middle Persian source for the chapter, it seems more likely that it was written by Ibn al-Muqaffaʿ. Inasmuch as it does not form part of the Old Syriac translation, and many of Dimnah's arguments in his own defense echo themes in Islamic theology current in Ibn al-Muqaffaʿ's time—for example, the roles of predestination and human autonomy, the relation between physical endowments and moral qualities, and the duty of self-defense against unjust accusations—the likelihood is that even if there was a Middle Persian source for the chapter, Ibn al-Muqaffaʿ considerably adapted and expanded its text. Brockelmann's attribution of it to Ibn al-Muqaffaʿ is more likely.[20]

THE FRAME STORY

Another change that presumably had already taken place in the Middle Persian from which Ibn al-Muqaffaʿ translated was the reworking of the *Panchatantra*'s overall frame story of a king commissioning a famous Brahmin sage to instruct the king's three sons. Instead, each chapter in the Arabic *Kalīlah and Dimnah* begins with a brief, formulaic conversation between a king, Dabshalim, and a philosopher, Baydabā.[21] No motive, other than the king's curiosity and desire for enlightenment, is given to explain the circumstances triggering these conversations. At the beginning of each chapter following the first, the king signals his comprehension of the moral of the previous chapter's story, and proposes a new subject for the philosopher to illustrate.

The introductory story of "The Lion and the Ox" may not serve as a frame for the later stories, but it does provide an ingenious transition between the world of human beings with its variety of characters (wise father, indolent sons, and one diligent son) and the world of animals with its own variety of characters. In the Arabic, the

story of the merchant and his sons serves as an introduction only for the chapter of "The Lion and the Ox"; it does not serve as an over-all frame for the successive stories, or even as a frame for the first story. The merchant and his sons do not reappear, either at the end of "The Lion and the Ox" or in the subsequent stories. This contrasts with the *Panchatantra*, where the overall frame story provides con-tinuity: at the beginning of each "book," the sage instructing the king's sons proposes an enigmatic verse to serve as introduction to a new tale. The sons ask for an explanation, and the sage begins to relate the tale.

There was a later attempt in Arabic to explain the circumstances behind the story of Dabshalim and Baydabā. An otherwise unknown author, Bahnūd ibn Saḥwān (also known as ʿAlī ibn al-Shāh al-Fārisī) composed a preface that appears in some manuscripts (de Sacy included it in his edition). It explains that Dabshalim, the king who appears in conversation with the philosopher Baydabā in the bridge passages of Ibn al-Muqaffaʿ's work, ruled India in the wake of Alexander the Great's conquests. At first he ruled justly, but then he became a tyrant who needed to be reformed. To avoid the dangers of direct confrontation, the learned men of the kingdom decided to proceed indirectly. One of their number, Baydabā, composed a series of fables to turn Dabshalim from his evil ways without incurring his wrath. The ruse succeeded: Dabshalim repented and Baydabā was rewarded.

Clever as this may be, there is no evidence in the *Panchatantra* or in *Kalīlah and Dimnah* itself that Dabshalim, the ruler to whom these fables are told, was a tyrant who needed to be restrained from wrongdoing or that his interlocutor, Baydabā, used fables because direct speech would endanger his life. Quite the opposite: in the surviving text, Dabshalim himself proposes the themes and Baydabā complies with his requests.

BARZAWAYH'S AUTOBIOGRAPHY

Chapter 3, "The Chapter of Barzawayh the Physician," contains Barzawayh's autobiography. Although some scholars have attributed

its composition to Ibn al-Muqaffaʿ, Theodor Nöldeke, who produced a separate edition and translation of it, argued convincingly that its origin as a composition in Middle Persian is historically plausible and that it contains material that would not have been available to Ibn al-Muqaffaʿ. This, however, does not rule out the possibility that Ibn al-Muqaffaʿ added material of his own, expanding on Barzawayh's religious ideas in the context of his own religious outlook. The chapter records Barzawayh's upbringing, his reasons for choosing medicine as a career, his devotion to his profession, his consciousness of the limitations of medicine, his increasingly ascetic religious outlook, and his agnosticism vis-à-vis existing religious traditions. Barzawayh distances himself from any existing religious community, having explored them all and found them wanting. It is this aspect that some readers have seen as having been highlighted or added in toto by Ibn al-Muqaffaʿ as a reflection of his own religious opinions.

It is tempting to read Ibn al-Muqaffaʿ into Barzawayh's biography, but this is speculative. We have little firm evidence about Ibn al-Muqaffaʿ's religious beliefs or the sincerity of his conversion to Islam. An anecdote in Ibn Khallikān's biography to the effect that Ibn al-Muqaffaʿ continued to recite Zoroastrian prayers on the eve of his formal conversion might be interpreted not as evidence of insincerity, but as evidence of a strongly religious personality, perhaps one likely to be as assiduous in observance of the rituals of Islam as he had been in the observance of those of his former religion. Ibn Khallikān cites a statement by the essayist al-Jāḥiẓ (d. 255/868–69) that Ibn al-Muqaffaʿ, along with the notoriously dissolute poets Muṭīʿ ibn Iyās and Yaḥyā ibn Ziyād, was suspected of heresy (zandaqah). Ibn Khallikān also cites a statement attributed to al-Manṣūr's successor, the caliph al-Mahdī (r. 158–69/775–85): "Never have I encountered a book of heresy whose source was not Ibn al-Muqaffaʿ." The contemptuous words that Ibn Khallikān attributes to Sufyān ibn Muʿāwiyah, the governor who oversaw the execution ("I have no qualms about rending you limb from limb,

because you are a heretic [*zindīq*] and have corrupted the people"), express the governor's long-held animus against his victim, but can hardly be taken as evidence of Ibn al-Muqaffaʻ's real opinions.[22] Some modern commentators, such as Brockelmann, have seen Ibn al-Muqaffaʻ as highlighting Barzawayh's religious skepticism; others, such as Gabrieli, are less certain, given that certain currents of religious skepticism were already active in Anūsharwān's Iran.[23]

THE MORALITY OF *KALĪLAH AND DIMNAH*

Franklin Edgerton initially characterized the moral world of the *Panchatantra* as follows: "Most of the stories remain true to the keynote of the book, its Machiavellian character; they are generally unmoral, and at times positively immoral, in the political lessons they inculcate."[24] Later in the same volume, he qualified this judgment:

> The Pañcatantra, like other books of the sort, often presents discordant views, evidently with intent; it arranges joint debates between characters in the stories. Thus it happens that at least one story occurs in it (Evil-wit and Honest-wit, I. 13)[25] which teaches, and is obviously meant to teach, the distinctly non-Machiavellian lesson that "honesty is the best policy." ... It is embedded in a long moral lecture read by the virtuous jackal Karaṭaka to the tricky Damanaka, in which he reproves him for his villainy, assuring him that he will live to repent it, in spite of its apparent success.[26]

This balanced assessment applies all the more to *Kalīlah and Dimnah*, especially in the recension here presented, with its distinctly Islamic overtones. Although the virtues the stories illustrate tend to be practical worldly skills, faithfulness, truthfulness, and trust receive their share of praise. Some of the stories celebrate successful friendships (Chapter 6, "The Ring Dove") or the overcoming of difficulties (Chapter 15, "The King's Son and His Companions"); characters who are scheming, ambitious, and unscrupulous are

presented as dangers to be avoided; ill-considered or impulsive actions are shown to have unsavory consequences (Chapter 9, "The Holy Man and the Mongoose").

If the dangers of life in this world are illustrated, this hardly amounts to a glorification of immoral behavior; rather, it is a frequent Islamic theme: the instability of this world, as contrasted with the permanence of the reward promised by God to the righteous. We are warned that friendships can succumb to the machinations of unscrupulous rivals (Chapter 4, "The Lion and the Ox"); alliances made for a specific end cannot be relied on once that end is achieved (Chapter 10, "The Cat and the Rat," with its decidedly unromantic ending: "I'll be your friend from a distance"); grievances are set aside, but suspicion persists (Chapter 12, "The Lion and the Jackal"). This world (*al-dunyā*, to use the Arabic term) is one of intrigues (Dimnah and his rival, the ox Shanzabah), innate antagonisms (owls and crows, cats and mice), and irreconcilable motives (in Chapter 8, "The Turtle and the Monkey," the turtle must decide between loyalty to his friend, the monkey, and loyalty to his wife, who has tricked him into believing that the only remedy for her disease is a monkey's heart). But for all these dark touches, evil never triumphs, except in embedded stories meant to be taken as a warning against thoughtless behavior.

A major theme of *Kalīlah and Dimnah* is a ruler's need for good counselors, of which there are many examples in the book. However, there are many warnings about the dangers lying in wait for anyone who would speak honest advice to power. One wonders whether Ibn al-Muqaffaʿ saw the dangers of his own position as a client of the caliphal family reflected in passages such as the following:

> "If this is your plan [that is, to enter the lion's service],"
> said Kalīlah, "I must warn you about the dangers of associating with rulers. Scholars say there are three things that only fools attempt and from which few escape unscathed: associating with rulers, trusting women with secrets, and drinking poison as an experiment. Scholars have likened a

ruler to a steep, rugged mountain where all sorts of pleasant fruit grow, but which is home to lions, leopards, and every kind of ferocious beast—the ascent may be difficult, but staying there is harder yet." (§4.13)

Or consider the following speech by the ox Shanzabah, upon being told by Dimnah (falsely) that the lion intends to make a meal of him:

> Can anyone serve a ruler and remain in his good graces? How right the one who said that rulers, in their scant loyalty to companions and abandonment of those they no longer need, are like a whore with her customers: when one leaves, another takes his place! (§4.65)

Or consider the pious jackal of Chapter 12 ("The Lion and the Jackal"), voicing his reluctance to serve at a lion's court:

> Only two sorts of people can associate with rulers and do their bidding . . . and I'm neither. The two sorts are an unscrupulous flatterer who gets what he wants through scheming and ensures his own safety through flattery, and a pitiful fool whom no one envies. Rarely do things turn out well for the person who would associate with a ruler on terms of truthfulness, sincerity, and modesty, untinged by flattery, for the ruler's foes and friends will join forces against him in envy, enmity, and deceit. The ruler's friends will compete with him for rank and envy him for it; the ruler's enemies will hate him for his good advice and service to the ruler. When both groups join forces against him, he is likely to perish, God forbid (§12.8).

Islamic Elements in the London Or. 4044 Redaction of *Kalīlah and Dimnah*

As might be expected of a text translated into Arabic in early Abbasid times and subjected afterward to a complex process of transmission and adaptation even before the earliest surviving Arabic manuscripts

were produced, the text of London Or. 4044 shows certain features that testify to the Islamic milieu in which it was produced and to the religious culture and philosophical interests of successive author-copyists and of the audiences for which they produced their texts. These features are subtle: there has been no wholesale rewriting such as one finds in the later Syriac version, with its explicit quotations from the Bible, or in various Arabic and Persian retellings that introduce quotations from the Qur'an, the Hadith, and even Arabic poetry. But Islamic overtones of various kinds are in fact present. First, there are turns of phrase that impart an Islamic patina to the work. In addition to the frequent contrast between the transitory, present world (*al-dunyā*) and the permanent afterlife (*al-ākhirah*), God is often referred to as *Allāh ta'ālā* (God the exalted) or *Allāh subḥānahu wa-ta'ālā* (God, glorified and exalted). One occasionally encounters predictions about the future qualified by the phrase *in shā' Allāh* (if God so wills)—such as in §9.2 and §13.28. The latter example is particularly striking, spoken as it is by a female dove telling her mate that his plan to store grain to tide them over the dry season will succeed, "God willing." Even the animals speak a language with Islamic overtones!

Closely related are the formulaic phrases addressed to rulers, examples of courtly etiquette not to be taken as having particularly deep religious or philosophical import. For example, when Queen Īrākht, at the prompting of the wise counselor Baylār, seeks to comfort the king, who has been terrified by his ominous dreams and by the frightful rites the Brahmins enjoin upon him to avert disaster, she begins by saying, "Do not be sad, blessed king. May God lengthen your life and grant you lasting joy" (§13.14). Later in the same chapter, the wise counselor, Baylār, begins an address to the same king with similar words: "May God grant Your Majesty long life, preserve you in health, and increase your judiciousness and nobility" (§13.76).

Sometimes the language reflects deeper Islamic religious and philosophical themes. This redaction frequently emphasizes the

doctrine that the ultimate agent in all human actions is God; human beings (and the animal actors in the fables) accomplish what they accomplish only with the help of God. In "The Cat and the Rat," the rat explains to the cat, "Each of us, with God's help, will be the cause of the other's salvation" (§10.5). In "King Haylār and His Minister Baylār," the malicious Brahmins explain that the catastrophes foreshadowed by the king's dreams can be averted only through a series of killings and bloody rites, after which "God will avert whatever He wishes" (§13.4). This emphasis on God's role contrasts with the Old Syriac version, which antedates the Arabic, where the rites themselves appear to be effective *ex opere operato*; no divine intervention is mentioned. Later in the same chapter, King Haylār attributes his escape from the clutches of the Brahmins first to God and second to the good judgment of the queen: "If God in His mercy hadn't restrained me through the advice of Īrākht, the best and most blessed of women, I should have perished, caused death, and lost all I have in this world and the next" (§13.19).

The combination of God's help and individual efforts sometimes leads to rather strange juxtapositions. For example, in "The Monkey and the Turtle," the monkey, shocked to learn that the turtle wants to extract his heart to use as medicine to cure his sick wife, exclaims, "The only thing to be done is to seek help from God and to use my own cunning" (§8.11). In "The Cat and the Rat," the rat, seeing himself surrounded on all sides by danger, exclaims, "I am surrounded by troubles . . . all in league to spoil my joy over the cat's distress. I see no recourse for me but to rely on God, and to use my intelligence and ingenuity" (§10.3). Something similar happens in "The Lion and the Jackal," where the pious jackal initially agrees to serve as the lion's adviser only if the lion promises not to believe any slanders circulated against him by envious courtiers: "Should one of them, be it with his own lips or through someone else, mention to the king something intended to turn the king against me, the king will not act hastily against me, but will investigate and

examine what has been brought to his attention and then do what God shows him to be best" (§12.10). In "The Trial of Dimnah," we meet a physician "who prospered because of the providential [that is, divinely decreed] cures that occurred at his hands through his treatments and drugs" (§5.29). In "The Owls and the Crows," the wise counselor tells the king of the crows: "I hope God will set in motion some good that will bring swift relief. Those in dire straits have often achieved through cunning what they could never have achieved in a contest of strength" (§7.20). Is it God's intervention, or is it cunning? Or are cunning and deception gifts imparted by God?

Finally, there is evidence in this redaction of a philosophical interest in the relations between individual volition and God's determination of events through His lordship over destiny and fortune (*al-qaḍāʾ wa-l-qadar*). In the world of *Kalīlah and Dimnah*, this divinely determined aspect of events operates through secondary causes (*ʿilal*, singular *ʿillah*). To naïve minds, these secondary causes appear to control the course of events; however, enlightened minds understand the role of divine providence in all things. Leaving aside the three introductory chapters, the first extended philosophical meditation on the subject occurs early in "The Lion and the Ox." The rich merchant's oldest son, heeding his father's warning about the need to pursue a gainful profession, loads an oxcart with merchandise and sets out for a land called Sūraqān to trade. On the way, one of the oxen, Shanzabah, sinks into a quagmire and, when extricated, is so exhausted that the son leaves him behind, instructing his assistant to wait for the ox to recover and then bring him to the city. However, the assistant tires, abandons Shanzabah, and tells his master that the ox has died. Shanzabah makes his way to a grassy meadow, where his bellowing eventually comes to the attention of the lion into whose court he will soon be introduced by Dimnah, thus setting the stage for the first story. We are told, however, that while Shanzabah, having been rescued from quagmire, stayed in the meadow, he was

fearful that some inevitable misfortune might yet befall him—as happened, for example, to a man who, they say, was cutting hay when a wolf attacked him. Only when the wolf was near did the man notice and flee in terror toward a village on the bank of a river. When he reached the river, he found the bridge in ruins. With the wolf catching up, he said to himself, "What shall I do? The wolf is right behind me, the river is deep, the bridge is in ruins, and I can't swim. The safest thing is to entrust my life to the water." So he jumped in. The villagers saw him and pulled him out just as he was about to drown. Back among the villagers, as he leaned against a wall and began to tell them what had happened, the wall collapsed and killed him. (§4.3)

Even the occasional satirical touches in this recension have an Islamic coloring. In the story of the partridge, the rabbit, and the pious cat (§§7.15–17), embedded in "The Owls and the Crows," a partridge and a rabbit lay claim to the same hollow as their home. The partridge suggests that they take their claims for arbitration to a pious cat:

"By the riverbank near us," said the partridge, "lives a cat who is an invalid. He fasts endlessly, prays night and day, harms no one, spills no blood, and is content to live on grass. If you like, we can go to him for arbitration and abide by his decision." (§7.15)

The cat, alas, turns out to be a hypocrite, but one skilled in the external observances of Islamic prayer. As soon as he sees the two potential victims approaching, he stands up on his hind legs in the posture of prayer. Then, having asked them to come closer, he being hard of hearing in his old age, he delivers a short sermon with Qur'anic overtones:

"Before pronouncing judgment, I'll start by giving you some good advice," he said. "I charge you to fear God and seek nothing but the truth: the seeker of truth prospers,

even if the judgment goes against him; but the seeker of falsehood loses, even if the judgment goes in his favor. The only things an inhabitant of this world takes with him from his earthly existence are neither money nor friends, but the good works he has done. A wise man should seek what endures and will bring him benefit tomorrow, and abandon everything else."

As he talked, they became more and more at ease with him and came closer and closer, until finally he pounced, grabbed them, and killed them both. (§7.17)

What stands out in this recension is how thoroughly and skillfully the Islamic elements, be they matters of vocabulary, turns of phrase, or more complex Islamic religious and philosophical arguments, are integrated into the dramatic structure of *Kalīlah and Dimnah*. Part of the pleasure for the reader lies in detecting these elements and in noting how ingeniously these sophisticated religious and philosophical ideas have been introduced into a dramatic situation or into the speech of animals.

Michael Fishbein

Agra
New Persian,
10th/16th c.

Ghazna
New Persian,
ca. 539/1144

Bukhara
Herat
New Persian,
4th/10th c.

Herat
New Persian,
ca. 910/1504

Constantinople/Istanbul
Greek,
ca. 1080 AD
Ottoman Turkish,
early 10th/16th c.

Konya
New Persian,
641-62/1244-63

Capua
Latin (from Hebrew),
ca. 1275 AD

Palermo
Greek (reworked from
earlier Greek version, with
additions from Arabic),
12th c.

Toledo
Hebrew,
12th c.
Spanish,
1251 AD

Principal Translations of the Arabic *Kalilah wa-Dimnah*

Design: Michael Fishbein
Cartography: Emily Bowe

0 500 1000 1500 2000 km

Note on the Text

The translation aims at a natural style. No attempt has been made to adhere exactly to the syntax of the Arabic or always to translate a given Arabic word by the same English word, as the result would produce a mechanical effect and hide the wide range of meanings of a given Arabic word. In dialogue, the aim has been to produce exchanges at once dramatic and expressive. The more philosophical speeches and orations have been rendered in a more formal English. For convenience, titles for some of the embedded tales have been added in the margin of the translation, although these are not in the manuscript. In these and other matters of style, the translator gratefully acknowledges that his inclination to prefer literalness over liveliness has been curbed by the efforts of his co-translator James Montgomery, whose mastery of English style matches his mastery of Arabic.

Notes to the Introduction

1 For further details about the life of Ibn al-Muqaffaʿ, see Gabrieli, "Ibn al-Muḳaffaʿ"; Sourdel, "La biographie d'Ibn al-Muqaffaʿ d'après les sources anciennes"; and Kristó-Nagy, *La pensée d'Ibn al-Muqaffaʿ*.

2 For a summary of Ibn al-Muqaffaʿ's works, see Latham, "Ibn al-Muqaffaʿ and Early Abbasid Prose," 53–77; and Kristó-Nagy, *La pensée d'Ibn al-Muqaffaʿ*, 81–107.

3 On these works and the nature of Ibn al-Muqaffaʿ's translations, see Hämeen-Anttila, *Khwadāynāmag: The Middle Persian Book of Kings*, 89–99, 106, 128–30.

4 The word translated as "conduct," *adab*, is perhaps to be read in the plural, *ādāb*. It originally meant something like "training, special skill," but soon came to mean "cultivation, general culture, education." See Hämeen-Anttila, *Adab (a) Arabic, Early Developments*.

5 For an account of the *Risālah fī l-Ṣaḥābah*, see Lowry, "The First Islamic Legal Theory: Ibn al-Muqaffaʿ on Interpretation, Authority, and the Structure of the Law."

6 So vocalized in the manuscript. Also read as Burzawayh or Burzōe.

7 Text from Marsham and Robinson, "The Safe-Conduct for the Abbasid ʿAbd Allāh b. ʿAlī," 256.

8 See Ibn Khallikān, *Wafayāt al-aʿyān*, 2:151–55.

9 For a description of the manuscripts de Sacy used for his edition, see *Calila et Dimna*, 57–64. His base text (1483A) is now catalogued by the Bibliothèque Nationale de France as Arabe 3465 and can be accessed online.

10 See the description of Rabat 3655 by Khouloud Khalfallah on the AnonymClassic website: http://www.geschkult.fu-berlin.de/en/e/kalila-wa-dimna/topics/Digital-Reconstruction.html. Many of its leaves are damaged or missing. A full copy of its text made in Egypt in 1175/1761 survives, now located in Paris (Bibliothèque nationale, Arabe 3475). Unfortunately, the copyist appears to have worked quickly and not very carefully, as is evident from a comparison of the copy with the surviving parts of the Rabat manuscript. Other early manuscripts are Riyadh King Faysal Center 2536 and Cambridge Corpus Christi College Parker Library 578, both fourteenth century. A comparison of the earliest texts for one chapter ("The Cat and the Rat") can be accessed on the website of AnonymClassic: http://www.geschkult.fu-berlin.de/en/e/kalila-wa-dimna/index.html.

11 The instability of the text of *Kalīlah and Dimnah* was recognized by scholars very early. In 1873, Ignazio Guidi documented it in a study of manuscripts of the work accessible to him in Italy. See Guidi, *Studii sul testo arabo del Libro di Calila e Dimna*. The situation as of 1924 was summarized by Martin Sprengling in his seminal article "Kalîla Studies. I."

12 Al-Yamanī, *Kitāb Muḍāhāt amthāl kitāb Kalīlah wa-Dimnah bi-mā ashbahahā min ashʿār al-ʿArab* (*How the Parables of Kalīlah and Dimnah Imitate Their Analogs in the Poetry of the Arabs*). Another early reference to *Kalīlah and Dimnah* can be found in the *Taʾrīkh* (*History*) of the third-/ninth-century historian al-Yaʿqūbī (d. 292/905), ed. Leiden, 1:97–99; trans., 2:351–52. Al-Yaʿqūbī lists ten of the chapters, with their titles, but does not mention Ibn al-Muqaffaʿ as translator.

13 The AnonymClassic project has classified the surviving manuscripts into two large groups or "continua," based on the presence and sequence of small units of the text. For a detailed description of the method and its provisional results, see Gruendler, "An Interim Report on the Editorial and Analytical Work of the AnonymClassic Project."

14 See Gruendler, "Les versions de *Kalīla wa-Dimna*: Une transmission et une circulation mouvantes."

15 On the tension between the native Arabic tradition and foreign, mostly Persian, cultural imports, see the article by S. Enderwitz, "al-Shuʿūbiyya," in *EI2*. For one major third-/ninth-century Arab author's view of the Persians, see Ibn Qutaybah, *The Excellence of the Arabs*, 1–103.

16 The *Panchatantra* underwent as many mutations in transmission in India as Ibn al-Muqaffaʿ's *Kalīlah and Dimnah* underwent in Arabic. See Edgerton, *The Panchatantra Reconstructed: An Attempt to Establish the Lost Original Sanskrit Text of the Most Famous of Indian Story-Collections on the Basis of the Principal Extant Versions*. Edgerton also discusses the relationship between the *Panchatantra* and the Middle Persian version translated by Ibn al-Muqaffaʿ; see *The Panchatantra Reconstructed*, 2:40–47. The earlier work of Johannes Hertel, *Tantrākhyāyika: Die älteste Fassung des Pañcatantra*, is still valuable, although many of his conclusions are contested by Edgerton.

17 Curiously, in Chapter 1 of the present text, Anūsharwān instructs his minister Buzurgmihr to prepare this biography; Chapter 3, however, is an autobiography narrated in the first person by Barzawayh. Various explanations have been proposed for the discrepancy.

18 Brockelmann dates it to around 570; see his article "Kalīla wa-Dimna." The Old Syriac also contains a chapter, "Mihrayār, King of the Mice," not found in London Or. 4044. As no Indian source for it has been found, it was probably an original composition in Middle Persian. See Nöldeke, "Die Erzählung vom Mäusekönig und seinen Ministern."

19 Hämeen-Anttila, *Khwadāynāmag: The Middle Persian Book of Kings*, discusses what can be determined about Ibn al-Muqaffaʿ's manner of dealing with his Middle Persian historical sources, and his conclusions can with caution be extended to apply to *Kalīlah and Dimnah*; see especially p. 130.

20 See Cheikho, *La version arabe de Kalîlah et Dimnah*, 49 (notes); Brockelmann, "Kalīla wa-Dimna."

21 The name was sometimes transliterated as Bidpai, and the whole collection has also come to be known as *Bidpai's Fables*.

22 Ibn Khallikān, *Wafayāt al-aʿyān*, 2:151–53.

23 See Brockelmann, "Kalīla wa-Dimna"; Gabrieli, "Ibn al-Muḳaffaʿ"; and Kristó-Nagy, *La pensée d'Ibn al-Muqaffaʿ*, 113–25.

24 Edgerton, *The Panchatantra Reconstructed*, 2:5.

25 In this translation, the story of the swindler and the simpleton (§§4.102–8).

26 Edgerton, *The Panchatantra Reconstructed*, 2:186–87.

KALĪLAH AND DIMNAH

How Anūsharwān Sent Barzawayh to India to Transcribe *Kalīlah and Dimnah*

God, who is blessed and exalted, created His creatures through His mercy, and in His beneficence gave them strength to serve Him. He provided them with the means to live prosperous lives in this world and to save themselves from punishment in the next. The most excellent gift that God bestowed is the intellect. It is the faculty appropriate to all things. Only by means of the intellect can a dweller in this world who aspires to the hereafter—by striving here to save his soul from the terrors of what comes next—live a prosperous life, increase his merit, and perform deeds that are appropriate for both worlds. Only by means of the intellect can those who strive to do good act effectively and be safe from fear of punishment in the afterlife; for the intellect is the means to every good and the key to every desire—none can dispense with it. 1.1

Acquired through experience, the intellect is a faculty hidden within a person, like fire latent in wood; the nature of fire is in the wood, but it only emerges by rubbing: it remains invisible until it is struck by something else, whereupon it ignites and burns. Similarly, the nature of the intellect is latent in a person: it is made manifest through education, and strengthened by experience. When it is strong, it is best at managing experiences and tempering behavior. It secures every benefit and repels every evil. Nothing, then, is better or more excellent for a person than the intellect, when it is supported by education and strengthened by experience. Someone who is endowed by his Creator with intellect and who 1.2

bolsters himself by diligently pursuing education will enjoy good fortune and fulfill his hopes in this world; and in the next world he will attain the most excellent lot, procure the greatest reward, and reach the most exalted station. What is more, intellect bolsters the state, upholds the realm, and ennobles the king. Only through it and under its guidance do both kings and commoners prosper.

1.3 God has bestowed on our fortunate king, Anūsharwān, the most excellent intellect and amplest fortune. He has also blessed him with a fine education, a thirst for knowledge, an extensive knowledge of philosophy, an inquisitiveness about the unknown, and a keenness for the truth of things. In these he has attained what no king before him ever has. During his quest for learning, he heard about a book by India's philosophers, one so prized by that country's kings and scholars that it was kept under guard in their royal libraries. This book was the foundation of all education, the pinnacle of every science, the guide to every benefit, and the key to salvation in the hereafter. It supported and aided kings in all the ways they needed in order to properly administer their realms, and it educated the common people in the ways to please their king and to improve their lives. This work was *The Book of Kalīlah and Dimnah.*

1.4 When the king got confirmation of what he had heard about this book and its usefulness in educating and fortifying the intellect, he could not rest until he had acquired it and examined it. Being a man of intelligence and education, he also asked the people of his kingdom to search the realm for a learned man, intelligent, educated, literate in both Persian and Sanskrit, eager for knowledge, devoted to perfecting his education, and diligent in examining and explicating works of philosophy. Such a man was brought to the king: a handsome youth, highly accomplished, and perfect in intellect and education. He was a renowned physician, proficient in Persian and Sanskrit. His name was Barzawayh the son of Azdahar.[1]

1.5 When Barzawayh came before the king, he prostrated, then stood with head bowed. "Barzawayh," said the king, "I have selected

you because I have been told of your superior learning and intellect, your fine education, and your eagerness to pursue knowledge wherever it may be found, and because I have received word about a particular book in India."

The king then told him the story, reported what he had heard about the book, and expressed a strong desire to obtain a copy. "Prepare to travel, for I am sending you to India. Use your intelligence and astuteness to extract the book from their libraries and get it away from their scholars, jurists, and sages. Transcribe it into Persian in its entirety, for your benefit and for ours, as there is no copy of this book in any of our libraries or anywhere in the kingdom.[2] Take as much money as you wish. If it runs out, send word and I will supply you with more. Hurry, and spare no effort in your pursuit of knowledge. Whatever the expense, everything in our treasury is at your disposal to cover your expenses in the pursuit of knowledge."

The king commanded the astrologers to draw up a horoscope and select a day of departure, an auspicious hour, and a precise time. Barzawayh took twenty-five saddlebags of money with him, each containing ten thousand dinars.[3]

Barzawayh departed with the money and traveled quickly, day and night. Once he reached India and had settled, he acquainted himself with the court and mingled in gatherings of nobles and commoners. He inquired about the king's favorites and assistants, and about the scholars and philosophers. He began paying his respects by visiting them in their homes, and would inquire about the court. He told them that he was a stranger who had come to their land to pursue knowledge and education, and that he needed their assistance in his quest. He asked for their guidance and prayers, but carefully concealed the goal of his journey, hiding any mention of it, and only alluding to it indirectly. Thus he continued for a long time, leading the scholars to believe that he was sharpening skills he already possessed and furthering his knowledge of subjects he already knew, but all the while he was surreptitiously inquiring about the object of his quest.

1.6

1.7 In the course of his long stay, he made many Indian friends—nobles, commoners, scholars, and masters of every trade. He made one friend his confidant and adviser, on account of his refinement, exceptional learning, and superior understanding. He sought his advice and felt at ease with him in every circumstance, and kept only the object of his quest concealed from him. He subtly probed and tested him, to determine whether he should be the one to whom he entrusted his secret during his stay there. He continued to examine his character and eventually came to trust him, realizing that he was indeed the right person to entrust with his secret, and that he would shoulder the burden of his request and assist him diligently in what he sought. So he treated him with more and more kindness. Given the length of his stay, by the time he hoped to achieve his purpose, he had incurred considerable expenses, entertaining people, and dining and drinking with them, in order to learn who was trustworthy and able to assist him in his objective. Of all his acquaintances, he felt at ease only with this one friend.

1.8 After Barzawayh had sufficiently appraised his friend's intellect to trust him, he said to him one day when they were alone, "My friend, I don't want to hide from you any more than I already have, or keep you in the dark about me. I want you to know that I've come to India for a purpose, and it isn't what it appears to be. I know that a man of intelligence needs only certain signs—a look, a gesture—to know the secrets of another man's mind and his innermost thoughts."[4]

1.9 "None of this was hidden from me," said the Indian, "even though I haven't broached the subject of why you're here and what it is you're after, or mentioned that you're concealing the real object of your search by pretending it's something else. I wanted to treat you as a brother, so I was reluctant to confront you with my sense that you were hiding something. Now your secret designs are clear. Since you have spoken first, I will tell you about yourself, your secret mission, and why you've come. You've come to our country to rob us of our priceless knowledge and prized treasures, and take them back

to your country to satisfy your king. Your presence here is a deception, and your friendliness trickery. But when I saw your patience throughout your stay, your dogged pursuit of your goal, and your care not to utter a single word that might hint at your secret, my admiration for your intellect grew, and I wanted to become your friend. Never have I seen anyone of more refinement, of greater resolve in pursuit of a goal, better able to keep something secret, or of finer character, especially in a foreign land among people whose nature and disposition are unfamiliar to you.

"A man's intelligence reveals itself in eight ways—first, in his kind- 1.10
ness and graciousness; second, in knowing his soul's inclinations and safeguarding his tongue; third, in his obedience to kings and endeavoring to please them; fourth, in knowing to whom he can confide a secret and how to go about revealing it to a friend; fifth, in decorous comportment, elegant behavior, and sweet speech at court; sixth, in keeping his own secrets and those of others; seventh, in controlling his tongue and not saying anything without careful consideration and deliberation; and eighth, in answering at gatherings only what he has been asked and revealing nothing he will regret. Anyone who unites these qualities will attract good fortune and profit, and avoid misfortune and loss, and they all are clearly discernible in you and apparent to me. God keep you and enable me to enjoy your friendship! Anyone in whom these eight qualities are found deserves assistance in his quest and in reaching his objective. But what you are seeking frightens me and fills me with anxiety and trepidation. We beseech God to keep us safe."

Barzawayh felt confident about accomplishing his mission when 1.11
he discovered that the Indian had answered him gently, without rebuke or chiding, even though the Indian had realized that Barzawayh's friendship with him was motivated by deception and cunning in pursuit of his objective and saw him as someone intent on plunder and theft. Barzawayh replied, "It turns out that I won't need to rely on the many types of learning in which I am proficient, the premises I've established, the ramifications I've detected, the

branches and details I've devised—you've already divined a great deal about my intentions and discerned much on the basis of the slightest evidence. By your God-given intellect and discernment, you've spared me the trouble of arguing. I have received a response in a few words that apparently you will assist me in my mission. When a scholar learns a secret, when it is confided to a person of intelligence and discretion, he stands firm and fulfills all the hopes of the confider of the secret, as strong as a castle with a stone foundation, as a palm tree with deep roots, or as a mountain that winds cannot unsettle or shake."

1.12 "Nothing is better than love," responded the Indian. "Whoever has love in his mind deserves to have a friend who shares his mind with him and doesn't hold back his thoughts. Good conduct begins with the keeping of secrets; when a secret is shared by two, it makes its way to three, and when it does, it becomes such common knowledge that its keeper will be unable to disavow it, like clouds when they are scattered—no one doubts that they are scattered, and anyone saying so will be believed by everyone who sees that they are. For my part, I am exceedingly happy and delighted with your friendship and company. What you seek, however, cannot remain concealed; it will inevitably leak out wherever people assemble, and when it becomes public, my life will be in such peril that no ransom, however great, could save it. Our king is harsh and severe. He punishes the slightest offense. Imagine what he will do in a case like this!"

1.13 Barzawayh replied, "Scholars have praised the friend who keeps a friend's secret. I rely on you in the matter that has brought me here. I've revealed it to you, and hope it will succeed because of you. It is serious business and I know the danger is great, but I trust your acumen, discretion, caution, and resourcefulness in devising a way for me to realize my hopes through your efforts and with your good fortune and blessing, even if you are troubled by fear. I know you aren't afraid that I'll tell anyone about it; you fear that your compatriots who surround the king might discover the secret. But I don't

expect it to be leaked, since I am leaving and you are staying. For as long as I am here, there will be no third party; and when I leave, you need have no fear that you will reveal it to your own detriment."

At these words, the Indian granted his request and gave him the books he wanted. Barzawayh went to work interpreting and copying them. The task took so long that his provisions and expenses mounted. He wore himself out, staying up at night and working all day, fearing all the while for his life. When he was satisfied with the job he had done with the book, and with other books besides, he wrote to Anūsharwān that despite fatigue and fear he had completed the book he had been sent to get, along with other books of Indian science that he knew the king would need, and would convey to the king everything he had acquired.

1.14

Anūsharwān rejoiced when he read the letter and knew that Barzawayh had indeed accomplished his mission. Fearing, however, that fortune might intervene and frustrate his joy by depriving him of what Barzawayh had obtained, he immediately ordered a letter to be written commanding Barzawayh to come home without delay. He wrote that Barzawayh could expect to be handsomely rewarded as a result of the king's renewed esteem; that as the king's favorite he would be appointed vizier. The king dispatched the letter with a trusted courier. He ordered him not to take the main highway, lest he be intercepted and the secret be divulged, in which case all his efforts would come to naught.

1.15

When the messenger reached Barzawayh, he delivered the letter in secret. Barzawayh read it, packed his bags, and left immediately for Anūsharwān's court. As soon as Anūsharwān learned of his arrival, he ordered that he be brought into his presence. When he saw how pale, fatigued, and exhausted Barzawayh was, he took pity and said, "Rejoice, faithful servant; you shall soon taste the sweet fruit of your devotion. Be glad, for you have earned the gratitude of the entire nation as well as a great reward from us." He commanded Barzawayh to rest mind and body for seven days, and then return, which Barzawayh did.

1.16

1.17 On the eighth day, the king summoned Barzawayh and commanded all the high officials and nobles to attend. When they had all assembled, the king commanded that the books Barzawayh had brought from India be fetched. The books were opened and their contents read before the audience. When they heard the contents—the learning, culture, intelligence, and marvels the Indians had recounted via the tongues of animals and birds—they rejoiced and thanked God for what He had bestowed on them through Barzawayh. They invoked God's blessing on him and showered him with praise for his painstaking efforts to acquire the books and bring them.

1.18 The king commanded that the storerooms of jewels, gold, silver, and garments be opened, and entreated Barzawayh to take whatever he wished. Barzawayh prostrated himself before the king, invoked God's blessing on him, and said, "May God in His generosity grant the king honor in this world and the next, and reward him with the greatest reward. By the king's approval, God has freed me of need for the goods of this world by means of what He has bestowed on me at your hands, O great, generous, and fortunate king. I have no need for wealth. Nevertheless, because complying with the king's wishes and doing what pleases him gives me joy, I will take a garment of Qūhistān weave to wear while serving the king and at court."

1.19 Barzawayh agreed to take the garment home, if only to impress the royal family and the courtiers. He then said, "May God prosper the king and grant him honor! When a person of intelligence and cultivation is honored, given gifts, and treated with favor, it behooves him to be thankful, no matter how much he may deserve it. In gratitude to the king, I pray that God will grant him lasting joy and happiness in all things. But I have one wish—may God increase the king's might—which, to my mind, is the greatest, most perfect, and loftiest thing I could hope for after the king's approval. If the king sees fit, it will be easy for him to grant my request, but it will be something of great value and importance to me."

"Ask and you shall be given whatever you desire," said Anūsharwān. 1.20
"Plead and your plea will be granted most generously, for we deem
you worthy of a great reward. Even if you ask to be made co-ruler,
we will not deny your request—let alone anything else. Speak!
Everything you ask will be given freely and generously."

"May God honor the king and reward him well on my behalf," 1.21
said Barzawayh. "I cannot reproach the king for my fatigue and
trouble; on the contrary, he deserves my thanks for having com-
pensated me and for allowing me to share in this benefit. The king's
generosity and good opinion are the best compensation. May he
then magnify his favor toward his servant and perfect his favor to
him and to his family by commanding and enjoining Buzurgmihr
the son of Bukhtigān to employ his talents to compose a chapter
about my life and character. Let Buzurgmihr deploy his choicest
language, his most elegant words, and his best style. May the king
command that this chapter, when completed, be placed with the
book's other chapters, to keep the memory of me alive as long as I
am in the world and after my death. Should the king do this, he will
have honored me and my family for as long as this book continues
to circulate and be read in this world."

When the king, along with his scholars and officials, heard 1.22
Barzawayh's words, they were pleased by his reasoning, high-
mindedness, and desire for enduring honor in this world. "Gladly
and with pleasure!" replied the king. "Your request deserves to be
granted. It may seem momentous to you, yet how small it is com-
pared to what you deserve!"

The king immediately sent for Buzurgmihr and said to him,[5] 1.23
"Buzurgmihr, you know Barzawayh's devotion to us: how he strove
to please us, exposed himself to perils and dangers for our benefit,
and wearied himself to make us happy. You know the favor he has
done us and the knowledge and wisdom we have gained through
him. You know that we offered him wealth and gifts from our trea-
suries, but he accepted none of this. What he desires of us and for
himself is something very small, something he sees as a reward and

an honor." The king then explained Barzawayh's request. "I want you to assist me in this matter, for I request it and it will bring me joy. I want you to exert yourself, however difficult it may be, and to write a chapter to go with the other chapters of the book, one that mentions Barzawayh's virtues, his early life, his distinguished lineage, his profession, his education, and his eminence, including how we sent him to India on our mission; the boons he brought back for us, for which we have honored and distinguished him; and the state he was in upon his return from India. Use the most laudatory language you can find. Spare no effort, so that you bring joy to Barzawayh, to me, and to the entire kingdom. It will bring joy to you, in particular, because of your love of learning and of scholars. You will be the most fortunate of people, for whenever the book is read and Barzawayh is mentioned, you will share in Barzawayh's fame and acclaim. Make it the first chapter of the book. Let me know when you have finished it and placed it where it belongs, so I can assemble the most important people in the kingdom and you can read it to them. In this way, the full extent of your judiciousness, learning, and effort to please us will become visible to them."

1.24 When Buzurgmihr heard the king's words and the great importance he attached to the project, he bowed low and said, "Your Majesty, may God make your joy, gladness, and happiness endure! May He grant you in this world honor exceeding that of all creatures, and in the hereafter the best of dwellings with the righteous who merit the Gardens of Bliss."

1.25 Buzurgmihr left the king's presence and began composing the chapter the king had commanded. He described Barzawayh's life from the time his father sent him to be educated[6] until the time the king sent him to India, and he returned with the book. In this chapter, he described as best he could what he knew about Barzawayh's education and way of life, his manifest contempt for the world, his asceticism, his desire for the hereafter, and what his soul longed for in its ultimate destination. He omitted nothing concerning Barzawayh's character and profession, all in his best style

and manner of composition. Then he informed the king that he had completed the chapter and had placed it at the beginning of the book.

The king assembled high officials, nobles, and common folk. He 1.26 summoned Buzurgmihr to bring the book and—in Barzawayh's presence—commanded that it be read aloud to the people. Buzurgmihr stood up, opened the book, and read "The Chapter of Barzawayh" to the people. The king and all the people rejoiced at Buzurgmihr's intelligence and learning, and at the effort he had expended to praise Barzawayh without engaging in fabrication or specious claims. The king and all the nobles commended him, thanked him, and praised him in the highest terms. The king bestowed a splendid reward of money, jewels, and clothing, but Buzurgmihr accepted only one garment. He donned it to impress his colleagues, as it was a garment such as the king himself might wear. Barzawayh thanked him, kissed his head and hand, and then turned to the king and said, "Your Majesty, may God make your honor and beauty endure, for you have honored me by what you have commanded Buzurgmihr to write in this book."

Here ends the Account of How Anūsharwān
Sent Barzawayh to India and What Happened to Him.

The Book of Kalīlah and Dimnah[7]

2.1 This book is a work of parables and stories composed by the people
of India, who sought to incorporate into it the most eloquent speech
they could find in the style they preferred. In order to make their
intentions comprehensible, scholars of every nation and tongue
have employed a variety of devices and means when presenting their
arguments. One device was to put eloquent and elegant language
into the mouths of animals and birds. This enabled them to accom-
plish a number of things: they found a way to speak indirectly and to
communicate through implication.[8] Because such a book combined
entertainment with wisdom, the wise would study it for its wisdom,
and the simple for its value as entertainment; young pupils and
others would be delighted to read it and it would be easy for them
to memorize. When the young person reached maturity and grew
in knowledge, he would ponder what he had memorized—as it had
been recorded and inscribed in his heart without his knowing its
true nature—and would come to realize that he had acquired a great
treasure. He would be like someone who, on coming of age, discov-
ers that his parents had unearthed treasures of gold and silver, and
had established a bequest for him, freeing him from the need to toil
and seek a living. As each type of learning has many branches and
nothing can encompass them all, therefore the means that schol-
ars use to express them also need to be numerous. The reader thus
needs to know the method used to compose the book, otherwise

he will not comprehend its intention or realize what can be gained from it.

2.2
*The Man
Who Found
a Treasure
but Could
Not Keep It*

The first requirement for anyone studying this book is to begin with a careful, deliberate reading: the objective should not be to get to the end of the book, but to uncover its meanings and to understand and reflect on what is being read. No one will benefit from the book if his sole concern is to reach its end without thoroughly understanding what he is reading. The person who finds something and rushes to get it all at once, without stopping to understand it bit by bit, is likely to suffer the fate of the man who discovered a treasure but couldn't hold on to it. This man, I was told, found a treasure chest in a desert. When he opened it and looked inside, he saw that it was greater than anything he had ever seen, and said to himself, "It will take a long time to carry it away little by little—even a small amount will take me days. I will hire men to bring it all to my house." And that is what he did. He brought the men, and each picked up what he could carry, heading—as the man supposed—to his house. When the job was done and the hoard had been removed, the man went home, where he found nothing. He realized that everyone he had hired had made off with whatever he could carry. All the man had to show for it was the trouble he'd taken to extract the treasure.

Similarly, you shouldn't pass from one thing to the next until you thoroughly understand the first thing; don't try to get to the end before you know the beginning. Once you are able to read this book properly, you must understand what you are reading and familiarize yourself with it, so that you can put each thing in its proper place and connect it with its meaning. You must not assume that if you have read the book through and know its outward sense, you are done with what you need to know. You must realize that the book has an inner meaning still to be learned and that you will not benefit from the outward sense until you become acquainted with the inner meaning—just as unshelled nuts bring no benefit until you crack them and extract their kernels.

2.4

*The Man Who
Thought He
Had Mastered
the Rules of
Good Arabic*

The book has a hidden sense that the reader must seek to know. He must not be like the man in the story, who, I've been told, in order to acquire proficiency in the art of eloquence went to a friend with a clean page and asked him to write down the rules of good Arabic. The friend did so and the man took the page home and read it, but he didn't know the meaning of what he was reading—he was only reading the words on the page. Thinking he had mastered the contents, he took a seat among a group of experts. When he spoke and made a mistake, one of the men said, "Sir, you have made a grammatical error." "How can I speak ungrammatically," he replied, "when I have my page at home?"

2.5 We ought to seek knowledge. When we have found what we seek—when we have understood it, become acquainted with it, and have reached our goal—we should derive benefit from what we have learned and be guided by the education we have acquired. It is said that there are two things we can never have too much of: intelligence, and provisioning for the hereafter. It is also said that there are two things required by all who would live a full life: sound education and great wealth. Education, they say, makes intelligence apparent in the way that grease increases the brightness of a dim flame. It raises the station of its possessor just as a poloball struck by a strong man soars through the air.

A man who has acquired knowledge but hasn't put it to good use is like the man in the following story. Once, they say, a burglar entered a man's house at night. The man woke up and said to himself, "I'll keep quiet and see what he does. I'll leave him be, and when he's done taking things I'll get up, stop him, and spoil his fun." So he kept quiet in his bed as the burglar began prowling around the house. Finally, just as the burglar finished gathering everything he wanted and left, the man grew drowsy and fell asleep. He woke up after the burglar had gone and, finding the house empty, began to chide and berate himself. He realized that because he hadn't used his knowledge, he hadn't benefited from it at all.

Only through actions can knowledge be perfected. Knowledge is the tree; actions are the fruit. A man seeks knowledge only to benefit from it; if he doesn't benefit from it, he has no reason to seek it. You would marvel at the ignorance of a man who was told that a road was known to be dangerous yet followed it and came to grief. And the person who does what he knows to be low and vile, with bad consequences besides, may be even more certain of what he is doing than the man who puts himself at risk out of ignorance and caprice. You might compare him to a sick man who knows the difference between heavy and light food, yet is led by appetite and gluttony to eat food that is heavy. There is little excuse for committing vile deeds when we know they are vile, and little excuse for failing to do praiseworthy deeds when we know their merits and benefits. Neither mistake can be excused. It is as if two men, one sighted and one blind, were to fall into a well and perish. The ability to see did not save the man who could see, for both are in the same predicament in terms of dying. But to the intelligent mind, the man with full use of his sight has less of an excuse.

Those who seek knowledge only to impart it to others or to acquire fame are like a spring from whose waters people benefit, but that gets no benefit itself. The seeker of knowledge should first use his knowledge to counsel himself; then he should impart it to others. There are three things in this world a man should acquire for himself and impart to others: knowledge, wealth, and a desire to do good.

It has been said that you should not seek a thing until you know its value. To exhaust yourself in seeking something that will not bring you any benefit must be deemed ignorant. We know that some readers of this book are guilty of this. Beware of being one of them; don't be like the blind man who reproached the one-eyed man for being blind in one eye.

No one with any intelligence should try to benefit himself by harming his companion, for treachery never goes unpunished. The treacherous are likely to suffer the fate of the sesame merchant and his partner in the story. Once, we are told, there was a

2.7

2.8

2.9

2.10
The Sesame Merchant Who Tried to Cheat His Partner

sesame merchant who had a partner. They kept their sesame in one room, but each man kept his stock separate. One of them decided to make off with his partner's sesame. As a way to identify it when he came to take it at night, he covered his partner's sesame with his coat. Then he went to a friend, told him his plan, and asked for his help. The friend refused until he was promised half of the take. Meanwhile, the merchant's partner went to the storeroom and saw his share of the sesame covered with his partner's coat. Thinking that the partner had covered it to protect it from dust and vermin, he said to himself, "How nice of my partner to cover my sesame and be concerned about it!—but it's more fitting for his sesame to be covered with his coat." So he moved the coat over to his partner's sesame. Once night fell, the merchant and his accomplice arrived. They entered the dark room, and the man groped about until his hand touched the covered sesame. Thinking it was his friend's stock, he took half of it and gave his accomplice the other half. The next morning, when the merchant and his partner entered the room, the partner saw that it was his sesame that was gone, but was afraid to say anything, lest the disgrace be worse than the loss of the sesame.

2.11 To seek you must have a goal to reach. An endless journey is only going to exhaust your mount. You should not set your mind on something that doesn't concern you, or seek what doesn't exist or what no one before you has been able to find; but you shouldn't despair of finding what can be found. You should give your life in the next world precedence over life in this world; the less attached you are to life in this world, the less distressed you will be when you must leave it. You shouldn't despair of success, even though your heart is troubled. Two things, it has been said, are an adornment for everyone: piety and wealth. An analogy for this is provided by the blazing fire: it consumes everything thrown into it and converts it into a substance compatible with itself.

Sometimes you obtain what you never hoped to obtain, as happened to the man in the following story. Once, I've been told, there was a man who was destitute and naked. He lamented this to his acquaintances and begged for something to wear. He begged and begged, exhausting himself in the process, but got nothing and returned home in despair. That night, noticing that a thief had slipped into the house, he said to himself, "There's nothing in my house for this thief to steal. Let him do what he wants and waste his energy." The thief prowled about but found nothing to take. Exasperated, the thief said to himself, "I don't see anything here, but I don't want my hard work to have been in vain." He approached a large jar of wheat and said to himself, "Since I've found nothing else, I'll just take these provisions." So he spread out his coat and poured some of the wheat onto it. When the man saw him pour out the wheat to make off with it, he thought, "This is too much to bear. If this fellow takes my wheat, hunger and nakedness will join forces. To fall victim to both at one and the same time is sure death." So he shouted at the thief, who fled, leaving his coat behind. The man kept the coat, put it on, and returned the wheat to the jar.

2.12

The Poor Man Who Received an Unexpected Boon from a Thief

You shouldn't despair of obtaining a reward, nor should you seek something unobtainable, but you also shouldn't rely on this example and cease to seek knowledge or make no effort to find it. Favor and sustenance sometimes come to the person who isn't seeking them, and are withheld from someone who is; however, if you consider the matter, you'll find that those who seek and find outnumber those who find without seeking. Therefore, don't emulate the few who find without seeking; rather, emulate the majority who seek and find.

2.13

Make it your practice to compare one thing with another and benefit from your experience. Be wary of things that harm you and of things that resemble them. Compare one thing with another, so as to beware of one thing as a result of your experience with something else. The person who guards only against things he has already encountered has not made experience the arbiter of his affairs; he

2.14

will continue to be exposed to things he has never actually encountered. Guard against the things that harm others, lest you suffer the same. Don't be like the dove who sees her nestlings snatched and slaughtered, but stays put until she herself is snatched and slaughtered in turn.

2.15 Everything should have a measure that you neither exceed nor fall short of; to exceed a measure is like falling short of it, inasmuch as both miss the mark.

2.16 Know that every man is striving for something. If he strives only for the sake of the hereafter, his life will be accounted to his credit; if he strives for the sake of both this world and the hereafter, his life will be accounted partly to his credit and partly as a loss; and if he strives only for the sake of this world, his life will be accounted as a loss. It is said that in this world we should work as hard as we can to set three things right: our life in this world, our means of livelihood, and our relations with others. It is said that our affairs will not go well if we are discovered to have three⁹ things: laziness, missing opportunities, and believing every informant. Sometimes we are told something unacceptable to our reason, the soundness of which we do not recognize, but we believe it anyway. Three kinds of people do this.¹⁰ Sometimes a person believes a thing because he sees someone else believing it and it is his habit to follow him. Sometimes a person believes a thing out of a desire to believe the thing he is told. An intelligent person is always suspicious of his desires: he shouldn't accept what anyone says, even if that person is truthful to his friends, nor should he persist in an error or hesitate to examine what he has been told. When he is uncertain, he should not undertake a thing or embark on it until the right way becomes apparent, lest he be like a man who strays from the road and gets more and more lost: the farther he travels, the farther he strays from the road. Nor should he be like a man who rubs a mote of dust in his eye until a white film develops over the eye and destroys it. The intelligent person acts resolutely and knows that there will be a

reward. Doing to a comrade something that would distress you if it were done to you is to act unjustly.

Let the reader take what is in this chapter as a model to guide 2.17 him. Let him begin with it, for it will, I hope, increase his insight and his understanding of what he reads. Once he is acquainted with it, it will suffice and he will need nothing else; otherwise, he will not profit from the book.

When I saw that the Persians, in disseminating and translat- 2.18 ing this book from Sanskrit into Persian, had added the Chapter of Barzawayh the Physician, but made no mention of any of the things we've just discussed, I decided that when I translated it from Persian into Arabic I would add a chapter, one that would serve as a foundation for understanding the book for all who decide to read it and gain knowledge from it.

The Chapter of Barzawayh the Physician[11]

3.1 Barzawayh, the chief physician of Persia, who copied out and trans-
lated this book of Indian provenance, related: My father belonged
to the military, and my mother to a family of Zoroastrian clergy.
A mark of God's great favor toward me was that I was my parents'
favorite child and that when I reached the age of seven, they sent me
to study medicine.[12] When I reached the age of ten and had become
better acquainted with medicine and its merits, I thanked my par-
ents for their decision and was eager to study it further. I applied
myself and acquired enough confidence to trust myself attending to
the sick, and was about to begin my practice, but then I stopped to
consider. I asked myself to choose among the four goals for which
men strive. Which of these four, I asked, should someone of my pro-
fession seek? Which, when pursued, is most likely to give satisfac-
tion: wealth, pleasure, fame, or reward in the hereafter? Medicine,
I found, was praised by all who possess intelligence and was cen-
sured by no religious community. I read in medical texts that the
best physician was the one who practiced his craft solely for heav-
enly reward, so I decided to seek heavenly reward through medi-
cal practice and demand no other payment. I didn't want to be like
the unfortunate merchant who, for a worthless bead, traded a ruby
that would have made his fortune forever. I also read in the medical
texts that the physician who through his craft seeks reward in the
hereafter is not precluded from achieving success in this world. He
is like a farmer who plows and cultivates his land to grow crops,

rather than grass; yet inevitably the land produces various kinds of grass, too.

I therefore set out to treat the sick with my hopes fixed on reward 3.2 in the hereafter. I never abandoned a patient whom I hoped to cure or, if that proved impossible, whose pain and suffering I hoped to alleviate, without treating him to the best of my ability. If possible, I attended to him personally; if I couldn't, I diagnosed, instructed, and dispensed medicine. Hoping for reward in the next world, I demanded no fee or remuneration from any patient. I envied none of my colleagues who equaled me in knowledge but surpassed me in wealth and prestige, except for the righteous intentions and kind-heartedness they displayed in word and deed. I restrained my soul whenever it incited me to envy such men and to desire a similar social standing. "Soul," I said, "can't you distinguish gain from loss? Will you not stop yearning for something the acquisition of which brings little enjoyment and great trouble and confusion, the loss of which brings great anguish, and the consequences of which after death are grievous?

"Soul, will you give no thought to what comes next, after this 3.3 place? Doesn't that make you forget the things you crave in this world? Will you not abstain from sharing the love that ignorant sinners feel for this fleeting and transient companion, where nothing you possess belongs to you or remains with you, loved only by the deluded and the heedless? Turn from this foolishness and levity, and strive with all your strength, energy, and wherewithal to lay up for yourself future blessings and reward. Beware of procrastination and indifference. Know that this fragile body is prey to infirmities; that it is filled with impure, corruptible mixtures bound together by four mutually antagonistic humors, all sustained by life; and that life will end. The body is like an idol made up of separate parts held together by a single nail: if the nail is removed, the parts will collapse.

"Soul, don't be beguiled by the companionship of friends and 3.4 loved ones, and don't yearn for it too strongly; though their companionship brings joy and happiness, it also brings much suffering

and pain, and ultimately ends in parting. It is like a wooden ladle, which can be used in a heated pot for as long as it lasts, but which ends up being tossed into the fire as soon as it breaks.

3.5 "Soul, don't let the desire to please your family and relatives lead you to destroy yourself by acquiring possessions. Don't be like a stick of incense that burns up while others enjoy its fragrance. Don't be beguiled by wealth and rank that lead people to insolence, not seeing the insignificance of the things they prize until they're gone, lest you be like hair on the head: cared for as long as it is there, but discarded as refuse once it is gone. Treat the sick diligently. Don't become discouraged and say that medicine demands great labor or that people are ignorant of its benefits and value. Consider that to relieve one person's distress, and rescue him so that he returns to his former state of comfort and ease, deserves the greatest reward and finest recompense. If doing this for a single person deserves such credit, then what about the physician who, in search of reward, treats ever so many patients—people who, after suffering pains and ailments that prevented them from enjoying the world and its pleasures—food, drink, spouses, and children—become even healthier than they were before? Surely such a physician should harbor great hopes and be certain of a fine reward for his knowledge.

3.6 "Soul, don't think that the everlasting world of the hereafter is far off. Don't be so inclined to the transitory world of the here and now that in your haste to make a paltry profit, exchanging much for little, you become like the merchant, who, they say, had a roomful of peaches and said, 'It'll take too long to sell them by weight!'—so he sold them in bulk for a pittance."

3.7 When I had disputed with my soul, cautioned it, and gotten it to see this, it could find no escape; it conceded, agreed, and turned away from its former desires. I made it my practice to treat the sick for the sake of a reward in the hereafter. This did not, however, prevent me from amassing a sizable fortune, even more than I deserved, from kings, friends, and colleagues, both before I went to India and after my return.

But when I thought about medicine, I realized that no physi- 3.8
cian could treat a patient with a drug that eliminated the disease
so thoroughly that it, or a similar disease, or an even more serious
one, would never recur. I didn't see how I could regard something
as a cure, when there was no guarantee the same disease wouldn't
recur or a worse one develop. On the other hand, I found that work
focused on the hereafter offered a deliverance such that a person
would obtain a cure that removed his fear of all diseases. My esteem
for medicine accordingly diminished and I turned to religion.

When this occurred to me, I was unclear about the subject of 3.9
religion. In no medical books did I find any discussion that could
lead me to the religion that was truest and offered the best guid-
ance. Religious communities were many and diverse, and their
adherents fell into three groups: those who inherited their religion
from their forefathers, those who had been forced by fear to adopt
their religion, and those who sought worldly pleasures, status, and
prosperity through their religion. Each group claimed that their
religion provided true guidance and that all who thought other-
wise were in error. They differed greatly about the Creator and cre-
ation, the beginning and the end of things, and other matters. Each
rejected the other and denounced its adherents as enemies. I there-
fore decided to examine the doctrines espoused by every religious
community and its leaders, and look into what they prescribed and
what they prohibited. In this way, I hoped to distinguish truth from
falsehood, and then choose the truth and cling to it with confidence
and certainty, rather than believing in something I didn't know
or accepting something I couldn't understand. I did this and con-
ducted inquiries, but I found that no one went beyond praising his
own religion and disparaging the religion of those who disagreed
with him. It became clear to me that their responses and arguments
were arbitrary and tendentious. In none of them did I find any mark
of impartiality and truth that could be recognized and accepted by
a reasonable person.

This being so, I realized that it was impossible for me to follow any of them. I saw that if I agreed with any of them on something about which I had no knowledge, I would be like the credulous dupe who went to commit a burglary. He and his companions climbed onto the roof of a rich man's house at night. The householder heard their footsteps, woke up, and sensed their presence. Realizing that no honest man would be on the roof at that hour, he roused his wife and whispered to her, "I think thieves have climbed onto our house. I'll pretend to be asleep. You wake me up in a voice loud enough to be heard by someone on the roof, and ask, 'Master of the house, won't you tell me where you got all your riches and treasures?' When I refuse, keep badgering me with questions."

The wife posed the question as instructed, and the thieves listened in. "Woman," said the husband, "destiny has led you to great prosperity, so eat, drink, and hold your tongue! Don't ask me to reveal anything that might be overheard and have unpleasant consequences for you and me both."

But the wife insisted: "Tell me, husband! By God, there's nobody here to hear our conversation!"

And he responded, "If you really want to know, I accumulated this wealth and these treasures by stealing."

"How could that be," she asked, "when everyone thinks you're honest and upstanding—a man no one mistrusts?"

"That," he said, "is because I became so adept at thievery and went about it with such ease and skillfulness that I was above suspicion."

"How so?" she asked.

"I would go out with my friends on a moonlit night," he replied, "climb onto the roof of the house I wanted to rob, and find the skylight through which the moonlight shone into the house. Then I would recite the charm '*Shawlam, shawlam*' seven times, wrap my arms around a moonbeam, and slide down—my landing would escape detection. Next, I would stand at the base of the moonbeam and repeat the charm seven times; any money or valuables in the

house would become visible, and I would take whatever I wanted. Then I would grab hold of the moonbeam, repeat the charm seven times, return to my friends, get them to carry all I had seized, and we would slip away."

When the thieves heard this description, they rejoiced: "This is even better than the money we were going to get from this house: we now have knowledge whereby God has banished our fears and rendered us safe from the authorities." They waited until they thought the man and his wife had gone back to sleep. Thinking that what they had heard was true, their leader went to the skylight, said, "*Shawlam, shawlam*" seven times, threw his arms around a moonbeam to lower himself into the house, and fell head over heels. The owner of the house jumped on him and gave him a thrashing. "Who are you?" he asked.

"I am a credulous dupe," answered the man, "and this is what comes of believing nonsense."

Wary of believing something that might have perilous consequences, I went back to investigating the various religions, seeking to justify adherence to any one of them. But from no one I questioned did I receive any answers that my reason found worthy of belief or adherence. So I said to myself, "If I can find no one I can trust, the sensible thing is to adhere to the religion of my fathers." But try as I might, I could find no justification for doing so. By this reasoning, I realized, the sorcerer who discovers his father is a sorcerer is justified in following his example—clearly a specious argument. I was reminded of the glutton who, when rebuked, excused himself by saying that his father and grandfather were gluttons.

Finding it impossible to adhere to the religion of my fathers or to justify doing so, I wanted to devote more time to religious investigations and inquiries, but it occurred to me how near my end might be and how swiftly earthly life ceases. For all I knew, my departure from the world might come faster than the flick of a wrist. I planned to perform what I hoped were good deeds, but perhaps my hesitation, my querying, and my prospecting would keep me from performing

3.11

3.12

3.13

The Perplexed Lover

those very deeds, and perhaps my time might come before I found what I was seeking. Through my indecision and vacillation, I might suffer the fate of the man who, they say, fell in love with a married woman. She dug him a tunnel from her house to the street and put the key by the water jar, for fear they might be surprised by her husband. One day, while she and her lover were together, word came that her husband was at the door, so she said to the man, "Hurry and leave through the tunnel by the water jar!"

The man rushed to the place, but found that the jar had been moved. So he came back to the woman and said, "I got to the tunnel, but the jar you mentioned isn't there."

"Fool!" said the woman. "Why are you worrying about the jar? I only mentioned it to help you find the way to the tunnel."

"Since there's no jar by the tunnel," he replied, "you shouldn't have mentioned it and gotten me so confused."

"Good grief!" she cried. "Save yourself! Enough of this foolishness and hesitation."

"But how can I leave," he said, "when you've gotten me so confused?"

So he carried on until the master of the house arrived, gave the wretch a thrashing, and handed him over to the authorities.

3.14 Anxious about indecision and vacillation, I decided not to expose myself to the risk I feared. I decided to limit myself to deeds universally regarded as righteous and on which all religions concur. I avoided murder, assault, extortion, theft, and treachery. I kept myself chaste with respect to women. I guarded my tongue from lies and hurtful speech. I refrained from insult, obscenity, falsehood, slander, and ridicule. I strove never to wish anyone ill. I would not deny belief in the resurrection and reckoning, the reward and punishment. I avoided evildoers and associated with righteous and virtuous people. I saw that no friend or companion compares to knowledge, and that—with God's help and assistance—acquiring it is easy. I discovered that it has more affection for and devotion to those who possess it than his own parents. I came to see

that dispensing it does not diminish it, but that instead it increases when dispensed. I found that, in spite of constant use and wear, it is always replenished. And I saw that one needn't fear that it will be confiscated by rulers, or damaged by disasters, floods, fire, invasions, thieves, or vermin.

The man who shuns righteousness and its reward and is distracted from it by a taste of the world's sweetness has spent his days, I realized, like the merchant in the following story. Once, they say, a merchant who possessed many valuable jewels hired a man for a hundred dinars a day to bore holes in the jewels and prepare them.[13] He brought the man to his house. When the man sat down, he saw a harp lying in a corner of the room. "Can you play the harp?" the merchant asked.

3.15
The Merchant and the Musician

"Yes," replied the man.

"Go ahead!" said the merchant.

So the man picked it up and skillfully played one beautiful, plaintive air after another until the evening. The merchant forgot all about his jewels and was completely absorbed by the music.

When evening came, the man said to the merchant, "Pay me my day's wages."

And the merchant replied, "Have you done anything to be paid for?"

"Yes," said the man, "I did what you ordered me to do."

So the merchant paid him a hundred dinars, and his jewels remained unworked.

The more I considered the world and its desires, the more I was moved to renounce them. I resolved to cling to acts of devotion and asceticism. I realized that asceticism smooths the path to one's ultimate state just as parents smooth the path for their child. I recognized it as a shield sure to ward off persistent evil, and as the gate that opens to the garden of bliss. I found that the ascetic, after meditating, is enveloped in tranquility; in his calmness, he becomes humble; in his contentment, he is free of want; in his satisfaction, he experiences no anxiety. He has cast off the world, and has escaped

3.16

from its evils; he has rejected cravings, and has become pure; he is spared sorrows, and is safe from regret; he inspires no fear, so men do not fear him; he commits no transgressions, so is in no danger. The longer I considered the ascetic life, the more I was drawn to it, to the point that I was on the verge of living among its devotees.

3.17 Then I grew fearful that I might not be able to endure the life of an ascetic; that I might be hindered by the habits I had been raised and nurtured on. I was afraid that if I renounced the world and embraced asceticism, I might be too weak to sustain it; and that, having renounced the work I had formerly pursued in hope of a good return, I would be like the dog who passed by a river with a bone in his mouth and, seeing its reflection in the water, jumped in to grab it, losing what he had in his mouth and not getting what he coveted. Thus, although I had great respect for the ascetic life, I feared that my soul might become distressed and impatient. So I decided to remain as I was.

3.18 It then occurred to me to weigh the suffering and privation of the ascetic life, which I feared I might be too weak to sustain, against the troubles that assail a man in this world, and it became clear to me that there are no worldly cravings or pleasures that do not turn into suffering and cause sorrow. The world is like salt water: the more you drink, the thirstier you become. It is like a bone picked up by a dog: he smells meat and gnaws at the bone until his mouth bleeds— the more he gnaws, the more it bleeds. It is like a kite that snatches a scrap of meat: other birds mob and harass her until, exhausted, she flees and drops it. It is like a jar of honey with poison at the bottom: your first taste is sweet, but death lurks below. It is like a dream that brings the sleeper joy but vanishes as soon as he wakes. It is like lightning that flashes for a moment and disappears, leaving in darkness the person who hopes for rain. It is like the silkworm: the more silk it wraps around itself, the more difficult it is for it to find a way out.

3.19 As I pondered these things, I again considered my decision about the ascetic life and striving to attain it. I debated with myself, saying,

"It isn't right to flee from the world to asceticism whenever I ponder the world's evils, and from asceticism to the world whenever I consider the hardship asceticism involves—always shifting, without ever making a decision or resolving on a course of action, like the judge of Marw, who listened to the first litigant and ruled against his opponent, then listened to the opponent and ruled against the litigant."

I reflected on the annoyance and privation that the ascetic 3.20 endures and said to myself, "How small and insignificant a hardship, compared to the rest and repose of eternity!" And I reflected on the worldly pleasures for which the soul hungers and said to myself, "How bitter and noxious they are, leading as they do toward eternal punishment and humiliation! Why not regard as sweet the brief bitterness that brings lasting sweetness in its wake? Why not regard as bitter the brief sweetness that brings a legacy of lasting bitterness?"

I thought, if a man were offered a hundred years of being cut to 3.21 pieces every day, revived, then suffering the same again the next day, with the promise that when the hundred years were over he would escape all suffering and attain peace and happiness, he would be right to consider those years as nothing. How can one refuse to endure a few days of asceticism and a bit of discomfort, when the world is nothing but suffering, affliction, and torment? Isn't man buffeted by affliction from the moment he's conceived till the end of his days? Medical books tell us that when the fluid destined to become a fully formed infant enters the womb, it mingles with a woman's fluid and blood; it curdles and thickens, and the wind churns the water and blood until they become like the fluid from which cheese is made.[14] Then it thickens like curds, and the infant's organs take shape at the proper time. If it is a girl, it faces its mother's belly; if male, its mother's back. After sixty nights, its formation is complete. It lies constricted within the caul as if bound in a sack, breathing with difficulty, as if every one of its members were in fetters. Above it lie the heat and weight of the stomach, and below it lie darkness and constriction. It is connected by a cord from its navel to

its mother's navel, by which it lives and draws on her food and drink. Its hands are on its cheeks, its chin on its legs. It remains in this state of distress, darkness, and constriction until the day it is to be born. When that process begins, the element of wind is given power over the mother's womb and the infant becomes strong enough to move. It turns its head toward the outlet, and because of its narrowness it experiences what a man held in the stocks experiences when they are tightened.

3.22 When the infant arrives on earth and feels the wind or the stroke of a hand, it feels pain like the flaying of skin. From then on, it suffers in all sorts of ways: it hungers, but cannot ask for food; thirsts, but cannot ask for drink; feels pain, but cannot ask for help. Add to this the experience of being picked up and put down, swaddled and unswaddled, anointed and wiped clean. If the infant falls asleep on its back, it cannot turn over—not to mention all sorts of other torments that continue while it is a nursling.

3.23 Having escaped the torment of being a nursling, the child begins the torment of discipline, purges, pains, and sicknesses. When he comes of age, there are worries about money, family, and children, along with fatigue, greed, covetousness, and the risks of buying and selling. In all this, his four enemies—gall, phlegm, blood, and black bile—are in a state of commotion within him, as well as wind; add to this deadly poisons, venomous snakes, and the fear inspired by men and by wild beasts; and he must also fear heat, cold, rain, and wind. Then come the pains of old age, for those who reach it. Even if he has no fear of these things and is guaranteed safety from them, he has to meditate on the moment of death, when he will bid the world farewell. He should meditate on what will descend on him at that moment: separation from family, loved ones, and kin, and from all that we cling to and desire in the world, and the impending terror to come after death. He would be deemed feeble and negligent if he did not make diligent provision and prepare in advance for its sudden appearance and reject the lusts and beguilements of

this world that divert him and distract him from preparing for what he must face.

3.24 This is especially true in this decayed age, which resembles nothing so much as dregs and mud. We see Time everywhere turn its back, so that it is as if Virtue had bidden its people farewell. Gone are the things whose loss we lament; present are the things whose presence is noxious. It is as if Good were wilting and Evil flourishing; as if Error were advancing in laughter, Integrity retreating in tears; as if Justice had set, Injustice risen; as if Knowledge had been buried, Ignorance resurrected; as if Love had been disinherited, Hatred and Resentment rewarded; as if Obscenity were awake, Shame fast asleep; as if Lying were fresh and fecund, Truth withered and dry; as if Capriciousness and Misrule had been given authority over rulers; as if the Oppressed had been cast deep into the earth, and the Tyrant had raised his head in exaltation; as if Greed, its maw agape in all directions, were devouring everything near and far, and Contentment had become unknown; as if the Ignorant were lifting their heads to the heavens, while the Pious and Good were sinking into the bowels of the earth. Virtue has been hurled from the loftiest height into the lowest abyss, Villainy is revered, and Authority has passed from people of merit to people of mediocrity. It is as if This World were proclaiming in joy and delight, "I have caused Good to disappear and made Evil manifest."

3.25 When I considered the world and its affairs and how man, its noblest and most excellent creature, wallows in evil despite his station, so that evil becomes his main characteristic, I realized that anyone with the least intelligence could comprehend this and make provision for his soul, work for its deliverance, and seek its safety, and I was utterly amazed. I pondered and perceived that the only thing standing in the way of achieving this was a paltry bit of pleasure that comes from the senses—smell, taste, hearing, sight, and touch—the chance of obtaining something pleasant or hoping to gain a trifle of indescribable slightness soon to be cut short and

wiped away. That is what distracts man from attending to his soul and seeking deliverance.

3.26

I have tried to find an analogy for this. It is like a man driven by fear to take refuge in a well. He lowers himself into it and clings to two branches on its edge.[15] His feet find something to support them. He looks down, and behold—his feet rest on four snakes that have thrust their heads out of their nests. He looks at the bottom of the well, and behold—a man-eating dragon with its mouth agape. He looks up, and behold—at the base of the branches are two rats, one white, the other black, gnawing away tirelessly. While he ponders his situation and tries to find a way to save himself, he sees some bees nearby that have made a bit of honey; he tastes it, and it distracts him from thinking about his situation and finding a way to escape. He forgets that his feet rest on four snakes—any of which, for all he knows, might attack him at any moment—and that the two rats are busily eating away at the branches, and that when they are cut he will fall into the well. And thus he continues, blissfully heedless, until he perishes.

3.27

I liken the well to the world, filled as it is with plagues, evils, perils, and dangers. I liken the snakes to the four humors, any of which, when excited, is like snake venom and deadly poison. I liken the two branches to life: the black rat to night and the white rat to day. I liken their constant gnawing at the branches to the cycle of night and day that consumes one's allotted time. I liken the dragon to destiny, from which there is no escape. I liken the honey to the scant sweetness a human being receives that distracts him from his soul, making him forget his condition, diverting him from his welfare, and turning him from the path of deliverance.

3.28

In the end, I found contentment with my situation and with performing my work to the best of my ability,[16] hoping to find in future days a guide to lead me aright, a ruler over my soul, and aides to help me in my affairs.[17] I remained in this state and returned home from India, having transcribed a number of their books, including this one.

The Lion and the Ox

A parable about two friends driven apart by the slander of a treacherous liar.

King Dabshalim of India said to Baydabā, his chief philosopher, 4.1
"Tell me a parable about two friends driven apart by a treacherous
liar who incited them to enmity and hatred."

And Baydabā the Philosopher said, "When two friends fall victim
to a treacherous liar who comes between them, they part company,
turn their backs on each other, and sever relations. Here is a story
to illustrate this."

In the land of Dastanābad there lived a rich merchant and his 4.2
sons. When they came of age, his sons proceeded to squander their
patrimony and pursued no gainful professions. Their father admon-
ished them, saying, among other things, "My sons, a man in this
world seeks three things, which can be obtained by only four means.
The three things are: an ample livelihood, honor among men, and
provision for the hereafter. The four means needed to obtain these
three things are: acquiring wealth honestly; managing it well, once
acquired; making it bear fruit; and spending it to enhance one's life,
to please God, one's family, and friends, and to benefit oneself in
the hereafter. If you neglect any of these four, you won't attain your
desires. If you don't acquire, you'll have nothing to live on. If you
acquire, but manage your wealth badly, it will soon disappear and
you'll be left with nothing. If you spend it without investing it to
bear fruit, it will be depleted quickly, however little you spend. It
will be like kohl: you might only use a speck of it, but it disappears

quickly. If you don't spend it where it ought to be spent, you'll be no better than a pauper; yet even this will not prevent your wealth from vanishing, be it by fate or by accident. It is like a cistern full of water: if more water pours in and there is no outlet to release the flow, the water will find a way to seep out, or it may even burst out all at once and everything will be lost."

4.3

The Man Who Escaped from the Wolf

The merchant's sons took their father's advice to heart. The eldest set out for a land called Sūraqān to trade. On the way, he came to a place that was very muddy. He had a cart with him, drawn by two oxen: Shanzabah and Nandabah. Shanzabah sank into the mud. With the help of his assistants, the man managed to extricate him, but Shanzabah was exhausted. So the merchant's son left behind a man who was under orders to watch over the ox for a few days; when the man saw that Shanzabah had recovered, he was to bring him and catch up. But the next morning the man, tired of waiting, abandoned the ox, caught up with the merchant, and told him that the ox had died. The ox, for its part, set off and plodded on until he came to a grassy meadow, where he stayed, fearful that some inevitable misfortune might yet befall him—as happened, for example, to a man who, they say, was cutting hay when a wolf attacked him. Only when the wolf was near did the man notice and flee in terror toward a village on the bank of a river. When he reached the river, he found the bridge in ruins. With the wolf catching up, he said to himself, "What shall I do? The wolf is right behind me, the river is deep, the bridge is in ruins, and I can't swim. The safest thing is to entrust my life to the water." So he jumped in. The villagers saw him and pulled him out just as he was about to drown. Back among the villagers, as he leaned against a wall and began to tell them what had happened, the wall collapsed and killed him.

4.4

Shanzabah soon grew fat and flourishing, and, with his belly full of food, he began bellowing loudly. Nearby there lived a lion. As king of that region, he had an entourage of many wild animals: wolves, bears, jackals, foxes, and so forth. He was proud and given to relying only on his own judgment, which was far from perfect.

When he heard the ox bellowing—he had never seen an ox or heard one bellow—he grew frightened, but not wanting his soldiers to notice, did not leave his place.

4.5

Among the animals in his entourage were two jackals, one named Kalīlah, the other Dimnah. Each was clever and intelligent, but of the two Dimnah was greedier, more ambitious, and less contented. The lion had not yet made their acquaintance. Dimnah asked Kalīlah, "Brother, what do you think is wrong with the lion? Why is he staying put, not stirring or showing his usual liveliness?"

"Why are you asking?" replied Kalīlah. "It's none of your business. Our situation here is good; here at the king's gate we find enough to eat. We're not the sort of people who converse with kings, discuss their affairs, and inquire into unknown matters. Enough of this! Anyone who interferes in things that are none of his business will suffer the same fate as the monkey."

"And what was that?" asked Dimnah.

And Kalīlah told the following tale: A monkey, so they say, once saw a carpenter splitting a log using two wedges, straddling it like a knight on horseback. Whenever he split a cubit's length, he would drive in a wedge, sitting astride the log like a rider on a mount. At one point, the carpenter got up to relieve himself, and the monkey dashed over to try his hand at something that was none of his business. He straddled the log, with his back toward the split and his face toward the wedge,[18] with his testicles dangling in the split, and pulled out the wedge. When the wedge came out, the log closed with his testicles deep in the split. He fell over in a faint, and the beating he received from the carpenter was worse still.

4.6
The Monkey and the Carpenter

"I see what you're driving at," replied Dimnah. "But people who approach kings don't do it only to fill their stomachs. Stomachs can be filled anywhere. People who approach kings seek eminence: a position that enables them to gladden their friends and rise above their enemies. The lowest sort of people, content with a pittance, are like the dog that rejoices at finding a dry bone. People of valor and merit aren't satisfied with little, or content with a pittance; their

4.7

ambition aspires to what they deserve—like the lion who catches a hare, but as soon as he sees a wild ass, drops the hare and pursues the ass. Haven't you seen that a dog will wag his tail until he is thrown a crust, but a full-grown elephant, conscious of his strength and worth, won't eat even the best fodder until he is stroked and coaxed? Anyone who does not live in obscurity, a credit to himself and to his friends, lives a long life, however short his years. Anyone who lives life in solitude and scarcity, of little use to himself or others, lives a short life, however long his years. The worst lot, they say, is a long life lived in scarcity and distress. They also say that anyone interested only in his stomach is no different from cattle and sheep."

4.8 "I understand what you're saying," replied Kalīlah. "But think it over and consider your situation. Everyone has his place and measure. A person ought to be content and satisfied if he can hold his own. Our position is not so bad as to make us despise our present circumstances."

"Positions," replied Dimnah, "can be contested and shared.[19] The industrious person's industry raises him from a lowly to a lofty place, but the person who lacks industriousness lowers himself from a lofty to a lowly place. It is difficult and taxing to rise from the depths to the heights, but easy to fall from a height. It is like a heavy stone: hard to lift onto your shoulder, but easy to drop. So we ought to aspire to a higher place, seeking it through our industry, and not stay where we are when we can rise higher."

4.9 "What have you decided to do?"

"I intend to present myself to the lion straightaway. He's indecisive, and he and his soldiers are at a loss. I may be able to offer him good advice while he is in this state, and gain honor and glory in his eyes."

"What makes you think the lion is at a loss?"

"I know it by insight and by inference. A perceptive person can tell his companion's inward disposition from his visible demeanor and actions, and can infer it from his behavior and appearance."

"How do you hope to gain a place at the lion's court, when you've 4.10
never rubbed shoulders with rulers and know nothing about how to
serve them or behave in their presence?"

"A strong person is equal to a heavy burden: if he can pick it up,
he can carry it. No burden is too difficult for the strong, no work too
arduous for the bold. An unfamiliar place poses no challenge for a
person of intelligence, and no one can resist the blandishments of a
person who pretends to be humble."

"A ruler doesn't bestow favor on the best of his courtiers; he 4.11
honors them according to their closeness. They say that in this
respect a ruler is like a grapevine, which clings not to the noblest
but to the closest tree, just as women cling to the closest man. How
do you expect to gain a place at the lion's court, when you've never
been close to him?"

"I understand what you're saying, and you're right. But you must
realize that those close to the ruler at present weren't always so:
they had been distant from him and then became close to him and
acquired standing. I, too, will make every effort to acquire standing
with the lion. They say that no one can fail to obtain what he wants
from the ruler if he perseveres at the ruler's gate, swallows his pride,
bears insults, controls his anger, and treats important people with
skill."

"I understand. But let's assume you've gained access to the lion: 4.12
what is this 'skill' you hope to use to gain a place at his court?"

"Once I'm close to the lion, I'll get to know his character. I'll
defer to his wishes, humor him, and rarely disagree with him. When
he wants something I think is right, I'll praise it, extol its benefits,
and encourage him, so his delight with it increases. If he wants
something I fear may bring harm and disgrace, I'll make him see the
harm and disgrace in it. I hope that in this way the lion will become
more and more fond of me and see in me what he sees in no one
else. If you're cunning and skillful enough, you can turn truth into
falsehood and falsehood into truth—like an accomplished artist
who paints a wall with designs that seem to jut out from the wall,

though they don't in reality, and designs that appear to recede, though they don't in reality. Once the lion recognizes my merits and knows what I have to offer, he'll be all the more eager to honor me and keep me close."

4.13 "If this is your plan," said Kalīlah, "I must warn you about the dangers of associating with rulers. Scholars say there are three things that only fools attempt and from which few escape unscathed: associating with rulers, trusting women with secrets, and drinking poison as an experiment. Scholars have likened a ruler to a steep, rugged mountain where all sorts of pleasant fruit grow, but which is home to lions, leopards, and every kind of ferocious beast—the ascent may be difficult, but staying there is harder yet."

"That may be true," said Dimnah, "but without risk there is no reward. If we abandon a promising enterprise out of timidity or fear of the consequences, we shall never attain greatness. Three things, they say, can be accomplished only with knowledge, lofty ambition, and great danger: serving a ruler, sailing the seas as a merchant, and fighting an enemy. They also say that there are only two places where a man of great valor should be found: as an honored companion of kings or as a hermit in the company of ascetics—just like the elephant, whose majesty and beauty belong in only two places: either roaming free in the forest, or as a mount for kings."

"May God grant you success in your decision!"

4.14 So Dimnah set out, and when he arrived he greeted the lion. "Who is this?" inquired the lion of his courtiers. They told him Dimnah's name and the name of his father, and the lion said, "I used to know his father." He told Dimnah to approach, then asked, "Where have you been living?"

"In readiness at the king's gate," Dimnah replied, "waiting for some matter to arise in which I could assist the king with my counsel and my services. There are many occasions when the assistance of someone who seems insignificant may be needed. No one, however lowly or insignificant, is without some use. A twig thrown on the ground can be used to scratch an itchy ear. A creature that

knows the difference between gain and loss is even more likely to be of use."

The lion liked what he heard. Thinking that Dimnah might be blessed with good judgment and the ability to give sound advice, he turned to his courtiers and said, "Someone of intelligence and virtue may be of low station and obscure origin, yet his virtue will shine forth and be recognized, like a torch whose flame rises even if it is pointed downward." 4.15

When Dimnah saw that the lion was pleased, he said, "The king's subjects and courtiers have a duty to acquaint him with whatever knowledge and virtue they possess and offer him their opinion and advice. Only in this way can the king know them and assign them to the positions they merit. They are like seeds of wheat or barley buried in the ground: no one can determine what kind they are until they sprout. Those attending the ruler should inform him of their usefulness and skills, and the ruler should assign each to his proper place, both according to that person's opinion and advice, and according to the usefulness and skills the ruler discerns in him. 4.16

"They say there are two things that no one, not even a king, should put in the wrong place or remove from where they belong: an ornament fashioned for the feet and an ornament fashioned for the head. Someone who puts a foot ornament on his head or a head ornament on his feet will be taken for a fool; someone who sets rubies and pearls in lead doesn't diminish their value, but he demonstrates his ignorance. They also say: Never take as your companion someone who doesn't know where to put his right foot and where to put his left. 4.17

"Only a ruler can know a man's true potential, only a general can know a soldier's, and only a jurist can interpret religious law. Three things, they say, differ greatly in excellence though they are called the same thing: one soldier and another, one elephant and another, and one scholar and another. Many inexperienced helpers harm an enterprise: success depends on good helpers, not on their number. It is like a man who weighs himself down by carrying a heavy stone 4.18

and gets nothing for it, while another carries a ruby that doesn't weigh him down and gets what he wants for it. Reeds, however many, are useless for a task that requires a beam. A ruler shouldn't despise anyone's virtues, however lowly, for something small can turn out to be of great importance, such as a sinew from a corpse used in a bow, which is then treated with dignity when brandished by a king in sport and war."

4.19 Dimnah wanted the courtiers to know that any honor he received from the lion had not been conferred on him because the lion had known his father, but because of Dimnah's own intelligence and merit, so he said, "A ruler doesn't bring men near or keep them at a distance because of the respective positions of their fathers; he employs them according to the benefits each can bring. Nothing is closer to a man than his body, but sometimes part of it falls ill and only a medicine brought from afar can dispel the illness. The rat lives as a neighbor in the house, but when he causes damage he is driven out. The goshawk may be wild and from a distant land, but people acquire it, keep it, and treat it with honor because of its usefulness."

4.20 When Dimnah finished his speech, the lion was even more pleased. Replying graciously, he said to his companions, "A ruler shouldn't deprive a deserving person of his due or lower the rank of a person of merit, and he should remedy any past negligence. He shouldn't be fooled by an aggrieved party's apparent acquiescence and acceptance. In this regard, people are of two kinds. Some are ill-tempered by nature, like a snake: if someone steps on it and it doesn't bite him, he shouldn't be foolish enough to step on it again. Others are easygoing by nature, like cool sandalwood; and yet, if rubbed too much, it becomes hot and noxious."

4.21 When Dimnah felt confident that he had secured the lion's favor, he said, when he was alone with him, "I've noticed that the king has stayed put in one place for some time and hasn't moved. Why is that?"

"That's true," said the lion. But not wanting Dimnah to learn of his cowardice, he added, "But there's nothing wrong."

Just as the lion was saying this, Shanzabah gave a loud bellow, startling the lion into revealing his state of mind to Dimnah: "That sound you hear, I don't know what it is, but the voice must be matched by the body, and the body be matched by its strength. If that's the case, we can't stay here."

"Has anything besides the voice troubled the king?" asked Dimnah.

"Nothing else," replied the lion.

And Dimnah said, "This sound shouldn't distress the king and make him abandon his home. As they say, water is the ruin of a weak dam, a leaky vessel the ruin of a secret, slander the ruin of friendship, and fright caused by a loud noise and commotion the ruin of a cowardly heart. There is a story that clearly demonstrates that not all noises are to be feared." 4.22

"What story is that?" asked the lion.

And Dimnah told the following tale: A fox, they say, once came to a forest where a drum lay by a tree. When the wind blew, the tree's branches would strike the drum, producing a loud noise. The fox heard the sound and headed toward it. When he approached the drum and saw how big it was and how loud the sound, he went to work on it, splitting it open in anticipation of a hearty meal. But when he discovered it was hollow, he said, "For all I know, the lowliest things have the biggest bodies and the loudest voices." 4.23 *The Fox and the Drum*

"I've told you this story because I expect that if we get to the source of this sound you find so disturbing, we shall find it to be less than we imagine. If the king wishes, he can send me to investigate, and stay here until I report back with information about the sound." The lion agreed, and Dimnah set off to find Shanzabah.

After Dimnah's departure, the lion thought things over and regretted having sent him to investigate. "I was wrong to trust Dimnah with such a mission. No ruler should hasten to befriend, trust, or confide in anyone who has stood waiting at the king's gate and long been treated coldly for no offence; or who has been harassed; or who is notorious for his greed and covetousness; or 4.24

who has suffered misfortune or deprivation without amends; or who has committed a crime and fears punishment; or who is wicked and no lover of the good; or who has been barred from some authority or stripped of some property that he possessed; or who has held an office that was divided, reduced, or shared with someone else; or who has offended along with his peers, but who was punished when they were pardoned, or who were all punished, but he most severely of all; or who has proved his valor as well as his peers, but they received a greater reward; or who has a hostile, quarrelsome rival promoted over him; or who cannot be trusted in matters of religion; or who has sought to benefit personally from something harmful to his ruler; or who fears harm to himself from something beneficial to his ruler; or who has been friendly with the ruler's enemy. Dimnah is clever and shrewd. He has been left to languish at my gate and may bear me a grudge that could lead him to betray me and seek to harm me. If he finds that the owner of the voice is stronger and preferable to me as ruler, he may find his prospects brighter and go over to his side and point out my weaknesses."

4.25 The lion pondered these things. Eventually he became so upset that he rose from his place and began pacing back and forth, watching the road. At last he caught sight of Dimnah approaching. When he saw that Dimnah was alone, he relaxed and made his way back, not wanting Dimnah to think that anything had prompted him to move. When Dimnah arrived, the lion asked, "How did it go and what did you see?"

"I saw an ox. His is the voice you heard."

"How strong and powerful is he?"

"Not strong at all!" replied Dimnah. "I saw no haughtiness that would indicate strength. I went up to him and addressed him as an equal. He wasn't strong enough or powerful enough to do anything to me."

"Don't let that fool you!" said the lion. "Don't attribute it to weakness! A strong wind doesn't uproot grass; it uproots mighty trees. Great warriors only challenge one another."

"The king should have no fear of him," said Dimnah, "nor exaggerate his importance. If the king wishes, I will bring him here to become Your Majesty's willing and obedient servant."

"Do it!" said the lion, delighted by Dimnah's words.

So Dimnah returned to the ox and said, with no fear or hesitation, "The lion has sent me to bring you to him. He has commanded me to say that if you come to him promptly and obediently, I am to promise you immunity for your past misconduct in lagging behind and failing to present yourself to him. If you delay, I am to hurry back and inform him accordingly." 4.26

"And who," asked Shanzabah, "is this lion who sent you to me? Where does he live?"

"He is the King of the Beasts," replied Dimnah. "He dwells nearby and has many fierce animals with him."

Frightened by the mention of the lion and the beasts, Shanzabah said, "I'll go with you if you guarantee my safety."

So Dimnah allayed his fears and they set out together. When they came before the lion, he asked Shanzabah politely, "When did you come to this land? What brought you here?" And Shanzabah told the lion his story.

"Stay with me," said the lion. "I will be generous and treat you well." Shanzabah invoked blessings upon the lion, praised him, and remained with him. The lion brought him into his inner circle, treating him with kindness and honor. Because he saw that Shanzabah had good judgment and intelligence, he trusted him with his secrets and consulted him in his affairs. Time only increased his admiration and esteem, and he drew Shanzabah closer and closer—so much so that Shanzabah's companions became envious of his closeness to the lion. 4.27

Dimnah was consumed with envy when he saw that the lion favored the ox over him and the other courtiers; had allowed the ox private access to him, as well as to his evening conversations and entertainments; and relied on him for advice. He became so upset that he complained to his brother, Kalīlah, "Aren't you amazed at 4.28

my foolishness, at what I've done to myself, how I only considered the lion's gain, overlooking my own gain and loss by bringing him an ox who has ousted me from my place?"

"You've suffered the same fate as the ascetic," responded Kalīlah. "And what was that?"

And Kalīlah told the following tale: An ascetic, so they say, once received a splendid garment from a king. A thief noticed the garment and wanted it. Hoping to make off with it, he devised a way to steal it. He went to the ascetic and said, "I want to become your disciple, learn from you, and acquire some of your erudition." The ascetic agreed. The thief became his disciple and looked the part. He was courteous and served his master well. Once the master was comfortable with him and trusted him, the thief caught the ascetic off guard and made off with the garment.

With both man and garment missing, the ascetic realized that the disciple must be the culprit. He searched his usual haunts, and then headed for the city in pursuit. On the way, he came across two wild goats that kept butting each other until they drew blood. A fox came to lap up the blood, and while he was busy lapping, the goats turned on him and butted him to death.

The ascetic continued on his way and arrived at the city. It was late in the evening, and the only lodging he could find was the house of a woman who kept prostitutes, so he stayed there. The woman had a maidservant, whom she used to hire out, but the girl had become so enamored of one man that she didn't want to go with anyone else. Faced with the loss of the girl's earnings, the woman developed a grudge against the lover and devised a plan to kill him, on the very night the ascetic became a guest. She plied the lover with undiluted wine until he passed out and fell asleep with the girl beside him. When both were sound asleep, she took some poison she had prepared and put it into a hollow reed in order to blow it into the man's posterior. She put one end of the reed into his posterior and the other end into her mouth, but before she could do anything, a puff of wind from the man's posterior drove the

poison back into her throat and she fell down dead. The ascetic saw everything.

4.32

The Shoemaker's Wife and the Barber's Wife

The ascetic set out early the next morning to find somewhere else to lodge. He was taken in by a shoemaker, who told his wife, "Watch over this ascetic; be generous to him and take good care of him. One of my close friends has invited me to a party." The shoemaker then departed. Now, the shoemaker's wife had a lover. Their go-between was a barber's wife.[20] The shoemaker's wife sent the barber's wife a message, asking her to go to the lover and tell him to come, as the shoemaker was out drinking with his friends and wouldn't be back until late, and would be drunk to boot. The lover arrived at dusk and sat by the gate waiting for the shoemaker's wife.

Late that evening, the shoemaker returned home drunk. He became suspicious and flew into a rage when he saw his wife's lover. He went into the house, grabbed his wife, beat her, and tied her to a post in the bedroom. When everyone was fast asleep, the barber's wife came over to her and said, "Your lover has been sitting by the door a long time! What do you plan to do?"

4.33

"Don't you see the state I'm in?" she replied. "If you'd be so kind as to untie me, I'll tie you up in my place for an hour, go to my lover, and come back as quickly as I can."

The barber's wife agreed, and she untied the shoemaker's wife and took her place. But the shoemaker awoke before his wife returned. He called out her name but the barber's wife, afraid he might recognize her voice, didn't reply. He called her and upbraided her repeatedly; still she made no reply. He got angrier and angrier, until he went at her with a knife and cut off her nose, saying, "Take this and go join your lover!"

When the shoemaker's wife came back and found her friend mutilated and her husband asleep, she released her friend and tied herself up in her place. The barber's wife picked up her nose and returned home. The ascetic saw and heard everything.

4.34

The shoemaker's wife raised her voice to God in prayer, beseeching Him, weeping, and calling to her husband: "If my husband has

treated me unjustly, give me back my nose, whole as it was!" Then she called out to her husband: "Get up, you evildoer! See how God has undone your work and has had mercy on me. He has given me back my nose, just as it was." The shoemaker exclaimed, "What is all this talk, you witch?" He got up and lit a lamp, and when he looked at his wife and saw that her nose was whole, he repented to God and apologized to his wife, asking her to forgive him.

4.35 Back home, the barber's wife turned over every conceivable scheme in her mind. "What explanation can I present to my husband and to people for the loss of my nose?" Her husband awoke at dawn and called out to her: "Bring me my things! I want to pay a visit to an important customer." But the only thing she brought him was his razor. "My whole kit!" he repeated, but again she brought just the razor. The barber flew into a rage and hurled the razor at her, whereupon she threw herself to the ground, wailing, "My nose, my nose!" And she kept on shouting and crying out until her kinsmen came and hauled her husband off to the judge, who asked the barber, "What led you to cut off your wife's nose?" He had no argument to offer in his defense, so the judge ordered that he be punished.

Just as the barber was being led to his punishment, the ascetic arrived, and approached the judge. "There isn't any doubt about it!" the ascetic said. "It wasn't the thief who robbed me, it wasn't the wild goats who killed the fox, it wasn't the poison that killed the woman, and it wasn't the barber who cut off his wife's nose—we all did it to ourselves!" The judge asked the ascetic to explain, which he did.

4.36 Dimnah said, "I understand the story, and it does resemble my situation. Indeed, no one has harmed me but myself. But what's to be done now?"

"Tell me what *you* think."

"For the time being, I'm not seeking a higher place than before; I only want to regain what I had. There are three things a prudent man must take into account and work out how to deal with. He

must consider past losses and gains, guarding against the recurrence of past losses and seeking ways to repeat past gains. Next, he must consider present gains and losses, striving with all his might for what results in profits and avoiding anything that results in losses. Finally, he must consider future gains he hopes for and future losses he fears, in order to obtain what he hopes for and guard against what he fears. When I consider how to recover the position that was wrested from me, the only remedy I can find is to scheme against this grass eater until the ox breathes no more. Once he has left the lion, not only do I regain my position, but it may also be better for the lion, as his excessive devotion to the ox is likely to disgrace him and spark resentment in most of his courtiers."

"But," said Kalīlah, "I see no disgrace or harm in how the lion views the ox or in the favored position he enjoys." 4.37

"Not so!" replied Dimnah. "Six things can destroy a ruler: privation, sedition, self-indulgence, brutality, the adversity of fate, and folly. Privation is the loss or dismissal of aides, advisers, and administrators who possess good judgment, courage, and trustworthiness. Sedition is civil war and the outbreak of fighting among the people. Self-indulgence is infatuation with women, conversation, drinking, hunting, or anything of that sort. Brutality is excessive harshness, the tongue quick to revile, the hand quick to strike at the wrong time. The adversity of fate includes disasters such as famine, plague, flooding, poor harvests, and the like. Folly is resorting to harshness when leniency is required, and leniency when harshness is required. The lion has become too fond of the ox, and that, as I said, is likely to harm and disgrace him."

"But how can you overcome the ox when he's stronger than you, 4.38 is shown more honor by the lion, and can count on more friends and supporters?"

"Pay no attention to my size. Things aren't always decided by strength and weakness. Many a small, weak creature has accomplished by cleverness, intelligence, and cunning what many strong,

powerful creatures were unable to achieve. Haven't you heard how a crow outwitted the cobra and killed him?"

"How did that come about?"

4.39

The Crow Who Outwitted a Cobra

And Dimnah told the following tale: A crow, so they say, had a nest in a tree on a mountain, not far from a cobra's den.[21] Whenever the crow had chicks, the cobra went to the nest and ate them. When the cobra had done this many times, the distressed crow complained to a friend of his, a jackal: "I've decided to ask you about something I intend to do, to see whether you agree with me about it."

"What is it?" asked the jackal.

"I intend to go to the cobra while he's asleep and peck out his eyes."

"That's not a good plan," replied the jackal. "Find a way to defeat the snake without risking your life. Beware lest you suffer the fate of the heron[22] who wanted to kill the crab but ended up killing himself."

"How did that come about?" asked the crow.

4.40

The Heron Who Would Kill a Crab but Killed Himself

And the jackal told the following tale: A heron built his nest beside a pond teeming with fish. He lived there for a time, but then grew old and could no longer fish. Weary and hungry, he looked for ways to cope with the situation. One day he sat himself down and made a show of sadness. From afar, a crab saw the state he was in and how sad he was, so he approached and said, "I see that you're very dejected."

"How could it be otherwise?" replied the heron. "Up to now, I've sustained myself by catching one or two fish every day. It was enough for me to live on, and it didn't decrease the fish population. But today I saw two fishermen come by, and one said to the other, 'I think there are lots of fish here. Why don't we catch them?' His companion said, 'I know a place with fish farther on. I think we should begin there; when we finish there, we can come back here.' I know that when they finish there, they'll come back and catch every single fish in this pond; if this happens, it will be the end of me."

The crab went to the community of fishes and informed them. 4.41
They in turn went to the heron to seek his advice. "We've come for
your advice," they said. "An intelligent person doesn't fail to ask his
enemy for advice, if the latter has good judgment and both stand to
lose or gain in the affair. Your judgment is good, and our survival is
to your advantage, so give us your advice."

"I don't think we can take on the fishermen and fight them," said
the heron. "The only solution I can think of is a nice pond I've dis-
covered with plenty of water, reeds, and vegetation. If you move
there, you'll thrive and prosper."

"Who but you can do us that favor?" they asked.

"I will," he said.

So each day the heron would pick up two fish and carry them off 4.42
to a hill, where he ate them. The rest of the fish had no idea what
was happening.

Then one day the crab came to the heron and said, "I, too, am
worried about staying here. Take me to that pond."

The heron picked up the crab, planning to make him his meal for
the day; but when he came to the hill where he would eat the fish,
the crab looked down and saw piles of fish bones. Realizing that the
heron was the offender and that he intended for him the same fate as
the fish, he said to himself, "When you meet your enemy in a place
where you know you'll die whether you fight or not, fight to save
your honor." So he gripped the heron's neck with his pincers and
squeezed so hard that the heron fell to the ground, taking the crab
down with him. The heron died, but not the crab, who went back to
the fish and told them what had happened.

The jackal said, "I've told you this tale to teach you that some 4.43
schemes are fatal to the schemer. But I'll show you how you can
bring about the cobra's death."

"How?" he asked.

"Fly off and see if you can get hold of a valuable piece of wom-
en's jewelry. Snatch it and fly away in short bursts. Fly, then land,

then take off again, so the people chasing you can keep you in their sights. When you reach the cobra's den, drop the jewelry there. When the people get there, they'll retrieve the jewelry and rid you of the cobra."

4.44 So the crow flew off and circled the sky looking for jewelry. He found a woman on a rooftop who had taken off her clothes and jewelry to bathe. He snatched a necklace and flew away, alighting from time to time so that he could be seen. When he reached the cobra's den, he dropped the necklace in full view of the people following him. They went to fetch the necklace and discovered the cobra there. They killed it and took their necklace.

4.45 Dimnah said to Kalīlah, "I've told you this tale to demonstrate that ingenuity can accomplish what force cannot."

"That would be so," replied Kalīlah, "if the ox didn't possess good judgment as well as strength, but he has good judgment and intelligence in addition to strength. How will you deal with that?"

"The ox, as you say, may be strong, powerful, and intelligent, but he's not on his guard against me and has no fear of me, so I'm likely to vanquish him, just as a rabbit once vanquished a lion."

"And how did he vanquish him?"

4.46

The Rabbit Who Vanquished a Lion

And Dimnah told the following tale: Once, they say, there lived a lion in a well-watered, fertile, grassy land. The animals there were surrounded by streams and pastures, but couldn't enjoy these blessings because of their fear of the lion. So they conferred among themselves, then went to the lion and said, "Every day you wear yourself out trying to catch one of us. We have an idea that will make things easier for you and for us. If you guarantee our safety and stop terrifying us, we promise to provide an animal every day and send it to you for your lunch."

The lion agreed. He made peace with them on these terms, and they honored their end of the bargain for a time. They drew lots every day and sent the unfortunate animal to the lion to be eaten, accompanied by an escort.

One day, a rabbit drew the short straw and she said to the others, 4.47
"If you do me a favor—it won't harm you at all—I may be able to rid
you of the lion."

"What sort of favor?" they asked.

"Very simple," she said. "Command my escort not to hurry me
along; I'll take my time, and the lion's lunch will arrive late. Also,
tell my escort to lag behind, so I arrive alone."

"Agreed," they said, and the rabbit set off, taking her time. When 4.48
it was past the lion's lunchtime, she approached at her leisure. The
lion, hungry and angry because his lunch was late, had risen to his
feet and was pacing back and forth. When he saw the rabbit, he said,
"Where have you come from? And where are the animals?"[23]

"I am the animals' messenger," she replied. "They dispatched me
with a rabbit, but when I was close, a lion turned up and snatched
her away, saying, 'I have a better claim to this land and its animals!'
'But this is the king's lunch!' I said. 'The animals have sent it to him.
Don't make him angry!' But he cursed and reviled you. I've come as
quickly as I could to bring you this information."

The lion grew angry. "Come with me," he said, "and show me this 4.49
lion." So she took him to a deep well filled with clear water. "This,"
she said, "is the lion's lair. I'm afraid of him, but if you hold me in
your arms I'll show him to you." So he held her in his arms. "Look
down into the well," she said, "and you'll see the lion." He looked
down and caught sight of his own reflection and the reflection of the
rabbit in his arms. When he saw his and the rabbit's reflection, he
leapt into the well and drowned, and the rabbit escaped.

Kalīlah said, "If you can destroy the ox without harming the lion, 4.50
go ahead and do it; his position has harmed me and you, as well as
members of the army. But if you can't do it without harming the
lion, don't do one at the expense of the other: that would be both
betrayal and villainy."

Dimnah avoided the lion for a few days; then, with a show of cau- 4.51
tious reserve, he turned up when the lion was alone.

"What's kept you away?" asked the lion. "I haven't seen you for a long time. Is everything all right?"

"I wish!"

"Has something happened?"

"Yes. Something neither of us wanted, Your Majesty."

"What is it?"

4.52 Dimnah replied, "A speaker who dares to deliver an unwelcome message is acting foolishly unless he trusts the intelligence of the person he is addressing. The person addressed, if intelligent, will tolerate the message and listen to it because it might alert him to a potential disaster. The speaker will bear with any frightful consequences for the sake of fulfilling a duty incumbent upon him. Trusting in Your Majesty's excellent judgment and patience, I dare to inform you of something that has come to my knowledge. Unwelcome as it may be, I am confident that you know my devotion to you and how I put your welfare ahead of mine. You might not believe what I'm about to tell you; nonetheless, when I call to mind how our lives as animals are bound up with your life, I can do no less than fulfill my duty to inform you, even though you haven't asked it of me and even though I fear you might not be pleased. To withhold advice from your ruler, conceal illness from your physicians, or withhold an opinion from your brethren is to betray yourself."

4.53 "What is it?" asked the lion.

"A reliable source has informed me that Shanzabah met secretly with your chief officers and said to them, 'I've gotten to know the lion and put his judgment, strength, and shrewdness to the test. As a result, it's clear to me that he is weak and lacks judgment, and that he and I are bound to have a falling out.' When I heard this, I realized that Shanzabah was a deceitful traitor. You've honored him in every way and have made him your equal—this has finally incited him to this clear treachery and malice. He hopes that your kingdom will become his once you're out of the way, and he's sparing no effort in scheming against you. He has intelligence, good judgment, friends, and accomplices. They say that a king should strike down

anyone he discovers who rivals him in rank, appearance, wealth, and followers; otherwise, he'll be the one who is overthrown.

"Your Majesty is experienced in worldly affairs and a good judge 4.54 of them. I advise you to deal with the matter before it reaches a crisis. Don't wait for it to happen, lest it escape your control and cause irreparable damage. They say there are three kinds of people: prudent, quick-witted, and feckless. One kind of prudent person isn't confounded when trouble comes. He isn't thrown into confusion; he doesn't falter in his judgment, resourcefulness, and ingenuity— he hopes thereby to find a way out of trouble. Even more prudent is the person who is ahead of events and is prepared, who foresees an event before it happens, sizes it up, and looks for the means to deal with it as if it were already upon him. He stops the disease before it strikes and wards off trouble before it happens. The feckless person, on the other hand, hesitates and entertains vain hopes until he perishes. The story of the three fishes is an example of this."

"What happened to them?" asked the lion.

And Dimnah told the following tale: They say there was a pond 4.55 where three big fishes lived: one quick-witted, one prudent, and *The Three* one feckless. The pond was on a highland that was hardly ever vis- *Fishes* ited. One day, however, two fishermen passed by, saw the three fishes, and decided to return with their net and catch them. At the sight of the fishermen, the most prudent of the three fishes became apprehensive and fearful: she immediately left the pond by following its outlet to the river. The quick-witted fish, less intelligent, put off devising anything until the fishermen returned. At the sight of them, she realized what they intended to do, but discovered that they had blocked the outlet. "I was careless," she said, "and this is the result. Now that I've been so careless, how can I save myself? Desperate last-minute schemes rarely succeed! But someone with intelligence doesn't despair or give up looking for a solution!" So she played dead and floated on the water, belly up. The fisherman took her and, assuming she was dead, set her down on the ground between the pond and the river. She then jumped into the river and

escaped. As for the feckless fish, she swam back and forth and was caught.

4.56 "I understand what you're saying," said the lion, "but I can't believe the ox would deceive me and wish to harm me after I've treated him so well. Why would he, when he has experienced no mistreatment at my hands?"

"But that," said Dimnah, "is the very thing driving him to it! Seeing as you've never mistreated him, and have favored him in every way and raised him to every rank, the only rank left for him to covet is yours! A low, incompetent person remains a useful counselor until he rises to a rank he doesn't deserve, but as soon he reaches it, he becomes dissatisfied; his loyalty turns into duplicity and his benevolence into treachery and harm, and he uses duplicity, treachery, and disobedience to seek an even higher rank. Such a low, ungrateful person serves the ruler and is loyal to him only out of fear or need; as soon as he feels himself secure and loses his fear, he reverts to his original nature—like a dog's curly tail that has been tied straight: as long as it is tied, it stays straight, but once released it goes back to being bent and crooked.

4.57 "Your Majesty, remember that anyone who doesn't accept the advice of his loyal advisers will regret his decision. He will be like a patient who abandons his doctor's prescription and follows his own appetites instead. A minister's duty is to inform the ruler of the facts, to benefit him and increase his renown, and to abstain from anything that would harm or disgrace him. The best brother flatters least when giving advice, the best deed has the most pleasing consequences, the best praise comes from the mouths of the righteous, the best governance is not mingled with arrogance, the best wife agrees with her husband, the richest of the wealthy aren't held prisoner by greed, the best friend never quarrels, and the best character traits promote the fear of God. They also say that a man who lays his head to rest on fire and lies on a bed of snakes is more likely to enjoy a sound sleep than someone who senses that his companion

harbors enmity against him day and night. The weakest king is the most remiss and least attentive to his affairs; the one who, like an elephant in rut, pays no attention to anything. He makes light of anything unexpected, and if an affair goes awry, he vents his wrath on his companions."

"You've spoken harshly," said the lion, "yet harsh words from 4.58 a sincere adviser must be borne. But even if Shanzabah were my enemy, as you say, he couldn't harm me. How could he, a grass eater, harm me, a meat eater? For me, he's nothing more than food! I'm not afraid of him. What's more, how can I betray him when I've given him a promise of safety, honored him, and praised him in front of all my troops? If I begin to behave differently, I make myself look like a fool and break my own promise."

"Don't delude yourself," replied Dimnah, "by saying that he's nothing more than food for you and that you do not fear him. Even if Shanzabah can do nothing to you on his own, he'll use others to scheme against you. They say that if a guest of unproven character asks you for an hour's hospitality, beware lest evil befall you because of him, as happened to the louse."

"What happened to it?" asked the lion.

And Dimnah told the following tale: A louse, they say, lived for 4.59 a time in a nobleman's bed. She would sip his blood while he slept *The Louse and* and would crawl over him so gently that she escaped notice. One *the Flea* night, a flea asked to be her guest and the louse agreed: "Spend the night with us. You'll enjoy tasty blood and a soft bed." So he did. But when the man got into bed, the flea gave him such a vigorous bite that it woke him up. The man ordered that the bed be thoroughly checked. During the search, the flea got away, but they found the louse and killed her.

"I've told this story to show Your Majesty that one can never be 4.60 safe from a troublemaker; even if he's too weak to do anything himself, disaster may come about because of him. Although you don't fear Shanzabah, I worry about those in your army whom he has

incited to hostility and emboldened against you. Still, I know that he himself will inevitably clash with you and will entrust the affair to no one else."

Dimnah's words made a deep impression on the lion. "What do you advise?" he asked.

"A rotten tooth," replied Dimnah, "causes pain until it is pulled. The way to get relief from a food that makes you nauseous is to throw it up. The remedy for an enemy you fear is to get rid of him."

"You've given me doubts—I don't want Shanzabah living anywhere near me. I'll send him a message about how I feel and command him to go elsewhere."

4.61 Dimnah wasn't pleased. He knew that if the lion spoke with Shanzabah and heard his defense, he would realize that there was no substance to the matter; that Dimnah had been lying, and his scheme would be exposed. So Dimnah said to the lion, "I don't think it wise to send Shanzabah a message and bring up his offense. Consider the matter, Your Majesty. You have the advantage as long as Shanzabah has no idea that you've received word of his actions. If he senses that you have, I'm afraid he'll immediately try to get the better of you. If he fights you, he'll fight well prepared; if he leaves you, he'll leave in a way that shows his superiority and that brings you shame. Furthermore, prudent kings do not inflict public punishment on those whose offense has not become public. Every crime has its punishment: secret punishment for a secret crime, public punishment for a public crime."

4.62 "A king who punishes or humiliates someone on suspicion," said the lion, "without being certain about the crime, punishes and humiliates no one but himself."

"In that case," replied Dimnah, "let Shanzabah come into your presence only when you're ready. Don't let him catch you off guard. If you look at him when he arrives, I'm sure you'll see that he's planning to do something terrible. Look for these signs: see if his color changes and his muscles twitch; see if he looks right and left, waving his horns as if preparing to gore."

"I'll be on the alert," said the lion. "If I see the signs you've mentioned when he enters, there'll be no doubt about what he intends."

Once Dimnah had incited the lion against the ox and was satis- 4.63
fied that he had put the thoughts he wanted into his mind, so that
the lion would be alert and ready for the ox, he wanted to go to
Shanzabah to incite him against the lion. But he wanted this done
by the lion's command; he did not want the lion to learn about the
meeting from someone else and become suspicious. So he said to
the lion, "Why don't I go and see Shanzabah and listen to what he's
saying? Maybe I can learn some of what he has in mind." The lion
gave his permission.

Dimnah set off. He appeared before Shanzabah, pretending to 4.64
be sad and dejected. Shanzabah welcomed him as soon as saw him:
"I haven't seen you for days! What's kept you away? Is everything
all right?"

"How can everything be all right," replied Dimnah, "when you're
not your own master; when your fate lies in the hands of a person
who can't be trusted and of whom you're in such constant fear and
danger that not a moment goes by without you fearing for your life?"

"What has happened?" asked Shanzabah. 4.65

"What was fated to happen has happened—and who can fight fate?
Can anyone attain greatness in this world without being destroyed
or becoming insolent? Can anyone follow desire without coming to
a bad end? Can anyone keep company with women without being
seduced? Can anyone beg from churls without being humiliated?
Can anyone consort with evildoers and escape safely without regret?
Can anyone serve a ruler and remain in his good graces? How right
the one who said that rulers, in their scant loyalty to companions and
abandonment of those they no longer need, are like a whore with her
customers: when one leaves, another takes his place!"

Shanzabah responded, "Your words make me fear that some-
thing has filled you with misgivings about the lion."

"Something has indeed filled me with misgivings, but it doesn't
concern me personally," said Dimnah.

4.66 "Who then?" asked Shanzabah.

"You know the claim you have on me," said Dimnah, "and the affection between us, and the promise of protection I gave you when the lion sent me to you. So now I must protect you and tell you what I've learned that makes me fear for you."

"What is it?" asked Shanzabah.

"A reliable source has informed me that the lion said to one of his companions, 'I like how fat this ox has become. Since I don't need him, I think I'll eat him and we can feed his meat to my companions.' As soon as I heard this, I realized his ingratitude and wickedness. I've come to inform you and do my duty by you, so that you can devise a subtle and clever plan for yourself."

4.67 When the ox heard these words, he recalled the solemn promise Dimnah had once made to him. Thinking about the lion and believing that Dimnah had given a true account of his intentions, he became worried. "It isn't right for the lion to act so treacherously when I've never offended him or any of his troops. Lies must have turned him against me and made him suspicious. The lion has bad companions, and they've made him believe what has been reported to him about others. Bad company often makes you suspicious of good people; it leads you to make the same mistake as the duck who, they say, saw the reflection of a star in the water and, thinking it a fish, tried to catch it. After repeated tries, she realized that it was nothing. The next evening, she saw a fish there, but didn't try to catch it, thinking it was like the previous occasions.

4.68 "It is understandable if the lion has believed the lies he has been fed about me because of his prior experience with others. But it is utterly amazing if he has received only good reports about me and wishes me ill for no reason. They say that it is strange when you seek to please your companion and he isn't pleased, but even stranger when you seek to please him and he becomes angry. Reconciliation can be hoped for when anger occurs for a cause; but there is no hope for reconciliation when it occurs without a cause. If anger is occasioned by the occurrence of a cause, then reconciliation can be

hoped for when the cause ceases. Causes come and go, and exist for a while, but what is gratuitous lasts and never ceases.

"When I reflect on the matter, I can find no offense I've caused 4.69 the lion, and if there was one it must have been small. By God, if you associate with a companion for a long time, you can never be so cautious as to avoid inadvertently doing something, small or great, that will displease him. A reasonable person ponders the magnitude and seriousness of an offence or mistake; he considers whether it was intentional or accidental, and whether pardoning it may incur some harm or shame. He will not hold anything against his companion that he can possibly forgive.

"If the lion thinks I've committed an offense, I don't know what 4.70 it could be, other than opposing him in some of his ideas, out of consideration and in the form of sincere advice. Perhaps he takes it as insolence or disobedience when he says no and I say yes, or when he says yes and I say no. But I don't think I should be faulted for that. I disagreed with him only when by doing so I could foresee success, benefit, and renown for him. I never spoke to him about such matters openly in the presence of his soldiers or before his companions; I met him privately and spoke to him as a respectful servant obedient to his master. I know that to seek to be indulged by comrades when asking for advice, or by doctors when one is sick, or by scholars over an obscure point of religion, is to fail to benefit from their advice.

"If it isn't this, perhaps it's the sort of thing rulers do in moments 4.71 of intoxication. Sometimes, in such moments, they favor those who deserve their anger and become angry with those who deserve their favor—all for no discernible reason. As has been said: To sail the sea is to run a risk, but to be a ruler's companion is to run an even greater risk. Though you attend on him with loyalty, uprightness, affection, and good counsel, you're still liable to stumble and fall, or to be lifted only when you're on the verge of destruction.

"If it isn't this, perhaps some excellence of mine has been my 4.72 downfall. A heavily laden tree may be ruined because of its load,

and the sweetness of its fruit may become its undoing. A peacock's tail—his pride and glory—may be his undoing as it weighs him down when he needs to escape his pursuers. A sturdy steed may be ridden so hard and become so worn out that he perishes. A virtuous man's excellence may cause his downfall because so many rogues envy him and seek to do him harm. Those who lack excellence are more numerous than those who possess it; the wicked everywhere outnumber the good and soon destroy a good man if they turn against him.

4.73 "If it's not this, then it is fate, which cannot be repelled. Fate strips the lion of his strength and vigor, and puts him in a cage. Fate mounts the weakling on the elephant's back, and gives the charmer mastery over the snake, extracting its venom, and playing with it as he pleases. Fate renders the resourceful inept and the inept resourceful. Fate frustrates the bold and emboldens the timid; it enriches the poor and impoverishes the wealthy; it instills courage into the coward and makes cowards of the courageous. Predetermined events take place in accordance with the means, occasions, and causes by which their courses have been determined."

4.74 "The lion's designs on you are not due to any of the reasons you've mentioned," replied Dimnah, "such as incitement by villains, the intoxication of power, or anything of the sort. Rather, they are due to his treachery and injustice. He's a treacherous tyrant: one's first taste of him is sweet, one's last taste bitter—a lethal poison."

"Yes," said Shanzabah, "I tasted the sweetness and found it delicious, but now I see that I've reached the lethal part. I don't think my staying with the lion was a good idea, he being an eater of meat, I an eater of grass. A plague on greed and expectation! They've made me fall into this quagmire and kept me from going my way—like a bee on a lotus flower: delighted by the scent, she becomes oblivious to when she needs to fly away, before the lotus closes its petals, so she is caught and dies. A slave to greed, who isn't satisfied with what is sufficient for this life, but sets his eyes on excess and fails to see the perils lying before him, is like a fly that isn't content with trees and

herbs, but seeks the liquid that flows from the ears of an elephant in rut, and the elephant kills it with a flap of his ear. To offer advice to an ungrateful person is like sowing seeds in brackish ground: the advice is offered to a self-satisfied know-it-all; or it's like engaging a deaf man in debate."

"Enough talk!" said Dimnah. "Do something to save your life." 4.75

"How can I save myself if the lion wants to kill me?" said Shanzabah. "I know his character and how he thinks. I also know that even if he only wished me well, his wicked companions, with their guile, would prevail if they incited him against me and wanted me to perish at his hands. When crafty villains unite against an innocent blameless person, they are likely to destroy him, even if they are weak and he is strong—just as the wolf, the crow, and the jackal destroyed the camel when they turned their wiles and deceptions against him."

"And how did they do that?" asked Dimnah.

So Shanzabah told the following tale: Once, they say, there lived 4.76
a lion in a forest beside a well-traveled road. He had three compan- *How the Wolf,*
ions: a wolf, a jackal, and a crow. One day, when some merchants *the Crow, and the*
were passing along the road, one of their camels lagged behind and *Jackal Destroyed*
wandered into the forest and encountered the lion. "Where have *the Camel*
you come from?" asked the lion, and the camel told him his story.
"What do you want?" asked the lion. "Whatever Your Majesty commands," replied the camel, and the lion said, "If you wish to become my companion, do so and enjoy abundance, safety, and comfort."

The camel lived with the lion until, one day, the lion went out 4.77
hunting and encountered an elephant in rut. They fought fiercely. Wounded by the elephant's tusk, the lion returned bleeding and fell sick, unable to hunt. The wolf, the jackal, and the crow became emaciated with hunger because they could not enjoy the lion's leftovers on which they usually dined. The lion, who realized what was happening, said, "You are suffering and need something to eat," and they replied, "When we see the king's condition, we do not worry for ourselves. If only we could find the king something to restore

his health!" The lion said, "I don't doubt your loyalty. If you can, spread out and search. Perhaps you'll find some game nearby. Let me know, so I can provide us all with sustenance."

4.78 The wolf, the crow, and the jackal left the lion and went aside to confer. "What do we have in common with this grass eater, this camel?" they asked. "His nature isn't like ours, nor are his habits. Why don't we convince the lion to eat him and feed us some of the meat?"

To which the jackal replied, "We can't propose this to the lion, because he has promised the camel safety and granted him protection."

"Stay here," said the crow, "and let *me* deal with the lion."

4.79 The crow went to the lion. "Well?" asked the lion on seeing him. "Have you spotted anything?"

"You can't find if you can't seek," replied the crow, "and you can't see if you don't have sight. We're so hungry that we can hardly walk or see. We do, however, have a proposal on which we're all agreed. If Your Majesty approves, we shall all have much to eat."

"And what is it?" asked the lion.

"This grass-eating camel," the crow answered, "who lazes about among us with nothing to do!"

4.80 This made the lion angry. "Shame on you! What a sinful thing to say! What a terrible idea! What happened to loyalty and mercy? How dare you confront me with such a proposal! Don't you know that I solemnly promised the camel safety and protection? Haven't you heard that a benefactor can bestow no gift, however great, more meritorious than to extend protection to a fearful soul and save its life? I have granted the camel my protection; I will not betray him."

The crow said, "I understand what Your Majesty is saying, but a single life is sacrificed to save a family, a family to save a tribe, a tribe to save a city's inhabitants, and a city's inhabitants to ransom a king. Now that need and disaster have descended on both the king and us, I will give the king a way out. Your Majesty will not be personally responsible for any betrayal of the camel, nor for commanding

it. We will devise a way for the king to keep his promise and for us to obtain what we need." The lion kept silent.

Interpreting this as a sign of agreement, the crow returned to his 4.81 friends. "I talked to the lion until he agreed to some such thing. But how do we deal with the camel if the lion refuses to kill him himself or to order his companions to do so?"

"We'll rely on your skill in the matter," replied his friends.

"Here is my plan," said the crow. "We meet with the camel. We mention the lion's hunger and exhaustion. We say, 'He's given us everything we need and been generous to us. If in his day of need he doesn't see how worried we are about him and how concerned for his welfare, he'll take it as ingratitude and baseness on our part. Let's go before the lion and speak of the favors he's bestowed on us; let us describe how, if we can acquire anything that will be of use to him, we will bring it to him, holding nothing back; and how, if we fail, our very lives are his to dispose of. Let's each of us offer himself, saying, "Eat me, Your Majesty! Don't die of hunger!" When we say this, the others will respond with a reason to reject the offer, and so we shall all be safe. In this way, we shall have fulfilled our duty to the lion and he will be pleased with us.'"

They met with the camel, and he agreed to their plan.

When they came before the lion, the crow spoke first: "Your 4.82 Majesty, you need something to sustain you in your distress, so it behooves us to offer up our lives in order to preserve yours. After all, it is through you that we have lived and through you, we hope, that our offspring may live. If you perish, none of us will survive and our lives won't be worth living."

"Shut up," replied the wolf and the jackal. "How will offering your life do any good, when there isn't enough in you to satisfy the king's hunger?"

"But I will satisfy the king!" said the jackal.

"Your breath is putrid and your belly is filthy," said the wolf and the crow.

"I'm not like that!" said the wolf. "Let the king eat me!"

"Anyone looking to commit suicide should eat wolf meat. He'll choke to death on it!" said the crow and the jackal.

4.83 The camel thought that if he made the same offer, they would find him an excuse, just as they had done for themselves; he would be safe and the lion would be pleased. So he said, "There is enough in me to satisfy the king's hunger; my innards are tasty and my flesh is wholesome."

"Well spoken!" said the wolf, the crow, and the jackal. "How noble! You've said what we know to be true!"—and they pounced on him and tore him to pieces.

4.84 Shanzabah said, "I've told you this parable with reference to the lion and his companions because I know that if they unite to destroy me I couldn't protect myself, even if the lion's opinion of me were not what it has been until now. The best rulers, it is said, are those who are like vultures surrounded by carrion, not those who are like carrion surrounded by vultures.[24] Even if the lion's heart harbored nothing but benevolence and mercy, much malicious talk would soon erase those feelings and replace them with cruelty and harshness. Water, you know, is softer than speech, and rock harder than the heart, but if water drips long enough on rock, it soon makes its mark."

4.85 "What do you intend to do?" asked Dimnah.

"I see no way but to fight him," said Shanzabah. "You can devote your whole life to prayer, almsgiving, and asceticism, and still not obtain the reward obtained in a mere two hours by a just fighter defending his life. Whoever fights to defend his life from someone who would wrongfully deprive him of it achieves great reward and great renown: if he is slain, he achieves Paradise; if he slays, he achieves reward and victory."

"No one should risk his life unnecessarily," replied Dimnah. "If you perish, you've thrown your life away, and if you're victorious, it is due to the workings of fate. The wise man makes fighting his last resort, preferring skill and cunning whenever possible. I don't think you're right. You should fight your enemies only after exhausting every other strategy. Hastening to fight before it is warranted

is overconfidence, rashness, and light-headedness; you should fight only in response to an opponent who makes the first move. Otherwise, if you kill your enemy you will be thought to have acted rashly, and if you are killed you will have sinned and earned punishment in the afterlife. It has been said: Don't disparage a lowly, weak opponent, especially a crafty one—let alone the lion, with all his boldness and strength! I have learned that to disparage an enemy for his weakness is to suffer the fate of the Sea's Custodian at the hands of the shorebird Ṭīṭawā."[25]

"And what was his fate?" asked Shanzabah.

And Dimnah told the following tale: They say that a shorebird, the kind called Ṭīṭawā, had his nest by the sea with his mate. When it came time for them to raise their brood, the female said to the male, "It's time for me to lay eggs. Find me a safe place—I am fearful of the Sea. If he comes with the full force of his water, he'll sweep away our chicks."

4.86
The Shorebird Ṭīṭawā and the Sea

"Why not right here?" replied the male. "We have water and reeds nearby; our home here is very comfortable."

"Fool, consider what you're saying! I'm afraid of this place—if the Sea rises, he'll carry off our chicks."

"I doubt the Sea would ever act so recklessly against us, because of the punishment he fears," replied the male.

"What boastful words!" said the female. "Aren't you ashamed of threatening the Sea? Have you so little knowledge of who you are to threaten him? How true what they say—nothing is harder than self-knowledge. Mark my words and move away from this place."

But the male refused to obey her. She repeated her request many times, but still he wouldn't listen. Then she said, "Those who disregard good advice are likely to suffer the fate of the turtle when she didn't accept the advice of her friends."

"And what was her fate?" he asked.

And the female told the following tale: They say that a pond was home to two ducks and a turtle. Being neighbors, they had become fast friends. One season, the water in the pond sank dangerously

4.87
The Ducks and the Turtle

low. When the ducks saw the water recede, they said, "We'd better leave this pond and move elsewhere."

They said goodbye to the turtle: "Farewell! We're leaving."

And the turtle said, "Drought is an especially great hardship for a poor creature like me who can only live in water. You, however, can live wherever you go. Please find a way to take me with you."

"We'll take you with us on one condition," they replied. "Promise that if we carry you up into the air and people see you, talk about you, and shout at you, you won't answer."

The turtle promised not to reply to anyone. "But how," she asked, "will you carry me?"

"Bite onto the middle of a stick," they said, "and we'll take hold of the ends and lift you into the air."

The turtle agreed, and off they flew. When people saw them, they cried out, "Look at that marvel! A turtle in the air, between two ducks!"

When the turtle heard their words, she became angry and said, "May God poke out your eyes!" As soon as she opened her mouth and spoke, she fell to the ground and died.

4.88 The male Ṭīṭawā said, "I hear what you're saying, but you needn't be afraid of the Sea." So the female hatched her chicks where they were.

Now, when the Sea's Custodian heard of this, he wanted to determine the extent of the male Ṭīṭawā's ability to protect himself and how he would manage to do it, so he waited until the tide rose, and carried off the Ṭīṭawā's chicks, along with the nest. Bereft of her chicks, the female said to the male, "I knew from the start that this would happen and that your lack of self-knowledge would cause us harm. Just look at what's happened to us!"

"I said to you at the beginning, and I say it to you now," replied the male, "that if the Sea behaved foolishly toward us, I would take revenge. You'll see what I'm going to do and how I'm going to get even."

4.89 He went to his comrades and complained about how he had been treated by the Sea: "You are my brothers, comrades I trust to help

me seek redress. Assist me. Devise a plan for me. What happened to me today might also happen to you."

"We'll help you to get what you seek," they replied, "but what can we do to the Sea?"

The Ṭīṭawā said, "Let's assemble all the birds and complain to them about how the Sea has treated us. We'll say to them, 'You are birds like us. Help us, because what has happened to us today might happen to you tomorrow.'"

So the male Ṭīṭawā assembled all the birds in one place and com- 4.90
plained to them about how he had been treated by the Sea. "We're ready to help you," they said, "but what can we do to the Sea?"

"We birds will go as one to the palace of the Phoenix of the West," said the Ṭīṭawā. "We'll cry and cry as loudly as we can, and call out to her until she sees us and forces the Sea to make amends!"[26]

That is what they did, and the Phoenix responded to them with 4.91
a question: "What has brought you together, and why do you summon me?" They complained to her about the Sea. "You are our leader," they said, "and the king who rides mounted upon you is stronger than the Custodian of the Sea. Go and ask him to help us against the Sea!"

And the Phoenix did so. She went to the king who rides her and asked him to fight the Sea. When the Sea realized his weakness compared with the strength of the king who rides the Phoenix, he immediately returned the Ṭīṭawā's chicks and never again touched the Ṭīṭawā's home.

"I've told you this story because it wouldn't be good for you to 4.92
fight the lion, and I don't think you should do it."

"I won't fight the lion," said Shanzabah, "or make any hostile moves, either secretly or openly. I'll be on my best behavior toward him, unchanged in any respect, unless there is an obvious threat to me."

Dimnah was displeased when Shanzabah said that he wouldn't change his behavior toward the lion. He thought he would fall under suspicion if the lion didn't see in Shanzabah any of the signs he had

described, so he said, "Go! As soon as you look at the lion, you'll see things that will make you uneasy."

"How will I know?" asked Shanzabah.

"If when the lion looks at you," said Dimnah, "he sits up on his haunches, raises his chest, stares at you, pricks up his ears, opens his mouth wide, and beats the ground with his tail, you can be sure he intends to kill you."

"If I see these signs in him, what you're saying will be beyond a doubt," replied Shanzabah.

4.93 Dimnah went to Kalīlah as soon as he was done turning the lion against the ox, and the ox against the lion. "How has your project progressed?" Kalīlah asked.

"It's about to turn out just as I wish," Dimnah replied. "No doubt about it! Don't imagine that the brotherhood between friends can hold. When a clever schemer uses his wiles to separate them, he can slice them apart just as a stone slices through water."

4.94 Kalīlah and Dimnah went together to visit the lion. Shanzabah entered just as they arrived. When the lion saw him coming, he sat up on his haunches, pricked up his ears, opened his mouth wide, and beat the ground with his tail. The ox, certain that the lion intended to kill him, said to himself, "A ruler's companion is never safe from the shifts in his master's moods and the changes in his attitude due to the influence of malicious liars. He is like a man who shares his bed with a snake, not knowing when it will attack him, or one who lives with a lion in his den, or one who swims in a lake with crocodiles— he doesn't know when he will be attacked." Such were his thoughts as he prepared to fight the lion, should the lion so desire.

4.95 As soon as the lion saw how the ox was behaving and perceived all the signs mentioned by Dimnah, he was certain that the ox had come to fight him. So he pounced on him and a fight ensued. The lion and the ox fought long and hard, until both were covered in blood.

When Kalīlah saw the lion bleeding and understood what he had endured from the ox, he said to Dimnah, "You wretch, look at your clever scheme now! How despicable! What an evil outcome!"

"And what evil outcome do you see?" asked Dimnah.

Kalīlah replied, "The lion's disgrace, the ox's destruction, and the 4.96
sowing of discord in the army—to say nothing of your evident clum-
siness in matters where you claimed to have skill. Don't you know
that the worst foolishness is that which leads to unnecessary fight-
ing? Don't those in a position to fight often avoid it, in fear of danger
or defeat, hoping to attain their objective by other means? A minis-
ter who orders war when the objective can be achieved peacefully is
more harmful to his ruler than an enemy. Just as the tongue can be
crippled by a disorder of the heart,[27] so can courage be crippled by
misjudgment. Courage and judgment need each other: alone, with-
out their comrade, they are useless in battle. But good judgment is
superior to courage, as there are many matters in which good judg-
ment will serve without might, whereas might alone can achieve
nothing in the absence of good judgment. Someone who wants to
use cunning, but doesn't know every detail of a matter he embarks
on, will act as you have in your insolence and conceit.

"Ever since I saw your greed and heard your talk, I have been
expecting you to bring disaster and disgrace on us both. A wise man
begins by reflecting on matters and actions before embarking on
them: he proceeds with those he hopes will work out as he wishes
and avoids becoming embroiled in those he fears will not.

"The only thing that prevented me from restraining you from the 4.97
start and acquainting you with your faults was that it was something
I couldn't make public for want of witnesses and supporters. Also,
I knew that my words wouldn't make you a better person or turn
you away from your desires. Now, however, I will tell you about
yourself and acquaint you with your faults, for your misjudgment
and clumsiness have become clear to me and I have seen their evil
consequences. You are good at talking, but bad at action. Nothing,
they say, is more dangerous to a ruler than a companion who is good
at talking, but bad at action. Your fine words beguiled the lion, but
your ineptitude caused his downfall. Words without deeds; theory
without experience; wealth without generosity; friendship without

loyalty; abstinence without piety; almsgiving without good intentions; and life without health, safety, and happiness—there is no good in any of these.

4.98 "You have stirred up an affair that only the wise and skillful can remedy—just as only a skilled physician can cure a patient who suffers from corruption of the bile, the wind, the blood, and the phlegm all at the same time. Learning sobers the wise, but intoxicates the fool—just as daylight sharpens the sight of every creature that can see, but dulls the sight of a bat. A wise man is not puffed up by office or honor, however great: he is like a mountain, unshaken even in a gale.

4.99 "Your case reminds me of something I've heard: They say that a ruler's goodness will be inaccessible if he is good but his ministers are evil, as no one will dare approach him. He will be like a pool of pure water harboring a crocodile: you can't enter it, even if you can swim or need water. A numerous and prosperous entourage is a king's crowning glory, but you have desired that only you, and no one else, should have access to the lion. You wanted no one else to enjoy any standing with him, whereas the ruler and his companions are like the sea and its waves. How stupid and foolish it is to seek friends by means of disloyalty, seek reward by means of hypocrisy, seek a woman's love by means of boorishness, seek one's own benefit by means of harm to others, or seek knowledge and virtue by means of sloth and indolence. But what's the use of all this preaching and instruction? I know that it's just as when the man once said to the bird, 'Don't try to put straight what cannot be straightened, or instruct those who will not be instructed!'"

"And how was that?" asked Dimnah.

4.100

The Monkey, the Firefly, and the Bird

And Kalīlah told the following tale: Once, they say, a band of monkeys who lived on a mountain saw a firefly on a cold night.[28] Thinking it was a spark, they collected firewood, piled it on her, and began blowing on it with their mouths and fanning it with their hands. A bird sitting in a nearby tree called to them, "Don't tire yourselves out! What you saw isn't fire." But they wouldn't be deterred. Losing patience, the bird flew down to come closer to the

monkeys and set them straight. A man who happened to be passing said, "Bird, don't try to set straight what cannot be straightened or instruct those who cannot be instructed! You don't test a sword on a rock that can't be split with an ax, and you don't try to bend brittle wood. To labor over what cannot be straightened is to regret it." But the bird refused to heed him. He approached the monkeys, and one of them grabbed him, dashed him on the ground, and killed him.

"This is exactly the way you are when it comes to how little you 4.101 benefit from instruction and admonition. Furthermore, deceitfulness and boasting are the keynotes of your character: both are bad, though deceitfulness entails worse consequences. This is illustrated by what happened to the swindler who was the simpleton's partner."

"And what happened to him?" asked Dimnah.

And Kalīlah told the following tale: Once, they say, a swindler 4.102 and a simpleton became business partners. While they were walk- *The Swindler* ing on the road, the simpleton lagged behind and found a purse *and His Partner* containing a hundred thousand dinars. He picked it up and told the *the Simpleton* swindler about it. They decided to head back home.

Close to town, they sat down to divide the money. "You take half, and give me half," the simpleton said to the swindler. But the swindler, intent on taking it all, said, "Let's not divide it: partnership and joint ownership are more conducive to familiarity and friendship. You take some, I'll take the same amount, and we'll bury the rest somewhere safe. When we need the rest, we'll come back together and get what we need."

"Fine," said the simpleton. So they took some of the money and buried the rest by the root of an imposing tree. Afterward, the swindler, unbeknownst to the simpleton, came back to the tree, made off with all the money, and leveled the ground over the spot.

A few days later, the swindler said to the simpleton, "We need 4.103 to pay some expenses. Why don't we go and get some more of the money?" So they set out together. They dug up the spot, but found nothing. The swindler began tearing his hair and beating his breast, and cried out, "Let no man trust his brother or be fooled by his

companion! Did you come back and take the money?" The simpleton became angry and swore he hadn't, but this only made the swindler more incensed. "Who else could have taken it?" he asked. "Does anyone else know about it?"

4.104 The swindler grabbed the simpleton and hauled him before the judge, and they told their story. The swindler claimed that the simpleton was the one who had taken the money.

"Have you any evidence?" asked the judge.

"Yes," said the swindler. "The tree where the money was buried will testify for me!"

The judge, incredulous and amazed at the idea of calling a tree to testify, ordered that the swindler place himself in the custody of a bondsman,[29] and said to the bondsman, "Bring him to me tomorrow, so I can learn the truth about his claim that the tree will testify."

4.105 The swindler then returned home and told his father the story. "Father," he said, "I called the tree as a witness because I have a plan. I'm relying on you: if you do as I say, we keep the money we have and we win as much again from the simpleton."[30]

"What do you want me to do?" asked his father.

"I buried the money," the swindler said, "at the foot of an imposing tree with a hollow a man can enter and hide in without being seen. I'd like you to go tonight and get inside the tree. Tomorrow, when the judge comes and asks the tree to testify, speak from inside the hollow, saying, 'The simpleton is the one who took the money.'"

"Son," said the swindler's father, "many a clever man has been undone by his own cunning. I'm afraid your cleverness will be like the heron's."[31]

"And how did his cleverness undo him?" he asked.

4.106 The swindler's father told the following tale: Once, they say, a
The Heron, the Snake, and the Mongoose heron had a snake for a neighbor. Whenever the heron had young to raise, the snake would go to the nest and eat them. The place suited the heron well, so he couldn't just leave it, but he was saddened by what the snake was doing to him. A crab, surmising what he was feeling, approached the heron and asked what was making him so

sad. The heron told him what the snake had done and the crab said, "Shall I show you how you can take revenge on the snake?"

"How?" asked the heron.

The crab pointed to a burrow in front of him. "See that burrow? There is a mongoose in it, an enemy of snakes.[32] Gather lots of fish; put some of them by the mongoose's burrow and line up the rest between the mongoose's burrow and the snake's den. The mongoose will then kill the snake."

The heron did this, and the mongoose followed the fish to the snake and killed it. But then, out of habit, the mongoose came back, searching for more fish. When he didn't find any, he kept searching until he stumbled upon the heron's nearby nest, and devoured both the heron and his young.

"I've told you this story to show that if you aren't careful you risk landing yourself in worse trouble than you planned to inflict on the other person." 4.107

"I hear what you're saying," said the swindler, "but don't be afraid! It's easier than you imagine."

So the old man, following his son's wishes, went to the tree, and got inside. The next morning, the judge, the swindler, and the simpleton came to the tree. The judge asked it, "Do you have any testimony?"

"Yes," replied the old man. "The simpleton took the money."

Amazed and incredulous, the judge began looking hard and trying to figure it out. He walked around the tree and noticed the hollow, but saw nothing because the man was too high up inside to be seen. So he ordered that firewood be gathered and lit, so as to fill the hollow with smoke. The swindler's father held out for a time, but finally, overcome, he cried out for help. On the judge's order, he was pulled out—just as he was dying. The swindler was punished, forfeited the money, and went home carrying his dead father on his back.

Kalīlah said, "I've told you this story to show you that someone who practices cunning and deception is often himself the loser. You, Dimnah, combine deceit and incompetence. Now you've 4.108

seen the consequences of your deeds, and you're unlikely to come out unscathed. Such is the end of people who act as wrongfully as you have. You are two-tongued, two-faced, and duplicitous. River water, they say, is sweet until it reaches the sea and mixes with it; a family lives in happiness, prosperity, and unity until a wicked man sows discord among them; and friends remain friends until a two-tongued person comes between them. Nothing is more like a snake than a two-tongued man. A snake has two tongues, and what drips from them is venom, just like yours. I've always been afraid of the venom of your tongue, fearful that it would infect me with evil; I've been reluctant to be near you, mindful of the warning of the wise: Keep away from dissolute people though they be your own kin or companions. Such a companion or friend is like a snake: its owner raises it and treats it with kindness, but all he gets from it is a bite.

4.109 "They also say: Cleave to the intelligent and generous man, cultivate his company, and don't part from him. There is no harm in associating with an intelligent man, even if his character leaves something to be desired: guard yourself from his vices, but benefit from his intelligence. Likewise, do not spurn the generous man, even if his intelligence leaves something to be desired: benefit from his generosity and help him with your intelligence. But shun completely the man who is both low-minded and foolish. Thus, it is right for me to shun and avoid you. How can your friends expect loyalty and generosity, now that I've seen what you have done to your king, who was generous to you and raised you to honor? In this respect, what the merchant said applies to you: 'In a land where rats can eat a hundredweight of iron, there is nothing preposterous about hawks carrying off elephants!'"

"And how does that saying apply to me?" asked Dimnah.

4.110 And Kalīlah told the following tale: In a certain land, they say,
The Mice Who lived a merchant who, having exhausted his wealth, decided to
Ate a Hundred- travel abroad to seek his livelihood. He had in his possession an iron
weight of Iron rod weighing a hundred *mann*,[33] which he left with an acquaintance for safekeeping, then set out. After a while he returned and asked

for the rod, but the acquaintance, who he discovered had sold the iron and spent the proceeds, said to him, "I put your rod to one side in the house but the rats ate it up."

"Indeed," said the merchant, "I've heard that nothing cuts iron better than rats' teeth. A small loss! Thank God you're well."

Delighted by the merchant's reaction, the acquaintance said, "Come stay with me today." 4.111

The merchant left, promising to come back. But he carried off his friend's young son, hid him, and then returned. The boy's father missed his son and asked him, "Have you seen my son?"

"As I was approaching your house," replied the merchant, "I saw a hawk carry off a young boy. Perhaps it was your son."

"Who has ever seen or heard of hawks carrying off young boys?" the man cried out.

"Surely," replied the merchant, "in a land where rats can eat a hundred *mann* of iron, there is nothing preposterous about hawks carrying off elephants!"

And the acquaintance said, "It was I who 'ate up' your iron—I consumed what wasn't lawful for me to take. Give me back my son, and take your iron."

Kalīlah said, "I've told you this story to demonstrate that if you can betray your king, who has shown you such favor, you're sure to betray others. I see that love means nothing to you. Nothing is more wasted than love bestowed on someone who knows no loyalty, than favors bestowed on someone who knows no gratitude, than instruction given to someone who won't listen or benefit from it, or than a secret entrusted to someone who knows no discretion. I have no illusions about changing your nature: I know that a bitter tree can be smeared with honey and butter but will still produce bitter fruit. I fear the effect your company might have on my judgment and character; for the company of the good bestows goodness, while the company of the evil bestows evil. It is like the wind: if it wafts over something rotten, it spreads a stench; and if it wafts over something fragrant, it spreads a fragrance. I know how heavy my words 4.112

will seem to you, but the foolish always make light of the wise, and the base make light of the noble. The crooked must be set straight by the upright, and impulsive fools brought back to their senses by the thoughtful. The low-minded never cease from attacking and denigrating the noble, the spineless from attacking the resolute, the rancorous from attacking the affectionate, the miserly from attacking the generous, and the vicious from attacking the righteous."

4.113 Kalīlah's words reached this point just as the lion finished dealing with the ox. After he had killed the ox and his anger had subsided, the lion thought to himself, "He was a creature of intelligence, good judgment, and character. For all I know, he may have been an innocent victim of injustice." And he became filled with sadness and regret.

When Dimnah noticed the lion's mood, he stopped talking to Kalīlah and approached the lion. "Now that God has given you the upper hand and enabled you to defeat your enemy, what is making you sad?"

"I grieve over the loss of Shanzabah's intelligence," replied the lion, "and I feel pity for him because of his good character."

4.114 "Don't feel pity for him," said Dimnah. "A wise man shows no mercy to someone he fears. Someone who is prudent sometimes takes a dislike and forms an aversion to a man, but then, albeit reluctantly, treats him generously, draws him close, and appoints him to office because he knows the man's usefulness and merit—just as you force yourself to swallow a loathsome medicine because of its benefit. And sometimes you like a man and esteem him, but then you banish him, cast him aside, and destroy him, fearing harm from him—just as someone whose finger has been bitten by a snake will cut it off and throw it away for fear that the poison may spread throughout his body and kill him."

The lion acknowledged the truth of his words. Later, however, he investigated the matter of the ox and how Dimnah had wronged him. Everything became clear to him, and he put Dimnah to a most horrible death.

Then the philosopher said to the king, "There are marvels for 4.115
intelligent people in this story of how Dimnah, young and weak as
he was and among the most contemptible and despised of beasts,
managed to separate the lion and the ox, so that they abandoned
their friendship, each turning against the other and becoming
filled with rancor and aversion. One learns to beware of slander-
ers, deceivers, sowers of discord, enviers, and insolent men, and
to guard against their falsities, deceits, trickeries, and calumnies.
Those with intelligence must guard against the fabrications and lies
of such people. They should scrutinize their actions and accept their
words only after proper investigation, and they should reject all
people they know to be of this sort. Sound judgment and prudence
lie in caution and in emulating people who are pleasing to God."[34]

Here ends the Chapter of the Lion and the Ox.[35]

The Investigation of Dimnah

5.1　The king said to the philosopher,[36] "I've listened to your account of how a crafty slanderer skilled at deception sowed so much unwarranted suspicion that he destroyed a friendship and replaced it with hostility. Now tell me how Dimnah defended his behavior to the lion and his entourage, and how the lion eventually changed his mind regarding the ox, became suspicious of Dimnah, and commanded that he be put to a most horrible death. Tell me how the lion learned about his enemy and what defense the latter offered."

5.2　The philosopher replied: The accounts tell us that after killing the ox, the lion regretted his haste. He remembered the ox's companionship and inviolability as a guest, and, to dispel some of his sadness and grief, he spent long evenings conversing with his companions. The lion's entourage included a leopard who, as one of the lion's most esteemed and distinguished companions, enjoyed access to the lion by day and by night. One evening after the ox's death, the leopard kept the lion company late into the night, before heading home. When he passed by the home of Kalīlah and Dimnah—they lived together in the same house—he overheard Kalīlah rebuking Dimnah for his treachery and deceit. Kalīlah was reminding Dimnah of how he had tried to restrain him and how Dimnah had rejected his advice. The leopard overheard the whole conversation.

5.3　Among other things, Kalīlah said, "You've done a terrible thing, an ugly thing, an appalling act of faithlessness. The consequences of your dreadful betrayal of the lion will soon bring about your downfall. When everything comes out, not one animal will defend your

conduct or come to your aid. They will unite one and all to destroy you. For my part, I no longer want to associate with you or be your partner."

"What's done can't be undone," replied Dimnah. "Brother, don't cause the two of us any more grief. Try to dispel the effect the affair has had on the lion's mood. Rest assured, I'm not going to praise what I did: greed and envy drove me to it."

After hearing their words, the leopard went back and paid a visit 5.4 to the lion's mother. After making her promise to reveal nothing, he told her what he had heard Kalīlah say and what Dimnah had confessed. The next morning, the lion's mother went to visit the lion. She found him sad and dejected over his thoughtless treatment of the ox.

"What is making you sad?" she asked.

"The death of the ox," he replied. "I keep thinking of his companionship and devotion, and how I benefited from his opinions and trusted his counsel and advice."

"A man's conscience is the most convincing witness against him," she said. "As your words indicate, your own heart testifies that you attacked the ox before you knew the truth about the matter. Haste is the root of error. When you received the report about the ox, had you restrained yourself, controlled your temper, and compared the report carefully with what you felt in your heart, your heart would have provided sufficient evidence regarding the report's truth or falsity. Hearts reflect each other; therefore, judge how things stood between you and the ox during his lifetime by what you feel about him now after his death."

"Since killing the ox," the lion said, "I've thought and thought, 5.5 trying to discover even one offense of his that ever excited my anger to confirm my suspicions; but the more I think, the better my opinion of him becomes. I can't recall any viciousness in his character that might have led to his envying me, or any hatred that might have caused him to try to overthrow me, and I see nothing on my part that might have provoked him. I want to investigate the case

thoroughly, although I know it won't undo my thoughtlessness; I want to know where I stand regarding the right or wrong of what I did. Tell me, have you heard anything?"

"I've been told something that I've been asked to conceal," replied the lion's mother. "I would tell you, were it not for what the sages have said about the shamefulness of revealing secrets."

5.6 "The sayings of the sages are ambiguous and can be taken in many ways," responded the lion. "In some circumstances the reasonable thing is to act on them; in other circumstances to refrain from doing so. The sages have said that covering up and hiding the doings of suspicious people is in itself suspicious, a kind of wrongdoing. Perhaps your informant acquitted himself of a responsibility by passing on the information; therefore, you too should help him by doing what is incumbent on you. He acquitted himself of his obligation to you by informing you; he removed the burden from his neck and put it around yours. Therefore, you too should remove it from your neck by explaining it to me, so we can do what we ought to do in a case like this."

5.7 The lion's mother said, "I know that what you say is true, but I also know that revealing the secret and burdening you with it would harm me in two ways. First, the person who told me the secret would hate me: he would take it as a betrayal of trust and ascribe it to weakness of character. Second, no one else would trust me with a secret after that."

"I understand," said the lion. "I don't want to look for a way out of my mistake by involving you in a betrayal of trust. If you're unwilling to divulge the informant's name and the details of what he told you, tell me about it in general terms."

She told him all about the conversation. Then she said, "I know very well that the sages have exalted the virtue of pardoning offenders, but that applies only to offenses less serious than the betrayal of the whole community or the betrayal of kings. Fools plead with this saying to excuse their evil deeds. But failing to punish those who

deserve punishment will corrupt the entire community. Do not, therefore, allow this traitor, this sower of corruption, to live."

The lion summoned his main companions, who were ushered 5.8 into his presence. Then he summoned Dimnah. Dimnah stood before him and saw from the demeanor of the lion and his companions that something was wrong. Turning to someone next to him, he asked quietly, "Has anything happened to make the king so sad? Has he summoned this gathering because something has happened?"

The lion's mother heard him. "What saddens the king is that he left you alive after seeing how you deceived him and incited him against his loyal adviser. He shouldn't allow you to remain alive a moment longer."

"What has changed his attitude toward me?" asked Dimnah.

"Your machinations," the king's mother answered. "Now he clearly sees how your lies incited him against Shanzabah."

"I think," said Dimnah, "that the first speaker has left nothing 5.9 for anyone else to say about the ironies of fate. As the saying goes, he who tries hardest to fend off the evils that men do is most likely to become the victim of evil. May this saying not apply to the king and his soldiers! I know the saying was only about associating with evil men: that no amount of wariness will save from their evil someone who knowingly associates with them. That is why ascetics have sequestered themselves and chosen solitude instead of human company, electing to work for God rather than for His creatures, for only God rewards good with good. Most people in this world don't act justly or reward each person as he deserves; indeed, they often inflict on the innocent punishment befitting sinners. But who is more likely to hit the mark than a king who flatters no one out of need and punishes no one out of fear?

"The virtue to which kings should most aspire is to reward those 5.10 who do good service; and what service has been more conspicuously good than my advice? The king, and everyone here, knows there was nothing between me and Shanzabah to cause me to

hold a grudge against him or seek his ruin. I had nothing to gain or lose. I advised the king and let him know what I had learned about Shanzabah. In the end, what he saw with his own eyes confirmed what I told him, and as a result he became more decisive and resolute in his judgment. I know that more than one scheming enemy of the king is afraid of me for the same reason, and so they've become my foes and have decided to destroy me. I never expected that the king's sorrow at letting me live would be my reward for sincere advice and good service."

5.11 When the lion heard Dimnah's words, he ordered him taken to the judge. "Investigate his case. I don't want to judge the right or wrong of any action without clearly establishing the truth and justice of it."

"Your Majesty," said the judge, "nothing can dispel blindness, clarify doubt, and uncover obscurities better than a rigorous, thorough investigation."

5.12 And Dimnah added, "Your Majesty shouldn't hasten to kill me on the word of a slanderer. Let him investigate the matter. The more he considers my case, the more certain he will be of my innocence and loyalty. As Your Majesty knows, fire dwells in trees and rocks; only through labor and effort can it be brought out and put to use. If I were a criminal, I would be as fearful of exposure as, knowing my innocence, I am now hopeful that the investigation will bring out the truth, just as perfumes diffuse their sweetness more widely when stirred. I would have found somewhere else to go if I were conscious of any crime or guilt; I wouldn't have stayed at the king's gate waiting for a reward. If he is in any doubt about me, I ask him to investigate. Let him entrust the matter to someone God-fearing and trustworthy, someone not swayed by slander, neither lenient nor arbitrary, for I held a position that others envied. Instruct that person to investigate and submit a daily report on what he finds out about my case and on the evidence I present. Let the king exercise his judgment, compare one part of the testimony with the other, and not hasten to act on the basis of dubious claims made by

malicious and hostile people. If he doesn't do this and instead coun-
tenances something unlawful, then I have no helper or refuge but
the One who knows the hidden thoughts and hearts of His servants.
As the sages have said: If you believe what deserves to be doubted,
and reject what deserves to be believed, you risk suffering the fate
of the woman who in her confusion gave herself to her servant, who
subsequently disgraced her."

"And what was her fate?" asked the lion.

And Dimnah told the following tale: They say that in a certain
city there lived a merchant whose wife was endowed with both
beauty and wealth. Next door lived a skilled painter who was the
wife's lover. She said to him, "It would make things easier for us if
you could devise something to alert me to your arrival when you
come at night, without calling out, throwing something, or arous-
ing suspicion."

"I have just the thing," said the painter, "a coat painted with
fantastic images, some white as heart of palm and some jet black,
brightly gleaming. Its whiteness will summon you on a dark night,
and its blackness will stand out on a moonlit night. I'll wear it when
I want to come to you. When you see it, know that it's your special
friend and come to me without any summons."

He wore the coat whenever he came to visit the woman; she
knew he was there, admired his skill and delighted in it, and he
could visit whenever he wanted. One of the merchant's servants
realized what was happening. A few days later, the servant—who
happened to be the painter's maidservant's lover—asked the maid-
servant to lend him the painted coat to show a friend of his, after
which he would return it immediately. She gave it to him, and he put
it on and visited the merchant's wife in the painter's guise. When
she saw him, she had no idea it wasn't her lover and gave herself to
him. He satisfied his lust and returned the coat to the maidservant,
who put it back in its place.

The painter had been away, but he came home later that night,
donned the coat, and went to visit the woman. When she saw the

5.13
The Wife and Her
Lover the Painter

5.14

5.15

coat, she came to him. "Why," she asked, "have you returned so soon after satisfying your desire?" The painter returned home in disgust, summoned his maidservant, and threatened to beat her, whereupon she told him the whole story. So the painter burned the coat.

5.16 Dimnah said, "I've told you this story to show you that sowing confusion is as bad as lying. Your Majesty—praise God—is unsurpassed in judgment, great in forbearance, and experienced in affairs. Despite the confusion that's being sown, you saw clear evidence of the ox's hostility and this justified killing him. This should prevent Your Majesty from putting me to death, for you know how sincerely I advised you and protected you from your ministers. Furthermore, Your Majesty knows how I regard my harsh life and meager fortune. You know that I cannot raise my rank above that of a servant and that I don't aspire to what those above me aspire. Though I may be insignificant in the king's eyes, I hope to be granted a portion of his justice in my lifetime and after my death. Death is of little importance to me. I would even welcome it if I knew that the king would find comfort, joy, and relief after killing me. The sages have said that a sinner who delivers himself up to death to protect the righteous will be pardoned on the Day of Judgment and escape everlasting suffering in the hereafter. Someone as contemptible as I, marked with the stigma of servitude, ought to give up his life for the benefit of a great, God-fearing king like you. He ought to prefer punishment in this world to punishment in the hereafter."

5.17 One of the king's attendants said, "Your Majesty, Dimnah isn't speaking out of reverence or respect for the king, but to escape the consequences of his mischief."

Dimnah replied, "Who will preserve my soul if I neglect it? Who will raise it up if I demean it? Have I any other soul to protect from perdition? Someone who doesn't protect his own life will never protect the lives of his kin. Don't you know there is nothing shameful in seeking to vindicate oneself? I've become the victim of your uncontrolled envy, evil, hatred, and hostility. Someone like

you isn't fit to stand at the king's gate, let alone to know him. You shouldn't even keep company with his riding animals."

The lion's mother said to Dimnah, "I'm amazed less by your pre- 5.18 vious faithlessness, deception, and corruption than I am by your preaching and reciting parables to those speaking about you."

"This," replied Dimnah, "is the place for preaching, if people would only accept it, and for parables, if people would only heed them."

"Sinful traitor," replied the lion's mother. "If you had any intelligence, you'd be too concerned about what you've laid up for yourself to busy yourself reciting parables."

"A traitor," replied Dimnah, "is someone who is given advice that enables him to triumph over his enemy and then shows no gratitude or joy; a traitor is someone who promises his enemy safety, but kills him though he has committed no misdeed when he gets his hands on him; and is someone who turns against the very person who revealed his enemies' hostility."

The lion's mother said, "Sinful traitor, you expect your devil to 5.19 help you argue with lies."

"A liar," replied Dimnah, "is someone who repays benevolence with malice, good with evil, and trust with fear. As for me, I've kept my promise and honored my oath."

"And what," asked the lion's mother, "is this promise you've kept and oath you've honored?"

"The king knows that if I were a liar I wouldn't have spoken these words in his presence about the imposters in his entourage," replied Dimnah.

The lion's mother saw that the lion hadn't replied to any of 5.20 Dimnah's arguments, so she began worrying that he might be swayed by some of his excuses and protestations of innocence. She gave voice to her misgivings: "Silence in the face of an opponent's arguments is like conceding the truth of his words. As the sages have said, to keep silent is to agree." And she left.

The lion commanded that Dimnah be made to post bond and be brought before the judge for investigation of his case.

Later, the lion's mother returned to the lion and said, "I've been hearing for a long time about Dimnah's deceit and corruption. Now his prolific lies, trumped-up excuses, and specious evasions have only confirmed this in my mind. If you give him a chance to speak, he will defend himself with lies and confusing arguments. Killing him will be a great relief to you and your soldiers. Kill him immediately! Don't be swayed by leniency or halted by doubt."

"Courtiers," replied the lion to his mother, "often compete among themselves for positions; envy and malice often develop among them, directed especially at judicious and intelligent colleagues. I know that Dimnah's position vexed more than one of my soldiers and my household. That might be the reason they're uniting against him, as I can well see and hear. So I don't want to act hastily in his case. A precious resource should be consumed only for a good reason and when one is clearly justified in doing so."

The judge ordered that Dimnah be sent to prison, and he was heavily shackled.

5.22 Because of their long companionship and close friendship, Kalīlah felt pity and a sense of responsibility, so he went to visit Dimnah secretly in prison. When he saw Dimnah's distress and wretched state, he wept. "Your condition," he said, "makes admonition unnecessary. But I must remind you of how I carried out my duty to give you advice and direction, for every utterance has its place. Had I failed to reprimand you when you needed it while all was going well, I would share your guilt today. But conceit took hold of you: it overcame you and confounded your judgment. I often cited the sages' maxim: 'The crafty man dies before his time.' By 'dies before his time,' they didn't mean that his life would end, but that he would suffer the things that ruin life, such as your present troubles, from which death would be a relief."

5.23 Dimnah said, "From our first acquaintance, you've always taken pains to speak the truth. Fulfilling your brotherly obligation, you reproved me and advised me, but greed and ambition ruined me and kept me from taking your advice. I was like a sick man who

craves food that he knows will harm him, but disregards that knowledge and surrenders to his appetite. I knew that I had sowed the seeds of trouble for myself and that, no matter how long ago they were planted, they would sprout in time—and the time has come for them to sprout. What torments me even more is my fear for you: that, because of our relationship, you might be suspected in my case and even tortured to make you confess anything I told you about my project. For me, that would be like dying twice, the harsh treatment you would receive being a kind of dying, for no one would doubt the truth of your words about others who have no ties to you, let alone about someone as close to you as I am."

"I understand what you're saying," said Kalīlah. "The wise have said that our bodies can't bear pain and won't hesitate to say anything, true or false, to avoid it. But I think you should repent of your sin and confess your wrongdoing, since you've been brought to this state. By repenting, you'll free yourself from the consequences in the hereafter. You're going to perish in any case. Don't add perdition in the hereafter to perdition in the here and now." 5.24

"You've given sound advice," answered Dimnah. "I'll ponder it and repay you for it."

Filled with grief, distress, and fear, Kalīlah wandered away aimlessly.

Nearby in the prison was another animal, who heard everything that had passed between Kalīlah and Dimnah. He committed it to memory, but kept it to himself.

When Dimnah learned of Kalīlah's flight, he wept for a long time in sorrow for him and in sadness at his departure. "What use is life to me, now that Kalīlah, my good brother and loyal friend, has left me? I see how true the saying is: When Fortune turns against someone in his afflictions and he sinks as low as once he was high, evil attacks him from every side; sadness and grief encompass him, and he is crushed by woes wherever he looks. Fate pursues him, however much he may guard himself against it. No sooner does one misfortune depart than another strikes, and he falls, just as I have fallen 5.25

victim to this blow. I have lost my comrades, my friends have abandoned me, and now I grieve for the loss of my brother. Misfortune has descended on me in the prime of life, in my days of vigor and the freshness of youth. Kalīlah, my brother and best friend, has departed from me in sadness and sorrow."

5.26 The lion's mother again brought up Dimnah and his betrayal of the lion. "Sparing sinners," she said, "is as bad as killing the innocent. Whoever spares a sinner's life becomes a partner in his sinfulness; whoever spares an innocent's life becomes a partner in his good deeds."

So the lion commanded the judge to investigate Dimnah's case without delay. He was to submit a report of every argument Dimnah used and every exculpation he presented. The judge put Dimnah on the stand in front of the dignitaries, and he informed the common people of the king's orders to investigate Dimnah's case; to seek out any knowledge that anyone, high or low, had of his actions; to ask Dimnah for his defense, if he had any; and to pass a just judgment. Dimnah would not be allowed to deceive the king or prevent the ruler from reaching a true judgment and obtaining whatever was necessary to vindicate it.

5.27 The judge addressed the court: "Let any of you who knows anything about Dimnah's case speak—and that for three reasons: first, to uphold justice and to provide true evidence, however it may fall; second, to enable verdicts to be pronounced that punish offenders, encourage the righteous, and protect the state from evildoers and the offspring of evildoers; and third, to free us from people of malice and deception and to prevent them from harming nobles and commoners alike."

Everyone remained silent. No one said a word, for they knew nothing certain about the case and were reluctant to give voice to suspicions.

5.28 When Dimnah saw their silence, he spoke up: "If I were a criminal, I would welcome your silence. But I am innocent. Either you know it, or you know of no offense on my part—and anyone not

known to have committed an offense cannot be called to account and is innocent. Therefore, you must say about me what you know. But anyone who speaks should realize that words have consequences, whether immediate or delayed. What he says about me will determine whether I live or die. Anyone who without knowledge condemns me to destruction or speaks about me merely on the basis of suspicion will suffer the fate of the physician who pretended to know something about which he really knew nothing."

"And what was his fate?" asked the judge.

Dimnah told the following tale: In a certain city there lived a learned physician who prospered because of the providential cures that occurred at his hands through his treatments and drugs. In time, this physician grew old and lost his sight. In the same city lived a fool who claimed to know the science of medicine and whose reputation spread among the people. The king of that city had a daughter whom he married to a nephew. She became pregnant and began to feel some of the pains that women experience in pregnancy, so the king sent for the blind physician. He arrived and questioned the young woman's family about her pains. They told him, and he prescribed a well-known medicine, which he named. However, when the king commanded him to compound some of it, he said, "Because I can't see, I can't gather the ingredients as I know they should be, and I don't trust anyone else to gather them." Then the quack came and told them that he was familiar with the medicine's ingredients and their preparation. The king ordered that he be admitted to the storeroom to take what he needed. When the ingredients for medicines were presented to him, he proceeded arbitrarily according to his pretentions, and chose ingredients with neither knowledge nor experience, merely using guesswork and conjecture. One of the things he chose was a bag of deadly poison. He mixed it in with the ingredients and gave it to the young woman to drink. She died within the hour. The king summoned the quack and made him drink some of the medicine he had prepared. He died on the spot.

5.29

The Quack Physician Who Claimed Knowledge

5.30 At that point someone spoke up: "Scholars and nobles, hearken to my words and ponder them with your understanding, your fullest intelligence, and your most diligent judgment. Scholars have said that the righteous can be known by means of certain things which they have described, written down, and revealed. Thanks to God's kindness and favor toward you in perfecting your intelligence, you learned men know the righteous by their distinguishing features and need no more than the merest indications. This wretch, on whom are visible the signs of evil and marks of sinfulness spelled out by the sages, is someone whose wickedness is beyond question for ordinary people and whose case is unequivocal for the elite."

5.31 "What are those marks and signs?" asked the judge. "You know more about them than we do."

And the speaker explained:[37] "They are as we read in scholarly books: Anyone whose left eye is smaller than his right, whose eye blinks constantly, whose nose bends to the right, who has a wide space between his eyebrows, whose body hairs grow in threes, who looks mostly at the ground as he walks and repeatedly looks back—in such a person treachery and wrongful conduct toward the righteous coalesce. All these signs are present in Dimnah."

5.32 Dimnah responded: "God's judgment upon His creatures is just and contains no injustice; it is true and contains no error. Rulers and judges who seek the truth would need no further evidence or argument if justice could be attained by means of such signs as you have mentioned. No one could be praised for doing good or blamed for doing evil, for no one could change any of the signs that determine his actions. Benefactors could be rewarded, and malefactors punished, merely on the basis of these signs. And if—God protect me!—I did what I am being slandered for based on these signs, then it was those signs that God decreed; there was no way I could have resisted what you have attributed to me and accused me of doing. Another indication of your ignorance of how to pass judgment is that, if what you said were true, my mere possession of these signs would entail no legal consequences for me; for such

signs are created with their possessor at the moment of his creation, and born with him at the moment of his birth. Their operations have no fixed date: no day or age at which they come into force or when judgment should be passed on those who possess them. And what about those who possess these signs but haven't reached the age of reason? This proves to intelligent people that you are an ignorant fool. You've heard something whose import you didn't understand, and you've applied it wrongly. You are no more learned or intelligent than those present, nor the most qualified to speak. You've spoken in error. What the man said to his wife applies to you: 'First cover your own nakedness, then ask others to cover theirs.'"

"And how did that happen?" asked the judge.

Dimnah told the following tale: A city called Burdjird was attacked by an enemy that killed some of its inhabitants and led others away as captives. As his share of the spoils, one of the victors received a plowman and his two wives. As their master, he gave them little to eat and drink and little to wear. One day, the plowman and his naked wives went out to gather firewood. One of the wives found an old rag in the field and covered her private parts. The other wife said to her husband, "Look at that hussy walking around naked!" And her husband replied, "A plague on you! Look at yourself! You are completely naked, yet you find fault and speak evil of someone who has covered her own nakedness. Unbelievable!"

Everyone fell silent when they heard how well Dimnah had replied to his accuser and saw the strength of his arguments. The judge ordered him returned to prison.

The next morning, the judge went before the lion with a group of dignitaries who had been present at the trial. The judge submitted a written account of the arguments that Dimnah had presented in his defense. The lion took the document and ordered them to leave. He then sent for his mother and read the document to her. Distressed to see that the lion was sympathetic to Dimnah, she said, "Don't be angry if I speak bluntly."

"Go ahead," replied the lion. "Say what you want to say."

5.33
The Plowman and His Two Wives

5.34

"I don't think you can distinguish what harms you from what benefits you," she said. "By dragging things out so long, Dimnah is going to stir up so much discord that you won't be able to contain it." And with these words she left in anger.

5.35 The next morning, the judge sent for Dimnah and made him stand before the full assembly. When no one ventured to say anything, the judge himself addressed Dimnah: "Although everyone here has kept silent and said nothing against you, they all suspect you are a criminal. Now that the charge against you has taken root in their hearts, I see no good for you in a life lived among those who think this way about you. I think it would be best for you to admit your guilt and through repentance save yourself from the consequences in the hereafter. You would thereby earn universal praise for two reasons: for your ability to find ways to escape, and because death in a state of grace is better than life in a state of disgrace."

5.36 Dimnah answered: "Righteous judges don't pass judgment on the basis of their own suspicions or the suspicions of others, be they dignitaries or commoners. They know that suspicion is no substitute for the truth. Even if you all suspect that I acted culpably, I know myself better than you, and my knowledge of myself is certain and is free of doubts. It is your suspicion that I slandered someone else that disgraces me in your minds. How then could I plead my own defense if I falsely slandered my own self and handed myself over to death in spite of knowing about my innocence? No life is more sacred to me than my own and no one else has a stronger claim on me. If I had done this to any of you, near or far, it would have accorded with neither my religion nor my mind and character. Therefore, refrain from speaking as you did. If you said it sincerely, it was misguided; if you said it with ulterior motives, deception and guile have no place in the character of the righteous. I know the truth of your words, but mischievous liars will construe them wrongly. I fear that your words will become a heavy burden for you. With the soldiers and the king, you've always enjoyed a reputation for good judgment and just decisions, but that has changed in my

case. You've always acted in accordance with a judge's obligation to refrain from people's errors and deceptions, yet in my case you've turned to acting on suspicions at complete variance with the facts. Haven't you heard what the sages said—that someone who claims to know what he doesn't know and attests to what he has never seen will suffer the fate of the falconer who slandered his master's wife, alleging that he had seen her fornicating with a man and doing what ought not to be done?"

"And what was his fate?" asked the judge.

And Dimnah told the following tale: They say that in a certain city there lived a distinguished man whose wife was of noble descent, beautiful, intelligent, and chaste. The man had a falconer whom he valued for his skill in training and handling hawks. The falconer had made advances to his master's wife but had been rebuffed, so he decided to defame her. He spread many rumors, none of which were taken seriously. When he saw the failure of his attempts to expose her to scandal, he devised a malicious stratagem to disgrace her. He went out hunting one morning and trapped two fledgling parrots, which he raised separately. He taught one of them to slander his master's wife by saying, "I saw the doorkeeper lie with my mistress on my master's bed." He taught the other to say, "As for me, I won't say anything!" The fledglings, after six months' training, had mastered what he wanted them to say—they said it in the language of Balkh. He then set them before his master and they cried out. His master liked the sweetness of their voices, although he didn't understand what they were saying, as they had been taught to speak the language of Balkh, which was the language neither of the master nor of his compatriots. He took the birds from the falconer, whom he rewarded with gifts, delighted as he was, and ordered his wife to keep the birds and care for them, which she did.

Sometime later, he invited visiting dignitaries from Balkh to his home, served them fine food, and gave them wine and such other items as one offers one's guests. When they took their places to drink, the man, who was a military governor, ordered the parrots

to be brought. They were set before him and cried out the phrases they had been taught. The guests, who understood what they said, looked at each another and hung their heads in embarrassment.

"Do you know what the parrots are saying?" asked one of them.

"No," he replied, "but I like their voices."

"We know what they are saying," the guests said.

The guests were embarrassed, but their host insisted they tell him. Finally, a guest told him, "One is saying, 'I saw the doorkeeper lie with my mistress on my master's bed.' The other is saying, 'As for me, I won't say anything!' It's not our custom, Governor, to eat in a house where there is fornication."

The governor was shocked to hear the guests' words. The falconer, who heard what they were saying, said, "I, too, testify to what the parrots testified."

5.39 Since the accounts agreed, the governor ordered that his wife be executed.

To this, the wife said, "Putting me to death without an investigation is likely to cause you even greater trouble. Look into the matter. Ask the parrots to say something else in this language. If they can say anything other than these two sentences, go ahead and do as you intend. If, on the other hand, that is all they can say, everyone here, including you, should know that they were trained by the deceiver who tried to seduce me to commit such a shameful deed."

5.40 The governor asked the visitors to question the parrots, and it turned out that they couldn't say anything but those two sentences in that language. The governor summoned the falconer, who entered confidently with a hawk on his arm, not at all like someone guilty or under suspicion. The wife called out from behind the curtain, "You villain! Did you see me do the foul deed you taught the parrots to describe?"

"I was asked," he replied, "and I said what I saw."

The hawk then leapt from his arm, grabbed his eyes with its talons, and tore them out.

"This," said the wife, "is God's punishment for bearing witness to something you didn't see."

Dimnah said, "I've told this story to impress on you the bitter consequences of false testimony in this world and the next."

The judge said, "A just judge needs to know the actions of those who do good in order to requite them for their deeds, and the actions of those who do evil to requite them for their misdeeds. If he deals correctly with both, those who do good will be more eager to do good and those who do evil will be more inclined to avoid evil. Alas, Dimnah, I think you had better consider the dire situation you are in and the sin you have fallen into. Repent, and confess the truth. As has been said: Better someone who turns away from his sin, admits it, and confesses than someone who persists in his sin or denies it. You will inevitably die someday, even if pardoned. Better the pains you suffer and endure as punishment for your crime than the torments of Hell, where there is no mercy, no rest, and no end to the torment."

5.41

Dimnah said, "Your Honor has spoken the truth in words befitting the righteous and God-fearing. But we also read in the scriptures: Blessed is he who is able to avoid performing with his body actions that harm his spirit. The scholars say that a wise man disregards harm to his body, but holds fast to his spirit. They also say that it is unseemly for loathsome words to be addressed to the undeserving. I despise the body and hold fast to the spirit, so I don't think I need fear the hereafter. Never have I lied in order to harm or insult anyone, and no one has ever seen me do so. How can I commit this gravest of sins, when we read in the scriptures of God's messengers: 'Do not lie or utter falsehoods'? How can a man lie about himself and say he did something he never did? The sages have said: When you are moved by intense fear or folly to ascribe to yourself a deed you did not do, you do not wrong your soul, nor do you place yourself in the hereafter among those who kill themselves.[38] I am innocent of the charges against me. If I am put to death as a result of this

5.42

slander, it will do me no harm, because of the great reward I shall receive in the hereafter."

5.43 The judge wrote down everything Dimnah said and delivered it to the lion. The lion examined the report, then summoned his mother and showed it to her. After considering Dimnah's words, she said, "Your Majesty, now I'm worried more by the prospect that Dimnah, through his deceit and cleverness, may contrive to kill you or drive you from power than by his past guilt in deceiving you and slandering your minister and guest, so that you killed him, even though he was guiltless."

Her words made a deep impression on him. "Tell me who gave you the information about Dimnah, so that I can use it as evidence for putting him to death."[39]

"I am reluctant to reveal something I've been asked to conceal," she replied. "My joy over Dimnah's death will give me no pleasure if I remember that I played a part in it by revealing secrets, something the sages have forbidden. However, I will ask the person who entrusted the information to me to allow me to name him or to inform you himself about what he heard."

5.44 She left and sent a message to the leopard. She reminded him of his responsibility to enhance the lion's prestige and of his duty to treat him well and guide him to the truth by delivering testimony that should not be concealed by someone like him. Both of them had a duty to side with the victim of injustice and exonerate a righteous person in life and in death. As the sages had said: Whoever conceals a dead man's vindication will fail to vindicate himself on the Day of Resurrection. Finally, after much persuasion, the leopard stood up and testified to what he had heard: that Dimnah, faced with Kalīlah's rebuke, had acknowledged coming between the lion and the ox.

5.45 After the leopard testified to what he had heard Dimnah say, the prisoner who had heard Kalīlah admonishing Dimnah on the night of his prison visit and Dimnah's admission sent a message that he had testimony to give. They brought him out of prison, and

he testified to what he had heard: that Dimnah, confronted with Kalīlah's rebuke, had acknowledged using slander and falsehood to come between the lion and the ox.

"What," asked the lion, "kept the two of you from testifying when you knew we had ordered an investigation into Dimnah's case?"

Each answered, "The testimony of a single witness wouldn't have brought about a conviction. Neither of us knew of the other's testimony, so we were reluctant to speak to no avail." 5.46

The lion was satisfied with their answer. On his orders, Dimnah was put to a most horrible death.

Here ends the Chapter on the Investigation of
Dimnah. Such are the consequences of wrong-
doing and the effects of envy and lying.

The Ring Dove

A parable about the circumstances that initiate friendships between sincere brethren and how each benefits by following the other's advice.

6.1 The king said to the philosopher, "Now that I've heard a parable about how a crafty liar can drive friends apart and incite them to become enemies, tell me one about how friendships between sincere brethren begin and how each benefits by following the other's advice."

"A wise man values nothing more than good friends," replied the philosopher. "Friends help us achieve good things and they console us in times of adversity. The story of the ring dove, the crow, the gazelle, and the turtle is an example of this."

"And what was their story?" asked the king.

6.2 The philosopher told the following tale: They say that in the Deccan, near the city of Mārūzūd, was a place abounding in game, where hunters would come to hunt. A crow nested there, in a great tree with many branches dense with leaves. One day, as he sat, he became frightened as he spied a hunter approaching, foul-faced, ill-tempered, and shabbily dressed, with a net on his back and a stick in his hand. "This man," he said to himself, "has come for a reason— whether it's to destroy me or someone else, I don't know, but I'll stay put and see what he does."

6.3 The hunter set up his net, scattered grain, and hid nearby. Soon a ring dove flew by, a leader of many doves, who accompanied her. She saw the grain, but not the net, and, along with the other doves,

swooped down and landed under the net. The hunter rushed up, delighted to have caught them. Each dove fluttered about separately, straining to free herself, but the ring dove said, "Stay true to one another! Don't focus more on your own life than on your companion's. Let's work together and perhaps we can lift this net."

So they worked together, lifted the net, and carried it high into the air. The hunter followed, hoping that the net would weigh them down and that they would land before they could go very far.

The crow, who saw what was happening, said to himself, "I'll follow them to see how their run-in with the hunter ends."

The ring dove looked back and saw that the hunter was following, still hoping to capture them, and she said to her companions, "The hunter, I see, is pursuing us. If we stay out in the open, we'll remain in his sight; let's head for the orchards and trees. He'll soon lose track of us and give up. I know a place by the fields where a rat has his den. He's a friend of mine. If we can get to him, he'll cut through the net and we'll be free." 6.4

So they headed for the place the ring dove had mentioned. When they disappeared from the hunter's sight, he gave up and went away. The crow, for his part, did not head back; he wanted to see whether the doves could manage to extricate themselves from the net, to learn how to do it himself and be prepared should a similar calamity ever befall him.

When the ring dove and her companions reached the rat's home, she ordered the doves to land, which they did. She discovered a hundred holes around the rat's den that he had prepared as a precaution. The ring dove called out his name, Zīrak, and he answered from his den: "Who's there?" 6.5

"Your friend, the ring dove."

He hurried out, and when he saw her in the net, he asked, "You're so quick-witted; how did you get into this predicament?"

The ring dove said, "Don't you know that everything, both good and evil, that befalls us is determined by destiny—the day, the season, the cause, the duration, and the magnitude? Destiny cast me

into this predicament: it made me see the grain clearly and blinded me to the net. My companions and I plunged into it, as you can see. There is nothing amazing about my inability to protect myself from destiny: things stronger and greater than I can't escape their destiny. When it is decreed, the sun and the moon are eclipsed, fish are caught in the depths of the sea, and birds are brought down from the air. The very means that enable the weakling to reach his objective can block the resolute man from his goal."

6.6 The rat began to gnaw at the knots that entangled the ring dove, but she said, "Begin with the knots ensnaring my companions; then attend to mine." She repeated this several times, but he paid no attention to what she said. Finally, after many such urgings, he said, "You seem to have no concern for your own life and not to recognize the claim it has on you."

"Don't chide me for my request," replied the ring dove. "I have a great responsibility as leader of this flock. They've fulfilled their duty of obedience, counsel, and assistance, and by that means God has delivered us from the hunter's snares. If you begin by cutting my bonds, I'm afraid you'll tire and neglect some of the others' bonds. But I know that if you start with them and leave me till last, you won't allow yourself, no matter how tired and weary, to stop cutting away my bonds."

"That," said the rat, "is what makes those who love you and desire your friendship love you and desire your friendship even more." He gnawed at the net until he was done, and the ring dove and her flock flew back home.

6.7 When the crow saw how the rat had freed the doves, he was keen to become the rat's friend. He said to himself, "What happened to them might happen to me, and I might need the rat and his friendship." So he approached the rat's den and called him by name.

"Who are you?" came the reply.

"A crow," he said, introducing himself. "When I saw your loyalty to your friends and how through you God helped the doves, I

became eager to spend time in your company and become friends. That's why I'm here."

"Friendship between us? Not a chance! Someone with his wits about him should seek only what he can obtain, otherwise he'll be considered as foolish as a man who wants to make ships sail on dry land, or carts travel on the sea. How can there be friendship between us when I'm the dinner and you're the diner?"

"Consider it rationally," said the crow. "Though you are my food, 6.8 eating you will hardly benefit me, whereas your life and friendship will bring me joy and safety as long as I live. Now that I've come to seek your friendship, I don't deserve to be sent away disappointed, for your fine character is obvious, though you weren't trying to display it. It is easier to hide musk, whose scent diffuses no matter how much you try to hide it and seal it up, than it is to conceal an intelligent person's excellence, try as he may to conceal it. Do not act out of character and deprive me of your friendship and kindness."

"The strongest enmity is that which is innate," responded the rat. 6.9 "It is of two kinds. In some cases, the hostility works both ways, as with the elephant and the lion; sometimes the elephant kills the lion, and sometimes the lion kills the elephant. In other cases, only one of the parties harms the other—as is the case between me and you. Our hostility isn't due to any harm we've done to you; it's due to the harm you've done to us. Truces between innate enemies eventually revert to hostility. No truce with an innate enemy can be trusted or depended on. Heat water as long as you wish; it will still put out fire. A person who tries to befriend his enemy is like someone who carries a snake in the palm of his hand. No intelligent person should ever try to socialize with a clever enemy."

"I understand what you're saying," said the crow, "but you ought 6.10 to follow your intelligence, recognize the merit of my words, and not make matters difficult between us by saying that there's no way for us to become friends. Intelligent people will find ways and means to a good act. Affection between the good is quick to be cemented,

slow to be broken. It is like a golden cup: slow to break, but easy to restore and mend if broken. Affection between the wicked, however, is quick to be severed and slow to be rejoined, like a clay cup broken by the slightest defect, never again to be put back together. After one meeting and a day's acquaintance, the noble love the noble; when the base form attachments it is from fear or desire. You are noble and I need your friendship. I will stay by your door and touch neither food nor drink until you become my brother."

6.11 "I agree to become your brother," answered the rat, "as I've never turned a needy person away from what he needs. I spoke to you as I did in order to leave myself an excuse, so that if you betray me, you won't be able to say, 'I found the rat weak in judgment and easily deceived.'" The rat came out, but remained by the entrance to his burrow.

The crow said to him, "What's keeping you from relaxing and enjoying my company? Are you still uneasy?"

6.12 "People in this world base their relationships on two sorts of things," said the rat. "Some relationships are based on feelings in the heart; other relationships are based on material goods. Those who share what resides in the heart are pure friends who regard each other with sincere affection. Those who exchange material goods are those who cooperate for an advantage and seek to profit from one another. Those who do good deeds only to gain a reward and acquire worldly benefits are like a hunter who scatters grain for the birds, not for their benefit, but for his own. The sharing of what resides in the heart is better than the exchange of material goods. I know how you feel toward me in your heart, and I feel the same toward you. No personal misgivings are preventing me from coming out and enjoying your company; however, I know you have companions whose nature is like yours, but whose view of me is different. One of them, I fear, might see me with you and kill me."

The crow answered, "The mark of a true friend is that he is a friend of his friend's friend, and an enemy of his friend's enemy. Those who neither love you nor wish you well are not companions

or friends of mine. It will be easy for me to break with those who think otherwise about you. The farmer pulls out the weeds when they grow among his plants."

So the rat approached the crow. They shook hands, became friends, and enjoyed each other's company. After a few days had passed, the crow said to the rat, "Your den is close to roads frequented by people. I'm afraid some fool will shoot at me and take me. I know of a secluded place with plenty of fish. I have a friend there, a turtle. I'll find things to eat there. I'd like to go and live with her in safety." 6.13

"Why don't I come with you?" said the rat. "I don't like my home here."

"What don't you like about it?" asked the crow.

"I'll tell you some stories when we reach our destination," replied the rat.

So the crow picked up the rat by the tail and flew off with him to the pond where the turtle lived. The turtle became frightened when she saw a crow approach carrying a rat; not realizing that it was her friend, she dove into the water. The crow put the rat down, perched on a tree, and called the turtle by name. Recognizing the crow's voice, she swam to the surface, greeted him, and asked where he had come from. The crow told her the whole story, from the time he first saw the hunter right up to the point of his arrival with the rat. 6.14

When the turtle heard the story of the rat, she marveled at his intelligence and loyalty,[40] and welcomed him. "What brings you to this land?" she asked.

At this point, the crow asked the rat, "What about the stories you said you were going to tell me? Tell them now, and answer the turtle's question, for the turtle, as my friend, is now your friend too."

The rat told the following tale: "My first home was in the city of Mārūzūd, in the house of an ascetic who had no family.[41] Every day he would be given a basket of food; he would eat from it and then hang up the basket with any leftover food in it. I would watch for the ascetic to go out, and when he did, I would jump up into 6.15
The Rat's Story

the basket, and, between what I ate and what I threw down for my fellow rats, there would be nothing left. The ascetic tried again and again to hang the basket out of my reach, but to no avail. Then one night a guest arrived at the ascetic's house. They struck up a conversation after they had eaten dinner together. The ascetic asked the guest what country he was from and where he was heading. The guest, it turned out, had traveled the world and seen many wonders. In the course of the guest's account, the ascetic kept clapping his hands from time to time to drive away the rats. This angered the guest. 'I'm talking to you,' he said, 'and you clap your hands as if making fun of what I'm saying! Why did you ever ask me your question?'

6.16 "The ascetic apologized. 'I was intent on your words, but was clapping to drive away the rats. They are a torment and eat any food I leave in the room.'

"'Is it one rat or many?' asked the guest.

"'Many,' said the ascetic, 'but one of them has left me at my wits' end!'

6.17 "'There must be a reason for this,' said the guest. 'You remind
The Woman me of what the man in the story said: "There must a reason why this
Who Traded woman has traded husked for unhusked sesame."'
Husked for
Unhusked "'And why did he say that?' asked the ascetic.
Sesame
"The guest told the following tale: 'Once I lodged with a man in a certain city. After dinner, he made up a bed for me and went off to bed with his wife. We were separated by a reed screen. Late that night, I heard the man and his wife talking and I listened to what they were saying. "Tomorrow," said the man, "I want to invite some people to eat with us."

"'"How can you invite people to dinner," asked the wife, "when you can hardly feed your own family? You're a man who never has enough to keep any surplus!"

"'The man said, "Don't regret what we spend on feeding others. People who hoard often suffer the same unsavory fate as the wolf."

"'"And what happened to him?" asked the woman.

"'Her husband told her the story of a hunter who went out one morning with his bow and arrows in search of game. He hadn't gone far before he shot and killed a gazelle. He picked it up to take it back to his family. On the way, a boar crossed his path and charged when it saw him. The hunter put down the gazelle, sharpened an arrow, and shot the boar, the arrow piercing its testicles. But the boar overtook the man and gored him with its tusks, sending the bow flying—and both fell down dead. A wolf came by, and when he saw the man, the boar, and the gazelle, saw promise for a life of abundance. "I should store whatever I can," he said. "It's an improvident person who fails to store things away! I'll treat what I've found as a hoard for the future; today I'll be satisfied with just this bowstring." So he approached the bow to eat its string, but when he snapped it the bow sprang back and dealt his throat a mortal blow. He died on the spot.

"'The husband said, "I've told you this story to bring home to you the unhealthy consequences of excessive thrift."

"'"You're right," said the wife. "We have enough rice and sesame to feed six or seven people. I'll start cooking tomorrow morning. Invite anyone you like for lunch."

"'The next morning, the woman took the sesame, husked it, and spread it in the sun to dry. She told her husband's apprentice to keep the birds and dogs away from the sesame; then she went off to see to her cooking. The apprentice paid no attention, and a dog crept up and began to eat. The woman saw this, and, considering the sesame unclean, was loath to cook it for food. So she took it to market and exchanged it for an equal amount of unhusked sesame. I was in the market watching what she was doing, and I heard someone say, "There must be a reason why this woman has traded husked for unhusked sesame!"

"'I say the same about this rat who you say jumps into the basket wherever you put it. There must be a reason why he alone among his companions is strong enough to do what you're complaining of. Get me a pickax. If I dig up his burrow, I might find a stash of something that gives him strength or discover what's so special about him.'

"So the ascetic borrowed a pickax from one of his neighbors and brought it to the guest. Meanwhile, I was in someone else's burrow listening to what they were saying. In my burrow there were a thousand dinars—I don't know who put them there—and I used them as my bed. They made me very happy and gave me strength. The guest dug down to the coins and took them. 'These,' he said to the ascetic, 'are what gave that rat strength to jump so high. Money increases strength and intelligence. You'll see that the rat will no longer have the strength to do what he used to do.'

6.21 "When I heard the guest's words, I felt my spirit break and my strength drain away. I moved to another burrow. The next morning, I noticed that the rats showed me less respect and deference. They had grown accustomed to me jumping up into the basket, but now that I could no longer do it, they abandoned me and said among themselves, 'He's finished forever! Soon he'll need one of you to take care of him.' They all rejected me and went over to one of my enemies. They began finding fault with me and disparaging me whenever I was mentioned. So I said to myself: 'I see that only money can guarantee followers, helpers, kinfolk, and friends. Only money can guarantee intelligence and strength.' Poverty, I learned, holds back from their aspirations the penniless who want to undertake a task, and so they fail to reach their goal. They are like water from summer rain that remains in the stream bed: it reaches neither the sea nor the river; it just stays put until it dries up in the ground because it has no strength to reach its goal.

6.22 "I discovered that the penniless have no intelligence: they have nothing in this world or the next. Without money, a man has nothing in this world: when poverty strikes, his brothers spurn him and his kin despise him. The need to support himself and his family often forces him to seek sustenance in ways that endanger his soul, so he loses both this world and the next.

"Nothing is worse than poverty. A tree growing in a salt marsh, eaten away on all sides, is better off than a pauper dependent on others. Poverty is the source of every woe: its victim is despised and

despoiled of intelligence and manliness; it banishes learning and good manners, brings suspicion in its train, deprives you of a sense of shame, and unites every woe. A man is forced to cast shame to the winds when poverty and destitution descend on him. He who loses his shame loses his dignity; he who loses his dignity is despised; he who is despised is insulted; he who is insulted grieves; and he who grieves loses his intellect: his mind is affected, and his memory and understanding become faulty. When a person is afflicted in intelligence, memory, and understanding, he does himself more harm than good by speaking and acting.

"When a man falls into poverty, I've learned, he is viewed with 6.23 suspicion by those who used to trust him; those who thought well of him think ill of him; offences committed by others are attributed to him, and he becomes the object of suspicion. Every trait deemed praiseworthy in a rich man is accounted a blemish in a poor one: if brave, he is called reckless; if generous, a spendthrift; if forbearing, weak; if dignified, dull; if articulate, garrulous; if taciturn, stupid. Death is easier to bear than poverty, which forces its victim to beg— especially if he must beg from those who are mean and miserly. It would be less onerous for a noble-minded man to be tasked with thrusting his hand into a dragon's mouth, extracting its poison, and swallowing it than to beg from a miserly scoundrel. They say that life is death and death a relief for the chronically ill, for those separated from loved ones and friends, for exiles in a foreign land without shelter by night or rest by day and with no hope of return, and for paupers forced to beg. Loath to beg, a poor man may be driven to treachery and robbery, which are worse than the poverty he tries to escape. Better, they say, to be mute than to be an eloquent liar, to be impotent than to be a lecher, to be poor than to live a life of ease from ill-gotten gains.

"After the guest had taken the coins from my burrow, I saw him 6.24 divide them with the ascetic, who put his share into a sack, which he placed by his head at night, and go to sleep. Eager to get some of them for myself, to restore some of my strength and to regain

some of my friends, I came out while the ascetic was asleep and approached his head, but the guest was awake; he picked up a stick and dealt me a blow that sent me running back to my burrow. When my pain subsided, greed and covetousness overcame my reason, so out I came again, hopeful as before, and advanced. But the guest was on the lookout and hit my head again and dazed me. I dragged myself back into the burrow and fainted. So severe was my pain that it made me hate money so much that today the mere mention of it frightens me.

6.25 "People's troubles in this world, I saw, stem from inordinate desire incited by greed. I perceived the great difference between the covetous and the generous. I learned that it is easier for a self-respecting man to brave terrors and dangers and undertake long journeys than to stretch out his hand to receive money from a covetous miser. I realized that satisfaction and contentment are true wealth. As the sages have said: There is no intelligence like good management,[42] no piety like abstinence, no lineage as distinguished as a good character, and no wealth like contentment. What cannot be altered is best endured. As has been said: Mercy is the best part of piety, love begins with openness, intelligence begins with knowledge of what can and cannot be, and contentment means to willingly relinquish the unattainable. In the end, I found satisfaction and contentment, and moved from the ascetic's house to the countryside.

6.26 "I had a friend, a dove, who through her friendship led me to the friendship of this crow. The crow told me about his friendship with you and that he wanted to visit you, and I wanted to accompany him. I didn't want to be alone, for no joy in this world can compare to the companionship of friends, nor any sorrow compare to their loss. Experience has taught me not to ask more of this world than what suffices to ward off need and suffering—and that isn't much: food, shelter, and simple clothing, accompanied by openness of hand and generosity of spirit. If a man were given the world and all it contains, he would benefit only from the few things by which

he keeps needs at bay; of all other things elsewhere he would have only what others have—namely, what the eye can see. This being so, I have come with the crow. I will be your friend. May my place in your soul be like his."

When the rat finished talking, the turtle answered him gently and kindly: "I understand what you are saying, and they are very fine words. Yet you seem saddened, saying that certain things still trouble you and that you have come to live among us as a stranger. You mustn't think that way. Know that good words find their completion only in action. Even if a sick man knows the remedy for his disease, his knowledge won't benefit him if he doesn't take the cure. Benefit from your intelligence and put your knowledge into practice. Don't grieve over your lack of wealth. A man of valor is honored without wealth, just as a lion is feared even when at rest. A rich man without valor is scorned despite his wealth, as a dog is scorned even if he wears a jeweled collar. Don't worry about being in a strange land. No land is foreign to a person of intelligence; even if he goes to a strange land, he has enough to sustain him, like the lion who takes his strength with him wherever he goes. Take care to provide your soul with whatever will make it worthy of good things; if you do, good things will come looking for you, as water seeks a hollow and as waterfowl seek water.

"Excellence is the lot of those who are perceptive, resolute, and prepared; it rarely keeps company with those who are lazy, vacillating, and listless—just as a young woman finds no delight in the company of an old man. Don't grieve yourself by saying, 'Once I was wealthy and now I've become poor.' Wealth and all the goods of this world come swiftly when they come, and depart swiftly when they depart—like a ball, swift to rise and swift to fall. As the sages have said: Things that lack stability and permanence are like the shadows cast by clouds, the friendship of evil men, the love of women, a liar's praise, and ill-gotten wealth. The wise man doesn't rejoice over an abundance of wealth or grieve over its loss; his intelligence and the good works he has performed constitute his wealth. He trusts that

6.27

6.28

his deeds cannot be wrested from him and that he will not be held accountable for what he hasn't done. The wise man mustn't neglect to make provision for the afterlife, for death comes unexpectedly, at a time that none can know. I know that thanks to your knowledge you don't need my counsel and that you understand what will bring you benefit, but I felt I had an obligation to exhort you to act wisely, for you are our brother and all that we have is at your disposal."

6.29 The crow was delighted to hear the turtle's kind and eloquent response to the rat. "You've made me rejoice," he said, "and done me a great favor. You should be as pleased with yourself as I am. The person visited constantly by righteous brethren and friends, surrounded by a throng of comrades whom he gladdens and who gladden him, attentive to them and to their needs, deserves great joy, contentment, and praise. When a noble person stumbles, he rights himself only with the help of the noble—just as an elephant that sinks into the mud can only be pulled out by other elephants. The wise man doesn't make much ado about any favor he has done, no matter how great. He sees nothing blameworthy in risking his life and exposing it to danger in doing good, for he knows that he has risked what is transitory in order to gain what is lasting, and that he has purchased something great at the price of something small. The most fortunate are those whose generosity is appealed to, from whom alms are requested, and whose help is sought. Only those who share their wealth can be considered rich. To live your life as an object of hatred and opprobrium cannot be said to be a life. Expense that brings profit in its wake is no expense at all, and profit that brings loss in its wake is no profit at all."

6.30 While the turtle, the crow, and the rat were speaking, a gazelle came running toward them. The crow, the rat, and the turtle took fright: the turtle jumped into the water, the rat ran into his burrow, and the crow flew up into a tree. The gazelle came to the water, drank a little, and stood looking around fearfully. The crow circled in the air to see whether he could spot anyone pursuing the gazelle; he looked in every direction, but saw nothing. So he called to the

turtle, who came out of the water, and called to the rat, "Come out; there is nothing nearby to fear." The crow, the rat, and the turtle rejoined each other. When the turtle saw the gazelle looking at the water but not drinking, she said to him, "Drink if you're thirsty. Don't be afraid; there is nothing for you to fear." The gazelle approached them, and the turtle, having welcomed him, asked, "What happened to you? Where have you come from, and where are you heading?"

The gazelle said, "I've been living in these plains, but archers kept chasing me from one place to another. Today I saw a shape that looked like a hunter. Afraid that it might be one, I came here out of fear."

6.31

The Gazelle's Story

"Don't be afraid," said the crow. "We've never seen a hunter here. We offer you our friendship and a place to live. The meadow is nearby. Stay and put yourself at ease. No harm will befall you."

The gazelle accepted their friendship and stayed with them. Every day, they went to a thicket to enjoy the shade, talk about events, and exchange pleasantries.

One day, the crow, the rat, and the turtle came to the thicket, but the gazelle was missing. They waited for a while, and when he failed to appear, they became afraid that he had met with harm. The rat and the turtle said to the crow, "Why don't you fly up and see whether you can spot the gazelle nearby." The crow flew up and looked around, and saw the gazelle caught in a snare. He swooped down and told the rat and the turtle.

6.32

The crow and the turtle said to the rat, "God help us! You're the only means to save him we can think of. Help our brother!" So the rat set out in haste. When he reached the gazelle, he said, "Brother, you're so quick-witted; how did you fall into such a plight?"

The gazelle replied, "Is quick wit of any use against events that proceed in accordance with God's hidden decrees?"

The turtle arrived while the two were talking. When the gazelle saw her, he said, "You shouldn't have come! If the hunter turns up when the rat finishes cutting the ropes, I can outrun him; the rat

6.33

can retreat to one of his burrows, and the crow can fly; but you are heavy and can't run. I'm afraid for you."

"A life of separation from one's friends is no life at all," said the turtle. "Anxiety is dispelled and the mind becomes calm when brother meets brother in time of trouble and each shares his thoughts with the other, but the heart aches, joy is banished, and the eyes are dimmed when friend is separated from friend."

While the gazelle and the turtle were speaking, the hunter came into view, just as the rat finished cutting the ropes. The gazelle ran off, the crow flew away, and the rat went into its burrow. When the hunter arrived and found his ropes cut, he stood looking around in amazement. Seeing nothing but the turtle, he tied her up.

6.34 They all became very sad at the sight. The rat said, "Barely do we cross one mountain of troubles before another looms. How true the saying, 'You walk straight ahead as long as you don't stumble, but stumble even once on rocky ground and you'll keep stumbling even when walking on level ground.' Not satisfied with separating me from family, wealth, home, and country, Fate has separated me from the companionship of the turtle, the best of friends, whose friendship asked for nothing in return, but was a friendship of generosity, intelligence, and loyalty; a friendship better than the love of parent for child; a friendship only death could end. Woe to this body prone to afflictions, constantly in a state of change and alteration, in which nothing is permanent or stable—just as a rising star must set, or a setting star must rise, undergoing change and alteration according to an appointed time and resting place set by the All-knowing.[43] The star that has risen sets, and the star that has set rises; the star in the east travels to the west, and the star in the west travels to the east until the appointed time.[44] The pain I feel now is like the pain of someone whose wound has begun to heal, but then his wound is struck a blow and he feels a double pain: the pain of the blow and the pain of the reopened wound. That is how a person feels whose wounds have been soothed by the companionship of brothers whom he then loses."

The crow and the gazelle said to the rat, "Our words and yours, 6.35
however well spoken, and our sorrow and yours, however intense,
won't help the turtle. Enough! Try to find a way out for the turtle.
They say that a soldier is tested only in combat; a trustee only in
financial matters; family and children only when one is in need; and
friends only in times of misfortune."

The rat replied, "I think we can manage it if you, gazelle, go lie
down in the middle of the hunter's path, as if you were wounded
or your leg broken. The crow will land on you, as if to feed on you.
I'll follow the hunter and stay close to him. If the hunter sees you,
I bet he'll scorn the turtle and turn his attention to you. As soon as
he approaches, run from him, pretending to limp, so that he keeps
hoping to catch you. Let him get close from time to time; then lead
him on as far as you can and elude him. I bet that before the hunter
returns I'll have cut the turtle's rope and rescued her."

The gazelle and the crow did as the rat said, and the hunter 6.36
behaved just as the rat thought he would. By the time he returned,
the rat had cut the turtle's ropes and both had escaped.

When the hunter found the rope cut and nothing there, having
previously seen a gazelle that seemed to be limping or dead by
turns, and a crow perched on top of it as if to eat but not eating—he
found the place uncanny and the sights made him uneasy. "This," he
said, "must be a land of jinn or enchanters!" and he fled in terror,
not stopping or turning aside to look at anything. The gazelle, the
crow, the turtle, and the rat safely returned together to their thicket.

The Crows and the Owls

A parable showing that even if your enemy assumes a façade of sincerity, friendship, and generosity, he should not be trusted.

7.1 The king said, "Now that I have heard a parable about true friends who love and help each other, tell me one about somebody misled by an enemy who assumed a façade of humility and flattery with the intention to deceive and beguile. Tell me what befell him because of his heedlessness."

And the philosopher said, "Anyone deceived by a clever enemy whose hostile intentions are well known will suffer the fate the owls suffered at the hands of the crows."

"And what was their fate?" asked the king.

7.2 The philosopher told the following tale: On a mountain, so they say, there stood an enormous banyan tree[45] that harbored the nests of a thousand crows ruled by a king. A thousand owls also lived on the mountain; they, too, were ruled by a king. One night, because of the long-standing enmity between owls and crows, the owl king and his followers made a sortie against the crows, killing and wounding many. The next morning, the king of the crows called a meeting of his followers. "See what you've suffered because of the owls! Many have been slain and many wounded; many have lost feathers from their heads, their wings, and their tails. What's worse, I think, is that the owls know where you live; they're bold and savage. I fear they'll return and won't leave you alone. So consider carefully what you want to do."

Five crows were recognized for their superior judgment, mature intelligence, penetrating insight, and skill at managing affairs. The king rarely disregarded their advice. He turned to one and asked, "What is your opinion on this matter?" 7.3

The first crow said, "My view accords with the scholarly consensus: The only way to deal with a bitter enemy against whom you are powerless is to flee."

The king asked the second crow, "What is your opinion?" 7.4

"As to my colleague's advice to flee," he replied, "I don't think we should abandon our homes or submit to our enemy at the first stroke of disaster. We should pull ourselves together, prepare to fight, and make sure we aren't caught off guard again, keeping a sharp lookout and sending out scouts. If our enemy advances, we meet them, ready to fight, but without submitting or rushing into the thick of the battle, allowing our contingents to engage theirs. We should prepare, but delay any fighting until an opportunity presents itself. If this doesn't work, then flight is justified."

The king asked the third crow, "And your opinion?" 7.5

"I don't agree with what they've said," he answered. "I would have you keep a sharp lookout and send out scouts to discover whether the enemy wants a truce or will accept a ransom. We should gather intelligence: if we detect a readiness to accept a generous but not excessive compromise, we shouldn't be averse to making peace with them by paying a tribute. That way we can keep violence at bay and live safely in our homes. It's good policy for kings to use money to protect their realms and peoples when they fear the enemy is strong."

The king asked the fourth crow, "What do you think of your colleague's idea of seeking a truce?" 7.6

"I don't think it's a good idea," he replied. "Better to leave our homes and be driven into exile than to dishonor ourselves by submitting to an inferior enemy. Besides, I know they'll make exorbitant demands if we sue for peace. They say: Concede an inch to your enemy and you'll get what you want; concede everything,

and you'll humiliate yourself, demoralize your army, and embolden your enemy. It is like a stick set up in the sun: bend it a little and its shadow lengthens; bend it beyond a certain point and its shadow shortens. Our enemy won't be satisfied with small concessions: our best course is to fight resolutely."

7.7 The king asked the fifth crow, "What do you think: battle, truce, or withdrawal?"

"We cannot fight an enemy that we cannot match in strength," he replied. "They say that if you don't know your capacity and your enemy's capacity and you go ahead and engage a foe you cannot overpower, you foolishly harm only yourself. A wise person doesn't underestimate an enemy; if he does so he lets himself be deceived, and the person who lets himself be deceived is vulnerable. I'm very fearful of the owls even if they don't attack us—I feared them even before they attacked us. A prudent person never trusts his enemy. If the enemy is near, he fears an assault; if the enemy is far off, he fears his sudden return; if the enemy shows himself in the open, he fears an ambush; if the enemy retreats, he fears he may wheel back to attack; and if the enemy is on his own, he fears his cunning. As long as he can find another way, the astute man avoids fighting. Fighting costs lives; other misfortunes only cost money, words, and labor. Don't resolve to fight the owls: anyone who gets into a kicking match with an elephant kicks with death and disaster."

7.8 "If we're not to fight," said the king, "what do you suggest?"

"Confer and consider," he replied. "By conferring with wise advisers, kings achieve victories beyond the means of a great army. By consulting the views of prudent minsters, kings augment their own judgment and prudence, just as the rivers that flow into the sea augment its waters. The prudent man knows his own capacity as well as his enemy's. He knows the opportune moment and the right time for deception. He reviews matters one by one; he considers which deserve priority and which can be postponed; he determines which subordinates he can rely on. Anyone who lacks such judiciousness and cannot heed the advice of wise ministers will soon

find himself on the losing side, even if fate has granted him good fortune. For fortune doesn't bestow favor on renown or beauty; it bestows it on the wise who heed their wise advisers. And you are such a person, my king.

"Regarding the matter on which you've sought my advice, I will 7.9 respond partly in public and partly in private. I can state publicly that just as I do not advise fighting, I do not advise stooping to pay tribute or to accept the humiliation of subjection. It is wise and noble to choose death with honor over a life of sorrow and humiliation. And I think we should consider the matter immediately, without hindrance or indifference. What I wish to impart in secret will remain confidential. Kings, it has been said, obtain victories only through prudent management of their affairs; prudent management depends on weighing opinions; and sound opinions depend on repeated examination and well-guarded secrets. He who guards his secret benefits in two ways: either he gains his objective, or, if he fails, he avoids shame and harm.

"If you have a secret project, you need a trustworthy counselor you can apprise, and who can help you make decisions. Even if the person seeking advice is superior in judgment to the person whose advice is sought, the latter's judgment will increase his judiciousness, just as adding grease to a fire makes it brighter. A counselor should agree with his patron in what he thinks correct, but be gentle when enlightening the patron about any error he might have made—that way, the correct opinion gains prominence when there is hesitation and uncertainty. By cooperating in this way, they will arrive at the correct opinion. A counselor who is not like this is on the side of his patron's enemies. This is like a man who utters a spell and sends a demon against someone: if he utters the spell incorrectly, the demon in his confusion may seize the reciter of the spell, unless God repels it. A king is unlikely to lose the good fortune he has been given if he guards his secrets, chooses his ministers well, is feared by the common people, takes care not to let his innermost thoughts be known, lets no good service go unrewarded, leaves no

criminal unpunished, and is moderate in his expenditures, neither a miser nor a spendthrift. Secrets differ in degree: some can be shared with kin and some with two men, while others require the cooperation of many people. Given the importance of this secret, I think that four ears and two tongues, no more, should be privy to it."

7.10
How the Enmity between Crows and Owls Began

The king rose immediately to address him in private. One of his questions was: "Do you know how the enmity between us and the owls began?"

"Yes, Your Majesty," he replied. "It was something a crow said."

"And how did that happen?" asked the king.

7.11

The crow told the following tale: Once upon a time, they say, the community of birds had no king. They had decided to make an owl their king, but during their assembly a crow appeared. "Let's wait for this crow," said one of them, "and ask his opinion about this." The crow arrived, and, when asked his opinion, he replied, "Even if all the other birds perished, and there were no longer any peacocks, cranes, ducks, and doves, it would be more honorable for you to live without a king than to make an owl your king—the ugliest, worst-natured, most irascible, least intelligent, and least merciful of birds—not to mention their midday laziness and daytime blindness. Their stupidity and bad character are the worst—unless, that is, you intend to crown him king, but manage affairs as you yourselves see fit, as did the rabbit who claimed that the moon was her king, then acted according to her own judgment."

"What do you mean?" asked the birds.

7.12
The Rabbit Who Claimed the Moon Was Her King

And the crow told the following tale: They say that a land where elephants lived experienced several years of drought. Water became scarce and the springs dried up. In their thirst, the elephants complained to their king, who sent out messengers and scouts in every direction to search for water. One of them returned and said that in another land he had found a spring full of water, called the Spring of the Moon. The king and his retinue set out for the land. It happened that the spring was located in a place full of rabbits, and the elephants trampled many of them to death in their burrows. The

rabbits assembled before their king and said, "See what these elephants have done! Devise something for us, because if they come back to their waterhole, they'll kill us all."

And the king said, "If anyone has a plan, let him bring it."

A young buck named Fayrūz—whose good judgment and courtly manner had already impressed the king—stepped forward. "If it please the king, send me to the elephants, along with someone the king trusts, to see and hear everything I say and do, and to report back to the king."

"You are someone I trust," said the king. "I am satisfied with your judgment and will hold your words to be true. Go to the elephants and in my name deliver any message you please. Do as you see fit, but remember that the sender's intelligence is judged by the messenger's judgment and behavior. Be gentle, agreeable, and calm; a gentle messenger softens the heart, but a rough one hardens it."

The rabbit set out just as the moon was rising. When he came to 7.13
the elephants, he didn't wish to get too close, lest they trample him to death, so he went to a spot overlooking the path and called to the king of the elephants, who answered. The rabbit then said, "The moon has sent me to you. Though the message be harsh, the messenger who delivers it is blameless."

"What is the message?" asked the king of the elephants.

"The moon says, 'Someone who, knowing himself to be stronger than the weak, imagines himself to be stronger than the strong, will be undone by his own strength. You know that your strength is superior to that of other animals, and this has deluded you with respect to me. You have gone to my spring, which bears my name; you have drunk from it, muddying it and polluting it with your elephants. I command you and warn you: Don't do this again or I will destroy you. If you have any doubt about my message, go to the spring right away, and I will accost you in a way that will leave no doubt.'"

Amazed at the rabbit's words, the king of the elephants set off with him to the spring. He looked into it and saw the moon's reflection.

"Take some water in your trunk," Fayrūz said, "wash your face, and bow down before the moon in worship."

When the king of the elephants put his trunk into the water, it seemed to him that the moon's reflection was trembling. "Why is the moon trembling?" he asked. "Could he be angry with me?"

"He is," replied Fayrūz.

So the elephant bowed down to the reflection, apologized for what he had done, and promised that neither he nor any of his elephants would ever return to that spring.

7.14 The crow said, "In addition to what I've told you about owls, deceit and guile are part of their nature. A deceitful, guileful king is the worst king of all. Those afflicted with a treacherous ruler or a deceitful judge will suffer the fate of the partridge[46] and the rabbit who took their dispute for arbitration to a cat who fasted and prayed."

"And what was their fate?" asked the birds.

7.15 The crow told the following tale: Once I had as neighbor a partridge who lived in a burrow near the tree where I had my nest. He and I were fond of each other and met often. One day I looked for him and couldn't find him. His absence dragged on, and I had no idea where he had gone. Meanwhile, a rabbit came to live in the partridge's home. I wasn't inclined to quarrel with him, because the partridge had been away so long that I thought he must have perished. The rabbit lived there for a time, but then the partridge returned and, finding the rabbit there, said, "This is my home. Get out!"

The Partridge, the Rabbit, and the Pious Cat

"I have possession," replied the rabbit. "You allege otherwise. If you have a valid claim, bring proof."

"I have clear evidence," said the partridge.

"First find a judge," said the rabbit. "Then we'll see about the evidence."

"By the riverbank near us," said the partridge, "lives a cat who is an invalid. He fasts endlessly, prays night and day, harms no one, spills no blood, and is content to live on grass. If you like, we can go to him for arbitration and abide by his decision."

"That's fine with me, if he is as you describe!" replied the rabbit.

So off they went, and I followed them to have a look at this pious 7.16
cat and to see how he would arbitrate between them. When the
cat saw the partridge and the rabbit approaching in the distance,
he stood up on his hind legs to pray. When they got close to him—
making sure to be cautious and respectful, and to acknowledge his
merit—they asked him if he would arbitrate. He asked them to tell
their story, which they did, and then he said, "Old age has overtaken
me; my ears have become so dull I can hardly hear. Come closer and
repeat your story." So they did.

"Before pronouncing judgment, I'll start by giving you some 7.17
good advice," he said. "I charge you to fear God and seek nothing
but the truth: the seeker of truth prospers, even if the judgment
goes against him; but the seeker of falsehood loses, even if the judg-
ment goes in his favor. The only things an inhabitant of this world
takes with him from his earthly existence are neither money nor
friends, but the good works he has done. A wise man should seek
what endures and will bring him benefit tomorrow, and abandon
everything else."

As he talked, they became more and more at ease with him and
came closer and closer, until finally he pounced, grabbed them, and
killed them both.

The crow said, "To everything else I've described, the owl adds
deceit, guile, and cunning. Therefore, you mustn't make the owl
your king."

The birds followed the crow's advice and didn't make the owl 7.18
king.

And the owl who had been chosen to be king said to the crow,
"You've done me a terrible injury. I don't know whether I did you
some wrong in the past for which I might deserve this treatment
from you. If that is the case, then so be it. If not, know that a tree
felled by an ax will sprout again; flesh and bone cut by a sword
will heal and mend, but wounds made by the tongue never heal.
An arrowhead that sinks into the body can be pulled out, but

arrow-sharp words that pierce the heart can never be pulled out. Everything that burns can be extinguished by something: fire by water, poison by an antidote, and sorrow by patience; but the fire of hatred never dies. You crows have planted a tree of enmity between us that will last for all time."

With these words, the owl left in a fury, thirsting for revenge.

7.19 The crow regretted his rashness. "It was stupid of me to say things that brought enmity on me and my people. I was neither the bird best qualified to speak about the subject, nor the one who had the biggest stake in the matter of the kingship. Many others may have thought what I thought and known what I knew, but, unlike me, they refrained from speaking, out of caution and consideration of the consequences. This is especially true when one speaks to someone face-to-face, as confrontation leaves a legacy of hatred and rancor. Even if as a speaker you are confident of your strength, ability, and virtue, you shouldn't let it lead you to expose yourself to enmity. My foolishness lay in venturing to speak on a weighty matter before giving it due consideration and before consulting those entitled to give advice. Failure to consult a wise counselor and act on his opinion, after thorough examination and reflection, guarantees unhappiness with the results. I little needed what I've acquired today and the distress I find myself in!" The crow chided himself at great length.

"This, to answer your question, was the reason for the enmity between the owls and us."

7.20 "Now I understand," said the king. "But tell me something more pertinent to today than the origin of the hatred between crows and owls."

And the crow said, "I've already told you what I think about fighting. You know how much I dislike it. But I hope God will set in motion some good that will bring swift relief. Those in dire straits have often achieved through cunning what they could never have achieved in a contest of strength—like the men who tricked the ascetic and made off with his goat."

"And how did they do that?" asked the king.

The crow told the following tale: An ascetic, they say, once bought a large, fat kid to offer as a sacrifice, and set off with it. Some sly fellows saw him and conspired to trick him out of it. One of them approached and asked, "Sir, what is this dog you have there?" The second then approached and asked, "Sir, do you intend to hunt with this dog?" Then the third approached and said, "You may be dressed as an ascetic, but walking with a dog isn't the sort of thing ascetics do." After hearing these remarks, the ascetic had doubts and became suspicious about the kid. "Perhaps," he said, "the vendor cast a spell on me." He promptly released the kid, and the men took it and divided it among themselves.

"I've told you this story because I think we, too, can attain our end through skill and cunning. Here's what I think: The king should fly into a rage in the presence of his soldiers and order that I be beaten, expelled from his presence, and cast down at the foot of the tree, all bloody, feathers and tail plucked out. The king should then leave with his soldiers, go to a place I'll specify, and remain there until I report back on how matters play out between me and the owls."

The king had this done to the crow and went with his crows to the specified place.

The owls came that very night. They didn't find any crows, and didn't notice the crow lying at the foot of the tree. Fearing they might leave before seeing him and that his self-imposed torments might have been to no avail, he began moaning and groaning until the owls heard him. When they saw him, they told their king, who approached, surrounded by owls, to question him about the crows. The king commanded an owl to ask him who he was and where the crows were.

The crow stated his name and then said, "You ask about the crows— I think you can see from my state that I am not privy to their secrets."

The king of the owls said, "This is the crow king's minister, confidant, and adviser. Ask him for what offense he has been treated in this way."

"The foolishness of my advice did this to me."

"Foolishness? How so?" asked the king.

7.23 The crow said, "After your attack, our king asked for advice. 'Crows!' he said, 'what do you think we should do?' As I was well-regarded by the king, I said, 'I don't think we can fight the owls: they're stronger than we are, and bolder. I think we should sue for peace and offer to pay tribute. If they agree, well and good; if not, we should flee the country.' I told them, among other things, 'Fighting the owls now would be worse for you and better for them. A truce is the best option.' I told them to submit, and drew an analogy. 'Nothing,' I said, 'repels a powerful enemy's strength and fury better than submission. Don't you see that the grass is safe from the gale because it is flexible and bends whichever way the wind turns?' They were enraged by my words and insisted they wanted to fight. They accused me of disloyalty and of turning against them. They rejected my advice and subjected me to every sort of abuse."

7.24 When the king of the owls heard the crow's words, he asked one of his ministers, "What's your opinion regarding this crow?"

"No two ways about it! Put him to death immediately. He's the crows' principal resource. Killing him earns us a great victory, as we will have deprived them of his expertise and cunning. His loss will be a blow to the crows. They say that when you hold the advantage at a critical moment and let it slip, you get no second chance; and that when you seek an opportunity to act, but neglect it when you get it, you're likely to lose the opportunity and never regain it. To catch your enemy weak and helpless and fail to get rid of him is to regret it when the enemy grows strong, readies himself, and becomes invincible."

7.25 The owl king then asked another of his ministers, "What's your opinion regarding this crow?"

"I think you shouldn't kill him. A humiliated enemy with no fight left in him deserves mercy and forgiveness; a frightened asylum seeker deserves safety and protection. Furthermore, a trivial matter will sometimes bring a person to show affection for his enemy—as

happened when the thief inadvertently caused the merchant's wife to show affection for her husband."

"And how did that happen?" asked the king.

The minister told the following tale: Once, they say, there was a man who was rich, old, and exceedingly passionate. He had a beautiful young wife with whom he was head over heels in love, but she detested him and wouldn't allow him to embrace her and satisfy his desires. The merchant knew how she felt, but this made him love her all the more. One night, a thief came to the merchant's house and found the merchant asleep and the wife awake. Frightened by the thief, she threw her arms around her husband. The embrace aroused the merchant, who exclaimed, "Whence comes this bliss?" When he saw the thief, he called out to him, "Man, feel free to take all the money and belongings you want. You deserve my thanks for getting this woman to embrace me."

7.26
The Thief Who Caused the Merchant's Wife to Embrace Her Husband

The king then asked the third minister for his opinion about the crow.

7.27

"I think you should spare him and treat him well, as he is likely to give you good advice. A wise man considers it a victory when his enemies fall out among themselves and are busy quarreling among themselves. This is exactly what happened when the ascetic escaped because the thief and the demon quarreled."

"And how did that happen?" asked the king.

The minister told the following tale: Once, they say, an ascetic set out to take to his home a milch cow he had been given. A thief, intent on stealing it, followed him, joined in turn by a demon in human form. "Who are you?" asked the thief. "A demon," came the reply. "I intend to follow this ascetic, and when he falls asleep, I'll take him." "For my part," said the thief, "I intend to follow him home and steal his cow." So together they followed the ascetic. When he arrived home that evening, he went into his room and put the cow in another room. When the ascetic went to bed, the thief feared that if the demon took the ascetic first, before he could steal the cow, the ascetic would scream; people would come running, and

7.28
The Ascetic Who Escaped When the Thief and the Demon Quarreled

he wouldn't be able to steal the cow. So he said to the demon, "Wait until I make off with the cow; then do as you please with the man." The demon, for his part, feared that if the thief stole the cow first, the ascetic might hear him, wake up, and rouse the family, and he wouldn't be able to do anything. So he said to the thief, "Wait until I take the ascetic; then do as you please with the cow." Each refused to yield to the other, and they kept arguing until the thief shouted to the ascetic, "Get up, man! This demon wants to take you!" The demon, for his part, shouted, "Get up, ascetic! This thief wants to take your cow!" The ascetic, his family, and his neighbors all woke up, and the thief and demon fled.

7.29 When the third minister finished speaking, the first owl, who had advised killing the crow, said, "I think this crow has deceived you with his graciousness, cunning, and entreaties. You're about to throw caution to the winds and expose yourselves to great danger. Be careful! Don't do it! Consider the matter intelligently, like those who decide correctly about their own and their enemies' affairs, like those who aren't deceived by an enemy's smooth words and abandon good sense because of an argument. Don't be like weaklings whose hearts soften toward their enemies at the slightest flattery and entreaty. Don't give more credence to what you hear than to what you know. Don't be like the carpenter who disbelieved what he saw and knew, but believed what he heard, and so was beguiled and deceived."

"How was he deceived?" asked the king.

7.30 The minister told the following tale: A carpenter, they say, had a
The Carpenter wife whom he loved. Another man fell in love with her, and some of
Who Disbelieved the carpenter's kin found out and told him. The carpenter, wanting
His Own Eyes to know for sure, said to his wife, "I'm going to a village a few miles away to do some work for a prince. I'll be there for a few days, so pack me some food." The wife did so and the carpenter left, saying, "Stay in the house and keep your door locked until I return."

7.31 As soon as he was gone, she sent her lover a message: "The carpenter has left on business and will be away for a few days." The

carpenter, however, came back surreptitiously, entered the house through a hidden entrance, and concealed himself under the bed on which he and his wife slept. When the lover arrived, the wife wined and dined him; then they got into bed and spent the night together. Toward the end of the night, the carpenter, overcome by sleep, stretched out his leg from under the bed. The wife saw it, and, recognizing him, knew it would mean trouble for her. So she said to her lover, "Raise your voice, and ask me, 'Whom do you love more: me or your husband?'" The man did so, and she answered, "Lover, why must you ask? Don't you know that we women take lovers only to satisfy our lust? We pay no attention to their achievements or character or anything else about them. As soon as we satisfy our lust, they become just like any other man out there. But a husband!—he is like one's own mother and father. God confound any woman who doesn't value the husband who toils and labors for her as much as her own soul! Never mention him again!"

The carpenter, moved by his wife's words, was overcome with compassion and tears. He was certain that his wife loved him. He stayed put until morning and when he was sure that his wife's lover had left, he came out from under the bed. His wife pretended to be asleep. Thinking she was sleeping, he sat beside her, fanning her face. When she stirred as if to wake, he said, "My precious, dear to me as my mother and father! You were up all night, tired out by that tedious man. I didn't want to upset you, otherwise I'd have reviled him. I desisted because of what I know about your affection for him." 7.32

"I've told you this story because I don't want you to be like the foolish carpenter who didn't believe what he saw with his own eyes but believed his wife's deceitful and lying words. Don't believe what the crow says. Remember that an enemy who can inflict no harm from a distance, often, if he is a smooth talker, tries to do it by drawing near and giving advice. I've never feared the crows as much as I do now, having seen this crow and heard his words." 7.33

But the king of the owls disregarded his advice and commanded that the crow be taken to his home, honored, and treated well.

7.34 The minister who had advised execution said, "If you don't kill this crow, at least treat him as an enemy to be feared and guarded against. He's cunning and deceitful. I think he's come here with a plan to do harm to us and to benefit himself."

But the king paid no heed, and the minister failed to stop him from treating the crow with honor and favor. The crow spoke courteously to the king when in his presence, and the king became more and more gracious, friendly, at ease, and credulously reliant on his advice.

7.35 One day, in the midst of the owls' assembly—with the owl who had advised execution present—the crow said, "One of you should tell the king on my behalf that the crows did me a great wrong by tormenting me and abandoning me. Tell him that my heart will never rest until I work my will on them. Tell him I've given much thought to the matter, and I see that it will not be possible as long as I remain a crow. I've heard on the authority of a learned man that anyone who willingly renounces his life and immolates himself in fire will have made such a magnificent sacrifice to God that any prayer he subsequently makes will be granted. Therefore, if the king permits, I will immolate myself and pray to the Lord to destroy the crows, thereby quenching my thirst for vengeance and achieving my objective, and I will pray to be turned into an owl, so I can join in your attack on the crows."

7.36 The owl who had advised execution said, "Like sweet-smelling, fine-colored wine in which poison has been dissolved, you appear to be good, but conceal evil. Do you think your vile nature and evil character will be consumed if we burn you in fire? No, they will accompany you wherever you go. If you know that your prayers will be answered, you will, I think, pray only for the destruction of the owls. You will remain true to your evil nature and character, like the lady mouse who was offered better and better husbands—the sun, the cloud, the wind, and the mountain—but scorned them all and chose to marry a rat."

"How did that come about?" they asked.

The owl told the following tale: Once, they say, there was a pious ascetic, one of the most distinguished of his time, whose prayers were always answered. While he was sitting by a riverbank, a kite flew by with a mouse in its foot, and it fell from the bird's claws and landed near him. Out of compassion, he picked it up and wrapped it in his cloak. He wanted to take it home, but concerned that raising it would be a burden on his family, he prayed to God to turn it into a young woman easy for them to raise. His prayer was answered, and the mouse turned into a beautiful maiden. He took her home and said to his wife, "Treat her as you would our own child," which she did.

7.37
The Lady Mouse and Her Choice of Husbands

The maiden lived with them until she came of age, at which time the ascetic gave her a choice of husbands. "You're of a marriageable age now," he said, and added, "The man in whose house a woman has not menstruated is most fortunate.[47] I wish to treat you as a father would his own child. Think about what you want in a husband; tell me, and I will do as you command."

7.38

"I want a husband who is strong, powerful, and invincible."

"I do not think," he said, "that there is anything stronger than the sun." And to the sun he said, "This beautiful maiden has been like a child to me. She has asked for a husband who is strong, powerful, and invincible—I give her to you in marriage."

And the sun replied, "I am powerful, but the cloud is more powerful, for he can block my rays."

So the ascetic said to the cloud, "This maiden has asked for a husband more powerful than anything else." And the cloud replied, "I am powerful, but the wind, which drives me this way and that, is more powerful."

7.39

The ascetic put the same proposal to the wind. And the wind replied, "I am powerful, but the mountain is more powerful, because I cannot move it."

The ascetic repeated his words to the mountain and the mountain replied, "I am powerful, but the rat is more powerful, because he bores into me and enters where he will, and I can do nothing to stop him."

7.40 So the ascetic said to the rat, "This maiden has asked for a husband who is the most powerful of God's creatures."

"How can I marry her," replied the rat, "when my burrow is so narrow? I am small and she is large and won't fit in there with me."

So at the maiden's request, the ascetic prayed to the Lord, who turned her back into a mouse, and she was married to the rat.

"Your case, deceiver, is just like hers."

7.41 Neither the king nor his companions heeded his words. The king ordered that the crow be honored, shown favor, given gifts, and treated courteously, which was done. As he grew in esteem, they all came to be on friendly terms. His wing feathers, tail, and plumage grew back and he became plump, strong, and healthy. He learned everything about the owls' vulnerabilities. He kept himself informed about their numbers and secrets and collected information about their affairs. Having learned all he wanted, he sneaked off and flew back to the crows. When he arrived, he greeted the king, who welcomed him and asked for a report.

"Good news! Rejoice in your victory and the owls' destruction."

"How so?"

"I've accomplished everything I wanted; the rest is up to you."

"We're ready and await your orders," replied the king.

7.42 "The owls," said the crow, "live in this location"—he named it. "By day they gather in a cave in a mountain there. I know of a place near the mountain where there is an abundance of dry wood. Each crow should carry as much wood as he can to the mouth of the cave where the owls roost during the day. There's also a flock of sheep near the mountain; I'll get fire from the shepherd, bring it to you, and drop it on the wood. Work together, flap your wings vigorously, and fan the fire until the wood blazes up. The owls who come out of the cave will be consumed by the fire and those who stay in the cave will be killed by the smoke."

And that is what they did. All the owls perished. The king and those with him returned safe and victorious.

Afterward, the king asked the crow who had brought about the owls' destruction, "How could you tolerate the company of owls so long, when the good cannot bear to keep company with evildoers? The good, so they say, would rather plunge into fire than live with evildoers."

"True, Your Majesty," replied the crow, "but a wise man doesn't fall to pieces when confronted with a disaster that threatens to destroy him and his people. He forces himself to be patient, in the hope that patience will bring relief and safety in its wake. He doesn't grieve at all or think himself above submitting to inferiors, provided that he can attain his objective and rejoice over the fruits of his action and patience."

"Tell me about the owls' intelligence."

"I encountered no owl of any intelligence or worth except the one who pressed for my execution," replied the crow. "Their judgment was too weak to believe him and recognize the merit of his opinion—to recall that I had been a crow of some standing and respected for my judgment, and that they ought to fear deception or trickery at my hands. He cautioned them about what I might have in mind. He gave them good advice, but they rejected it; their own intelligence wasn't adequate, and they wouldn't accept the advice of those whose intelligence was. They didn't fear me or keep secrets from me. A king, so it has been said, should keep his secrets and affairs from all who are suspect; only persons above suspicion should be allowed near where he keeps his secrets, plans, and letters; near the basin where he bathes, near his bed, blankets, and clothing; near his mounts and weapons, his food and drink, or his oils, perfumes, and herbs."

The king said, "It was pride and his ministers' bad judgment that killed the owl king."

"You're right," said the crow. "Rarely do the proud win a victory. Has eminence ever been attained without insolence ensuing? Can we eat to excess without falling ill? Can we covet without suffering disgrace? Can we trust the counsel of rogues and evil ministers

THE CROWS AND THE OWLS | 133

without falling into peril? It has been said: A proud man should not expect honest praise; a deceiver should not expect many friends; a churl should not expect honor; a miser should not expect charity; a covetous man should not expect to have few sins; and a haughty, negligent king who rarely consults his ministers should not expect his reign to last or his people to prosper."

7.46 "It must have been distressing," said the king, "to humble yourself before the owls."

"Yes, it was," said the crow, "but I bore it patiently because I expected a good outcome. As has been said: When certain of a good outcome, a wise man must not be too proud to carry his enemy on his shoulder. Those who hope for benefit bear hardship patiently—just as the cobra patiently carried the frog on his back."

"How did that come about?" asked the king.

7.47
The Cobra Who Stooped to Carry the King of the Frogs And the crow told the following tale: A cobra, they say, grew so old and feeble that he could no longer hunt and feed himself. So he said to himself, "Only by employing cunning and skill will I be able to find sustenance." One day, as he was out looking for some food, he happened upon a pool filled with many frogs, which he once used to catch. He lay down there, looking sad and dejected.

"Snake, why are you so sad?" asked one of the frogs.

"Who is more entitled to be sad than I?" he replied. "I used to live almost entirely on the frogs I caught, but now I'm in trouble. Frogs are off limits for me—I couldn't swallow one even if I had it in my mouth."

7.48 The frog went to his king and told him this good news. The king asked the cobra how this had come about.

The cobra said, "A few nights ago I was chasing after a frog. I drove him to a house. In he went, and in I went after him. The house, which was dark, belonged to a holy man whose son was in the house. I felt the boy's toe and, taking it for the frog, I bit it, and the boy died. I fled, with the holy man in pursuit, cursing me: 'If this snake has slain my son unjustly and wrongfully, send down shame and humiliation upon him and make him a mount for the king of

the frogs, able to catch only those the king gives him as charity.' As a result, I've come to you willingly so that you can ride me."

The king of the frogs was eager to ride the cobra—he considered it an honor that would bring him glory and prestige. After he had ridden the cobra for a few days, the cobra said to him, "Your Majesty knows that I've been cursed and placed under a ban; please give me some food to live on."

The king of the frogs said, "I swear that as long as you are my mount, you must have something to live on!" He ordered that every day two frogs be seized and given to the cobra. Thus the cobra lived out his life, and benefited by demeaning himself before a contemptible enemy.

"Similarly, I too patiently endured what I had to in order to obtain a great benefit for us: our safety and the enemy's destruction."

The king said, "I see now that a downfall effected through gentleness and skill eradicates the enemy more thoroughly than one effected through open conflict. For all its heat and fury, when fire attacks a tree, it burns only the part above the ground; but water, for all its gentleness and coolness, uproots the part under the ground. They say that four things should not be taken lightly even in small doses: fire, disease, enemies, and debt." 7.49

The crow said, "Everything I did was a result of Your Majesty's judgment, discipline, and good fortune. If two men seek a thing, they say, the more valiant of the two will win it; if they are equal in valor, the more determined; if they are equal in determination, the one with better helpers; and if they are equal in that respect, the one who is more fortunate. They also say that to try to get the better of a resolute, intelligent, fortunate king—one whom prosperity doesn't make overconfident and adversity doesn't dismay—is to invite your own death. All the more so when the king is like Your Majesty: knowledgeable about affairs, knowing the right time for severity or softness, anger or contentment, haste or deliberateness; a ruler who ponders today, tomorrow, and the consequences of his deeds—all of which leads to proper judgment." 7.50

7.51 The king of the crows said, "Not so! It was due to your judgment, intelligence, and advice, and at the risk of your life. One resolute man's good judgment can destroy a powerful enemy more effectively than many soldiers. But what amazes me most is how you were able to stay among the owls so long, listening to their furor, without uttering a word."

"I always followed Your Majesty's own practice of associating with everyone, high or low, with courtesy, gentleness, acquiescence, and complaisance," responded the crow.

7.52 "I see now that you are a master of action," said the king. "My other ministers are masters of fruitless words, for that is how the masters of talk are. We derived no pleasure from eating or sleeping before God gave you to us as a great blessing. A sick man, they say, finds no pleasure in sleep or food until he recovers his health; a greedy man promised office or wealth by his ruler finds no pleasure until the promise is fulfilled; and a man beset by an enemy whom he fears night and day finds no pleasure until he is rid of him. They say that the heart finds rest when worry departs; the back finds rest when a heavy load is removed; and the heart fills with joy when one becomes safe from one's enemy."

"I ask God, who has destroyed your enemy, to grant you enjoyment of your sovereignty," said the crow. "May He cause it to be for the benefit of your subjects and give them a share in the happiness of your reign."

And the king said, "If a king's subjects derive no joy from his reign, he is like a nanny goat's wattle, which the kid sucks, thinking it a teat, but gets no good out of it."

7.53 The king then asked, "Tell me, good minister, how did the king of the owls behave toward his soldiers?"

"With arrogance, insolence, boastfulness, conceit, incompetence, and poor judgment. All his companions and ministers were like him, except the one who advised them to kill me."

"What indications of intelligence did you see in him?" the king asked.

"Two things: first, his opinion that I should be executed on the spot; second, that he didn't keep his advice hidden even if it was made light of by his master. Furthermore, he spoke politely and gently, without harshness or roughness, so that he often apprised the king of a shortcoming without angering him. He would cite parables and speak of others' shortcomings, so that the king might recognize his own through theirs, yet find no way to become angry with him. This is one of the things I heard him say to the king: 'A king must not become negligent about his authority, for it is a momentous matter that few obtain and that prospers only through sound judgment.'"

Here ends the Story of the Crows and the Owls.

The Turtle and the Monkey

*A parable about someone who works hard to acquire a thing, but having
acquired it, doesn't know how to hold on to it.*

8.1 The king said to the philosopher, "Now that I've heard you speak
about people who harbor hostility, and how we should not be taken
in by them or trust them, even if they entreat us and court our affec-
tion, tell me a parable about someone who works hard to acquire a
thing, but having acquired it, doesn't know how to hold on to it, so
that he loses it and has nothing but grief and regret to show for his
efforts."

8.2 And the philosopher told the following tale: They say that by the
shore of the sea there was a land full of monkeys ruled by a monkey
king. Eventually the king became old and weak, and his throne was
coveted by a kinsman who so ingratiated himself with the monkeys
and won their affections that they made him king and banished
his predecessor. The old king fled to a place by the seashore where
there was a large grove full of all sorts of trees. He became fond of a
fig tree overlooking the sea and would eat its figs. There was a turtle
who liked to rest in the tree's shade and eat any figs that fell into the
water. One day, while the monkey was picking figs, one fell from his
hand, and he was so pleased by the sound it made as it fell into the
water that he began throwing figs into the water, delighting in the
sound. Convinced that the monkey was throwing them down for his
sake, the turtle began to eat them. Eager, therefore, to make friends
with the monkey, he addressed him politely and told him of his

desire for friendship. The monkey agreed, and each came to trust the other and enjoy his company. The turtle rejoiced to have the monkey as neighbor and friend, and each devoted himself exclusively to the other, to the neglect of family and friends.

The turtle stayed away so long and it was so out of character that 8.3 his wife became sad and complained to a friend of hers of her anxiety about her husband.

"May God not bring you shame or cause you sadness," replied the friend. "Don't be grieved, and don't worry about your husband. I've heard that he is living as the neighbor of a monkey. He likes his new friend so much that the friend has replaced you and his other kinfolk and friends in his affections. Don't be sad, but let's devise a way to destroy the monkey who has brought you so much heartache. If the monkey perishes, your husband will come home and resume his intimacy and kindness."

They devised the following plan. The turtle's wife pretended to 8.4 be sick and sent a messenger to inform her husband about her condition, asking him to come see her before her death.

When the messenger arrived, the turtle asked the monkey for permission to pay his family a visit, and the monkey agreed. When the turtle saw his wife's condition, he questioned her, speaking as gently as he could, but she didn't answer. The wife's friend was standing beside her, and the turtle, seeing that his wife would say nothing, asked the friend, "What's wrong? Why can't she say a word?"

"How can a sick person speak," replied the friend, "when she knows for certain that there is only one medicine for her illness, a medicine that can't be obtained here?"

The turtle was overcome by sadness and grief at these words. "Tell me what the medicine is and I'll gladly do everything to find it, even if I have to give up my life."

"We women are more knowledgeable than doctors about women's diseases, especially the internal pains that only women experience," replied the friend. "This pain involves her womb. The remedy for it is known; it just isn't available."

"What is it?" he asked.

"A monkey. She must eat some of its heart."

"Where can I find this?" asked the turtle. "How can we get it?"

"I've already told you the medicine isn't available. We have no choice but to endure patiently whatever happens to her."

8.5 The turtle was consumed with grief. He considered what he could do for his wife, but his only hope lay with his friend. He was tempted to trick the monkey and in this way obtain what was needed, but he rebuked himself for thinking this and reminded himself of the sacred bond of brotherhood and protection that existed between them, warning himself of the consequences of treachery. At the same time, he remembered how much his wife meant to him, the sweetness she brought to his heart, her helpfulness to him, and her superiority over other women. He began to weigh the two things. Treachery was a grievous sin in the eyes of God and unseemly by the standards of morality, but he could hardly abandon his wife, given his strong attachment to her. He pondered the matter for a long time. Finally, passion won the day and inclined him toward his wife and against loyalty to his friend, and he decided to kill the monkey. He reasoned that the way to do it was to work out how to transport him to the island where the turtle's home was located. "When we get there, he'll have no food or drink to nourish him; soon enough he'll perish of hunger and thirst, and when he dies I'll take his heart and give it to my wife to eat."

8.6 Having settled on this plan, the turtle went back to the monkey, who missed him and was eagerly awaiting his return. The monkey, joyful and relieved to see him back, asked after the turtle's family and children. The turtle filled him in, adding, "Because I longed for you so much, I got nothing from the joy of seeing my family and children. Everything was spoiled as soon as I remembered that you were alone and cut off from your own family and children. I could hardly wait to get back to you. Now I want you to strengthen our bond of friendship and honor me by accompanying me to see my family. They will see you, learn the place you hold in my heart, and

rejoice in our brotherhood, and you will partake of our food and drink. I wish to repay you for the kindness you've bestowed on me since becoming my neighbor."

The monkey said, "You mustn't think that I deserve any credit 8.7 for what I did for you. I've come to believe that I owe you more than you owe me. I needed you more than you needed me. Cut off from my kingdom, my family, my homeland, my friends, and my acquaintances, I had become a solitary outcast. If God hadn't granted me your companionship and friendship, I should have perished of grief and loneliness. Therefore, you deserve more than I can ever recount. However, if you would like me to visit your family and children with you, I'll come. But how can I cross this stretch of water?"

"I'll carry you on my back," said the turtle, "until we reach the island where I live. It is free from danger, with shady groves and many kinds of fruit trees. Affection increases when friends are at ease with each other, visit each other's acquaintances and family, and share food, and this hasn't happened between us yet."

The monkey finally gave in to his exhortations. The turtle had the 8.8 monkey mount his back, and set out on the sea toward his family. At one point, he stopped at a place that wasn't too deep and remembered the brotherhood that existed between them and thought of the treachery he had decided to commit. He felt deeply troubled and inwardly was very torn. He debated with himself, saying, "I am about to commit a terrible act of treachery. Women don't deserve to have people commit treachery and villainy for their sake. They're not to be trusted or relied on to keep a promise. Gold, they say, is tested by fire; an animal's strength is tested by a heavy load; a merchant's honesty is tested in transactions; but no test whatsoever yields thorough knowledge about women."

The monkey noticed that the turtle was debating with himself 8.9 and became uneasy. "Why do you seem worried and sad? Am I burdening you?"

"What have I done to make you feel this way?" asked the turtle.

"I see you're deep in thought," said the monkey.

"You're right," said the turtle. "I recalled that you are coming to visit my family while my wife is ill, which is going to curtail our kindness and hospitality considerably."

"What I've already experienced of your eagerness to show me kindness makes it unnecessary for you to go to any more trouble."

The turtle carried the monkey a bit farther. Then he stopped again to debate with himself. "How can I leave my wife in her present state? But how can I betray my friend?" Then, to absolve himself from a wrong decision, he told himself, "They say that if you can obtain a great reward only by means of a slight sin, then the right thing to do is to obtain the reward by means of the sin." The great reward he would obtain, so he thought, would be his wife's recovery; the slight sin, so he thought, would be to kill the monkey.

8.10 While the turtle was pondering these things and citing maxims to himself, the monkey, too, was pondering his situation. Full of misgivings and suspicions, he said to himself, "The sages say that you should use prudence and skill to protect yourself against misgivings about a friend who finds his way into your heart. If your suspicion is true, you achieve safety; if not, you practice prudence, which harms neither you nor your friend."

"Still so lost in thought?" the monkey asked the turtle.

"I became lost in thought when I remembered my wife's illness and the place she holds in my heart."

"Your anxiety about her saddens me," said the monkey. "And your grief troubles me. Let's find a way to help her. Anything that troubles you troubles me."

"Actually," said the turtle, "I've looked into it. The physicians have prescribed the only medicine that will heal her."

"And what is it?" asked the monkey.

"A monkey's heart," replied the turtle.

8.11 The monkey realized this spelled disaster. "This is what greed has done to me," he said to himself. "Desire overcame my better judgment—and I'm not the first to be undone by desire and greed. They

say that to be satisfied and content is to live a secure life, restful and at ease; but to be covetous and greedy is to live a life of weariness, fatigue, and fear. In any case, the only thing to be done is to seek help from God and to use my own cunning." So he said to the turtle, "The sages have said that those with means should spend it on three things: charity, if they desire a heavenly reward; service to their ruler, if they desire honor in this world; and women, if they desire a life of comfort.

"I know the place this woman holds in your heart. It isn't right for me to withhold what you need for her health, and I recognize the pain she's experiencing. Whoever prescribed the medicine did so correctly: the same pain sometimes affects our womenfolk, and one of us gives up his heart and she recovers. Our loss is small, and we tolerate it on account of the benefit it brings to our womenfolk. I would have brought my heart along if you'd mentioned this to me. I wouldn't withhold anything that would benefit your wife, especially since I've reached the age when I no longer need a heart for the rest of my life. I'm at the stage when nothing is more troublesome than my heart's companionship—it's where so many worries and sorrows dwell. I've been eager to part with it, but because of our long companionship, I was loath to do so except out of duty or as a favor. In any case, if it leaves me, most of my worries and sorrows will cease."

His hopes raised by the monkey's words, the turtle said, "Friend, 8.12 where is your heart?"

"I left it at home."

"And why did you do that?" asked the turtle.

"It has always been the custom among us monkey folk. We don't take our hearts with us when we go somewhere we expect to experience unbridled joy, because the cares and worries that have accumulated in our hearts would disturb us and cloud our happiness. Therefore, when I set out, wanting my joy and pleasure to be complete, I didn't want my heart to accompany me, so I left it behind. Now that you've mentioned your wife's illness and her sorry state,

however, I don't want her to think I failed to offer you my heart despite my debt of gratitude to you. She might even think I left my heart behind on purpose, begrudging it to you and her—women's minds have weak judgment. Let's go back to get it and bring it to her."

8.13 When the turtle heard this, his mind was set at ease and he became confident that he would obtain what he needed. He immediately turned back. When they reached the shore, the monkey jumped onto land, ran to the tree, climbed up, and stayed there. After a while, when the monkey hadn't returned, the turtle urged him to hurry.

The monkey replied, laughing, "I know you. Don't think I'm like the donkey who the fox told the lion had no heart and no ears."

"What do you mean by that?" asked the turtle.

8.14

The Donkey Who Had No Heart and No Ears

The monkey told the following tale: They say that in a jungle there lived a lion who came down with a bad case of mange. It wearied and weakened him, and so sapped his strength that he could no longer hunt. A fox, his devoted companion, lived with him and used to eat the lion's leftovers.

"Isn't there any medicine for this disease?" asked the fox.

"Yes," replied the lion. "But the medicine, simple as it is, can't be obtained."

"What is it?"

"A donkey's heart and ears."

"Surely it shouldn't be difficult for you to obtain this kind of medicine!" exclaimed the fox.

8.15 "You can see how I suffer from the mange," said the lion. "My hair is gone, I've lost my beauty, and I'm ashamed to leave the jungle and be seen by any of my colleagues."

"Well," said the fox, "I'll get you a donkey and bring him to you right here in your jungle if you're reluctant to go out because of your condition."

"How will you do it? Where will you get him?" asked the lion.

"There is a place with lots of water nearby. A fuller goes there frequently and his donkey carries the laundry. When he reaches

the spring where he washes the clothes, he unloads the donkey and frees it to graze in the meadow by the spring. I'll go there . . .[48] and bring you the donkey. But I think you should eat only what is needed for your recovery—the heart and the ears. The rest you should offer as a sacrifice."

"Very good!" said the lion.

The fox went to the donkey and spoke to him very politely. Then he asked, "Why are you so thin?"

8.16

"This fuller—you see him over there—works me to death and feeds me coarse fodder," replied the donkey.

"Why do you stand for such mistreatment, when you can just leave?" asked the fox.

"Who will help me?" replied the donkey. "Where can I go? How can I escape from men?"

"If you'll do as I say," said the fox, "I'll take you to a place with lots of grass and water and no people. I found my way there a few days ago. There is an animal there who has suffered even more grievously than you, but now she's living in utter luxury. She has put on weight and recovered her health. If you saw her, you wouldn't believe how fat and well off she is."[49]

The donkey became excited at the story of the animal and the fox's description of the good pasture. "Take me wherever you wish," he said. "I'm eager to go, even if by accompanying you I gain nothing but your friendship."

The fox brought him, much to his surprise, face to face with the lion. The lion attacked the donkey and struck a light blow, but was so weak and exhausted that he was unable to hold onto him, and the donkey fled as fast as he could back to where he had come from. The fox was left looking at the lion in amazement at his wretched condition. "Master," he asked, "what is this weakness? What have you done? Why did you put me to the trouble of finding the donkey if you meant to let go of him? If it was because you couldn't hold on to him, then I'm in real trouble, if my master can't hold on to an emaciated donkey with sores on its back."

8.17

8.18 The lion was very uncomfortable. "If I say I let him go intention-ally," he said to himself, "I admit my deceitfulness; if I say I let him go from weakness, I admit my impotence." He turned to the fox and said, "Subjects shouldn't trouble themselves trying to comprehend everything kings do in their affairs. Kings have a level of judgment and understanding not attained by subjects and commoners. Stop asking questions that shouldn't be asked by someone like you. Go back to the donkey, flatter him, and bring him back. If you do, I will extol your loyalty and superiority to all your colleagues in my entourage."

"The donkey has known treachery at my hands," said the fox. "But I'll go back and do my best to trick him."

8.19 The fox returned to the donkey, who immediately said, "What have you done to me?"

"I was only trying to look out for you," replied the fox. "The problem was an excess of lust. The animal that jumped onto you was indeed the one I told you about. You panicked when there was nothing to fear. When she saw you, she was so overcome by joy and desire that she jumped on you and did what she did. Had you waited a moment, she would have become your wife."

The donkey's lust was inflamed by the fox's story. He had never seen a lion before. The fox continued to deceive and mislead him until he believed him. At that point, trusting the fox and his words, the donkey returned with him. When the lion saw him, he approached stealthily, pounced on him, clung to him, and killed him.

The lion said to the fox, "Guard the body while I go wash. Then I'll eat its heart and ears, as prescribed."

8.20 The lion went off to wash himself, and the fox helped himself to the donkey's ears and heart and ate them.

When the lion returned, seeing no ears and no heart, he asked the fox for an explanation.

"Didn't you sense that this donkey had no heart or ears? Had he a heart with which to understand and ears with which to hear, he wouldn't have come back to you after what he'd experienced."

"I've told you this story," said the monkey to the turtle, "because 8.21 you tricked me with deceit and cunning, and now I've paid you back in kind, to show you that I'm not like the donkey the fox claimed had no heart or ears. As the scholars put it: Every evil has a counterpart, good or bad, by which alone it can be overcome."

The turtle said, "You're right. As they say, a wise man is sparing 8.22 of words, unsparing of deeds; he acknowledges a mistake when he makes one; he ascertains the facts before embarking on anything; and by his intelligence he seeks to undo any lapse of his intelligence—like a man who stumbles on the ground, but uses the ground to right himself and stand up. I confess my deed and acknowledge my guilt, though my plea cannot undo my treachery or excuse my wrongdoing. I want you to know that I recognize my wrongdoing, though I know that because of my treachery you aren't going to resume our former friendship. This pain has been brought upon me by my own soul, and I have lost a friend because of my own evil inclination."

The Holy Man and the Mongoose

A parable about the consequences of acting without deliberation, reflection, or clarity.

9.1 The king said to the philosopher, "I have listened to a parable that was truly spoken and hit the mark! Now tell me one about a man who acts too quickly, without reflecting or ascertaining the facts."

The philosopher said, "Anyone who does not ascertain the facts and approach his affairs with calm deliberation, but instead acts without careful reflection, will suffer the fate of the holy man who, to his grief and regret, killed the innocent mongoose."

"What was his fate?" asked the king.

9.2 And the philosopher told the following tale: Once, they say, a holy man had a wife whom he loved. She lived with him a long time without conceiving. Then, much to his joy, just when they had given up hope, she became pregnant, and he took to recounting his hopes for the child. "Rejoice," he said, "for you're going to give birth to a boy, God willing. I'll choose a beautiful name, give him the finest upbringing, and teach him all sorts of subjects, and we shall have a righteous legacy. I'll set out at once to find nurses for him."

9.3 "Stop going on about things you know nothing about and that you have no business talking about," replied the wife. "How do you know whether I'll give birth or not, what sex the child will be if I give birth, and how the child will turn out? Who except God—glory to Him—knows what is in the womb?[50] How do you know that I'll give birth to a healthy child? Stop chattering like this. You're likely

to suffer the fate of the holy man who spilled his butter and honey on his own head if you speak about outcomes you know nothing about."

"And what was his fate?" he asked.

The wife told him the following tale: A holy man, they say, used to receive an allowance of food from a butter and honey merchant every day; he would eat what he needed and store the rest in a jar he hung on a peg in the corner of his room. Eventually the jar was full of butter and honey. One day, while he was lying on his bed underneath the jar, he said to himself, "If I sell the butter in this jar, I can make ten dirhams, and use that to buy five female goats. They'll become pregnant, and after five months each will give birth; when their kids give birth in turn, they'll be a large flock." He calculated five years on this basis and reckoned that it would come to more than four hundred goats. "Then I'll sell them and use the money to buy a hundred head of cattle, an ox or a cow for every four goats. I'll get seeds, use the oxen to plow, and profit from the cows' milk and from their calves. Within five years I'll have lots of money, produce, and property. Then I'll marry a beautiful woman from a good family; I'll lie with her and get her pregnant, and she'll give birth to a strapping young lad. I'll choose a name for him, educate him, and teach him many subjects; if he becomes disobedient, I'll raise this stick of mine and beat him on the head." Whereupon he lifted the stick in his hand and waved it. The stick struck the jar and broke it, and the butter and honey poured down over the man's head.

"I've told you this parable," said the wife, "to keep you from rushing to talk about things you shouldn't talk about and which you don't know will happen or not."

The holy man learned a lesson from his wife's parable and thereafter kept silent on the subject.

It wasn't long before the woman gave birth to a son, and his father was overjoyed. When the days of her confinement were over, the woman wanted to become available for her husband, so she said, "I am going to do my ablutions. Sit by the child and take care of him

9.4

The Holy Man and His Jar of Butter

9.5

9.6

until I come back."[51] The wife left and the husband sat by the boy, to care for him, while his wife was busy. Before long, a messenger from the king arrived, summoning the holy man and urging him to make haste. There was no one else in the house to care for the boy, but he could hardly refuse. He did, however, have a tame mongoose that had proven useful on many occasions; so he left it with the boy, locked them in the room, and departed with the messenger.

9.7 After he had gone, a cobra came out of its hole and approached the boy. The mongoose pounced on it, killed it, and tore it to pieces. The holy man returned soon after. When he opened the door, the mongoose, stained with blood, came to greet him. When the holy man saw this, he lost his mind and thought the mongoose had killed the boy. He rushed at the mongoose and killed it without pausing to think or confirm his suspicions. Then he went over to the boy, whom he found alive, with a snake torn to pieces beside him. He beat his breast and face in grief over his deed. "If only this boy had never been born! If only I'd never committed such an act of betrayal! If only I hadn't behaved with such a display of ingratitude and without rewarding a favor!"

9.8 When the wife returned and saw how her husband was behaving, she asked, "Why are you crying? Why are the snake and the mongoose both dead?"

He told her what had happened and she said, "This is the fruit of haste."

The Cat and the Rat

A parable about someone beset by foes on every side, who fears for his life and is certain that he is about to perish, but finds a way to avoid disaster by befriending and making peace with one of his foes, and then keeps his promise to the foe he made peace with.[52]

The king said to the philosopher, "Now that I've listened to your 10.1
parable about rushing into action without ascertaining the facts,
tell me one about someone surrounded by many enemies, who, on
the brink of death, finds a way to avoid disaster by befriending and
making peace with one of his foes, and then keeps his promise to
the foe he made peace with. Tell me about truces and the circum-
stances when one should seek them."

The philosopher said, "Not all enmities and friendships endure. 10.2
Affection sometimes turns into hatred, and hatred into affection,
in response to changes in circumstances and conditions. The wise
man plans for every contingency: sometimes he seeks help from
an enemy; sometimes he despairs of receiving it from a friend.
Antagonism should not prevent a wise man from approaching an
enemy for help when he hopes to avert danger or attain an objec-
tive; under such circumstances he will have no qualms about chang-
ing his mind regarding rapprochement or mutual separation. If we
understand this clearly and act on it prudently, we can achieve our
ends. The story of the cat and the rat will serve as an example: they
concluded a truce when it was to their advantage, and it saved them
from the terrible predicament into which each of them had fallen."

"And how did that happen?" said the king.

10.3 The philosopher told the following tale: In a certain country, they say, at the foot of a banyan tree lay the den of a rat named Afrīdūn; nearby was the den of a cat named Rūmī. Hunters often came to the tree in search of game. One night a hunter set up his snares and the cat fell into them. When the rat crept out to find something to eat, looking warily in every direction as he advanced, he saw the cat entangled in the snares and rejoiced at the sight. But then he looked back and saw a weasel lying in wait; he looked up, and there was an owl in the tree, watching him. He feared that the weasel would pounce on him if he turned back and that the owl would snatch him if he turned right or left, and the cat was directly in front of him if he went straight ahead. "I am surrounded by troubles," he said to himself, "all in league to spoil my joy over the cat's distress. I see no recourse for me but to rely on God, and to use my intelligence and ingenuity.

10.4 "First, I mustn't become confused or distraught, for a wise man doesn't lose his composure and, whatever the circumstances, his intelligence never deserts him. Wise minds are like the sea, whose depths cannot be plumbed. Trouble cannot exhaust a wise man's intelligence and destroy him, nor is he so dominated by hope as to become reckless or blind." Then he thought, "The best strategy is to seek a truce with the cat. The cat is in deep trouble, but I may, God willing, be able to save him. If he hears me speak honest words, without guile, deceit, or reproach, he may appreciate what I propose; recognizing the benefit to be gained, he may desire my help in saving him and make peace with me for our mutual good."

10.5 So he approached the cat. "How are you?" he asked.

"In deep trouble," replied the cat, "just as you would wish."

"Truth be told," said the rat, "that's how it used to be: I was delighted if something upset you, and I welcomed it if it annoyed you. Today, however, I'm your companion in misfortune, and my only hope for salvation lies in what I hope will be your salvation, too. This has aroused in me sympathy for you. Rest assured that my

words contain no lies or deceit. Look: do you see that weasel lying in wait for me, and that owl up above? They are enemies both to me and to you, but they fear you. I'll come over to you, cut your cords, and rescue you if you swear not to harm me and promise to protect me as you would your own life. Trust what I say and rely on me, for no one is farther off the mark than two persons who, though of different character, are on equal footing: the person who trusts no one and the person whom no one trusts. Rest assured I'll keep my promise. Accept my offer and have confidence in me. And don't delay: the hunter may return and the outcome will be equally unpleasant for both of us. A wise person doesn't procrastinate. Take as much pleasure in my survival as I will take in yours. Each of us, with God's help, will be the cause of the other's salvation, like a ship and its crew: the ship brings the crew home, and the crew brings the ship home to port. All this comes to pass as ordained."[53]

The cat was delighted, recognized the truth of the rat's words, 10.6 and replied at once, "I agree with what you say, and I don't doubt your honesty. I agree to this truce, which I hope will save us both. I will thank you as long as I live, and will reward you well."

The rat said, "Embrace me gently when I approach. The weasel and the owl will go away when they see the evidence of our truce, and I'll start gnawing through your cords."

"With pleasure!" exclaimed the cat.

The rat approached, and the cat drew him close and made peace. The weasel and the owl left in disappointment and frustration.

The rat began to bite through the cords. The cat, thinking he was 10.7 working too slowly, said, "I don't think you're serious about cutting my bonds. If you've changed your mind now that you've gotten what you need and have become indifferent to what I need, that's not how generous, noble, and loyal people behave. My prompt display of affection benefited you by saving you from destruction, as you saw. You ought to reciprocate and not brood over our former hostility. What has happened between us should make you forget all about it. Think also of the merits of loyalty and the evil consequences of

treachery. A noble person is ever grateful, never malicious: a single favor makes him forget many insults. The swiftest punishment, they say, is the punishment of treachery and perjury, or of a merciless person who, entreated and begged for forgiveness, neither pardons nor forgives."

10.8 The rat said, "Friends are of two kinds: those who become friends freely and those who do so out of necessity. Each kind seeks benefits and protection from harm. One can feel at ease with someone who freely becomes a friend, and will accommodate that friend in any situation. Sometimes one can feel at ease with a friend acquired out of necessity, but sometimes one must be wary. The wise person always withholds the fulfillment of part of such a friend's needs as security against what he guards against and fears. Most people maintain relationships for the sake of immediate benefits. I will keep my promise, but will also be careful not to suffer at your hands the very thing that compelled me to seek a truce with you and compelled you to grant it to me. Be confident. Every action has its time and should not be undertaken at the wrong time. I'll cut your cords at the right time, but for now I'm leaving one knot as security: I'll cut it only when I know you're too preoccupied with saving your own life to think about me. That will be when the hunter approaches."

10.9 So the rat cut the cords, except for the last knot, and stayed by the cat, nobly fulfilling his promise. In the morning, the hunter approached from afar. The cat resigned himself to death. "This," said the rat, "is the time I was waiting for to cut the cord." And he began cutting the last cord. Before the hunter arrived, he was done cutting it—but the cat was all the while full of mistrust, apprehension, and mortal fear. When the cat escaped, he ran straight for the tree and climbed up it, and the rat dived into his hole. The hunter collected his mangled snares and left empty-handed.

10.10 Sometime later, the rat came out of his burrow. He saw the cat at a distance, but was reluctant to approach him. "Gallant friend," called the cat, "what is keeping you from coming near so that I can reward you for your good deed? Come! Don't break off our

friendship! Anyone who makes a friend and fails to cultivate his friendship and affection loses friendship's fruits and benefits, and his companions despair of deriving any benefit from him. I must try to reward you. The favor you did me can never be forgotten. As long as I live, fear no treachery from me. Everything I have will be given unsparingly." The cat solemnly swore to this.

"Many a friendship," replied the rat, "conceals hostility within and is even more dangerous than open hostility. If you're not skilled at soothing a friend's feelings after hostility or breaking up with an enemy after friendship, you'll make an enemy out of your friend and give your enemy power over you. The worst of enemies is the person who gives voice to fine words that are at odds with the deceit hidden in his heart, especially if the hostility is innate and the association and friendship were occasioned by necessity. To fail to be on guard against this is like riding on the tusk of a rutting elephant and falling asleep. Friends are called friends only because of the benefit we expect from them, and enemies are called enemies because of the harm we fear from them. If a wise man hopes to benefit from an enemy, he makes a show of friendship; and if he fears harm from a friend, he makes a show of hostility. 10.11

"Haven't you seen how young animals follow their mothers hoping for nourishment, and when that stops, they go on their way? The wise person changes his disposition in response to changing circumstances and the changing moods of his companions, just as clouds form one moment and disperse the next, shed rain one moment and withhold it the next. Sometimes he will be open, sometimes reserved; sometimes easygoing, sometimes cautious; sometimes pleased, sometimes angry; sometimes harsh, sometimes compliant. Sometimes friend is separated from friend by changes in circumstances, but the friend who has been separated from his friend will fear no evil, because there was no underlying hostility. But when hostility is the underlying reality, and friendship is occasioned by a need that drives the person to it, the relationship will turn into enmity and revert to its underlying reality as soon as the 10.12

cause occasioning the friendship disappears—just as water heated on a fire becomes cold once taken off the fire.

10.13 "It isn't a good idea to associate with someone whose enmity is innate unless you need to. No enemy can be more harmful to me than you. Misfortune forced us to call a truce for our mutual benefit. I'm afraid that hostility will return now that we no longer have a reason to need each other. The weak person stands to gain nothing by remaining in the vicinity of a powerful enemy; the humble person stands to gain nothing by remaining in the vicinity of a proud foe. I know of no need you have for me, other than a desire to eat me. I think you harbor evil intentions toward me when you address me with such gentle words. I don't think it's a good idea for me to trust you. As the saying goes, the weakling who guards against his enemy is more likely, God willing, to remain safe than a powerful enemy taken in by a weak foe. A wise man flatters his enemy, feigns affection, and pretends to be at ease with him when he must, but gets away from him as fast as he can when he has no further need. If we're too quick to let down our guard, we can hardly beg pardon for our downfall. A wise man keeps his promise to the one with whom he has made a truce, but doesn't trust anyone to do the same to him. As scholars have said, a wise man should make peace with a bold enemy and abase himself to him when there is a need to do so, but should avoid him when he has no need for him and should not trust him. They also say that above all you should prefer to keep as far as possible from your enemy. When it comes to the safety of my life and your keeping your promise, the most prudent course is for me to keep my distance from you; similarly, I think the safest thing for you is to keep away from the hunter. I'll be your friend from a distance, and there is no need for you to reciprocate. When all is said and done, there is no way for us to meet, except in the case of a misfortune like the one that previously brought both of us together."

The King and the Bird Finzah[54]

A parable about aggrieved parties who have reason to retaliate and how each should guard against the other.

The king said to the philosopher, "I have heard your parable about 11.1
someone surrounded by enemies, who saved himself from peril,
kept his promise, and remained safe by enlisting the help of and
making a truce with one of his enemies. Now tell me a parable about
aggrieved parties who have reason to retaliate against each other
and how each should guard against the other."

The philosopher told the following tale: Once, they say, there 11.2
was a king who had a bird named Finzah. The bird was clever and
could talk, and was the father of a chick. The king commanded that
Finzah and his chick be kept in his principal wife's apartment, and
ordered her to care for them. Then this wife gave birth to a son. The
chick became fond of the boy and they became playmates. Finzah
went to the mountains every day and brought back two mysterious
fruits; one he fed to his chick, and the other to the king's son. This
so hastened their growth and increased their strength that the king
noticed it and honored Finzah even more. One day, while Finzah
was away in the mountains, the chick hopped onto the lap of the
boy's nurse. The boy became angry, grabbed the chick, and dashed
it to the ground, killing it.

When Finzah returned and saw his chick lying dead, he cried 11.3
out in grief, "Fie on the companionship of kings, who know neither
trustworthiness nor loyalty! Woe to anyone who has the misfortune

to be their companion! They have no real friends, hold no one sacred, and love no one. They honor and cultivate only those whom they need or want to benefit from. But the moment their need is satisfied, it's farewell to affection and friendship! They reward no good deed and forgive no sin. Their life is nothing but pomp, ostentation, and acclaim. They dismiss their own crimes as trivial, but treat the slightest opposition to their whims as a crime." Then he said, "I will avenge my chick's death on that ungrateful, merciless wretch who killed his comrade, the playmate who shared his meals." So saying, he jumped onto the boy's face and scratched out the boy's eyes with his feet; then he flew away and perched beyond anyone's reach.

11.4 The king was overcome with grief at the report of this and determined to trick Finzah and trap him. So he rode forth and, halting where he could make his voice heard, called out, "You will be safe. Come to me!"

But Finzah refused and said, "King, traitors are punished for their treachery. Even if they escape immediate punishment, they won't escape it in the long run: punishment may even overtake their children and their children's children. Your son behaved treacherously to my son, and I exacted swift punishment."

"True, we did this to you," said the king. "But now that you've avenged yourself on us, you have no further grievance against us, nor we against you; so come back to us in safety."

11.5 "I won't come back," replied Finzah. "People who understand such things have forbidden us to approach people with an injury to avenge. The more kindness, gentleness, and hospitality displayed by someone with a rancorous heart, they say, the more uneasy you should be; you'll find no better way of keeping safe from someone with a grievance than fear, distance, and caution. A wise man, they say, regards his parents merely as friends, his brothers merely as comrades, his wives merely as companions, his sons merely as a memorial, his daughters merely as liabilities, his relatives merely as rivals, and himself as solitary and alone. Today I am sad and solitary.

Because of you I now shoulder a heavy burden of sorrow that I alone carry. I am leaving. Goodbye!"

The king said, "It would be as you say had you not repaid us for what we did to you, and had you not reacted to our prior treachery. But since we acted first, what wrong have you done? What prevents you from trusting us? Come back!" 11.6

"Grudges hide in the heart and fester," replied Finzah. "Men's tongues don't speak the truth about their hearts. The testimony of the heart about the heart is truer than the testimony of the tongue. I know that my heart doesn't testify to the truth of your tongue, nor your heart to the truth of my tongue."

"Surely you know," responded the king, "that although resentments and grudges exist between many people, a wise man is more eager to quell hatred than to nurture it."

"It is indeed as you say," replied Finzah. "Nonetheless, it's unwise to suppose that an injured party full of resentment will simply forget and turn away from his injury. A wise person fears deceit and cunning; he knows that many enemies who cannot be overcome by brute force are ensnared by gentleness and mildness, just as a wild elephant is ensnared by using a tame one."

The king said, "Even if he fears for his life, a man of noble character doesn't leave his friend, abandon his brothers, or allow the memory of friendship to fade. We find this virtue in even the lowliest of animals. Some people in Sind are notorious for slaughtering dogs and eating them; even though a canine companion may see this, his friendship for them will keep him from leaving them." 11.7

Finzah said, "Hatreds are to be feared wherever they exist, but the strongest hatreds are those that dwell in the minds of kings. Kings make a religion of revenge; they see vengeance as a noble deed worth boasting about. A wise man shouldn't be fooled when hatred is quiescent; as long as it finds nothing to stir it, hatred in the heart is like a hidden coal without wood to burn. Hatred constantly yearns for pretexts, just as fire yearns for wood; and it flares up in 11.8

the slightest breeze. Water quenches fire, but no water, words, softness, gentleness, entreaty, or humility—nothing less than people's lives—can quench hatred. In spite of this, those who have caused injury, hoping for benefits or protection, are often eager for the aggrieved party's return. I, however, am too weak to do anything for you that will dispel your feelings. And even if you felt toward me as you say, it would be impossible for me to know; if I returned, I should live in fear, disquiet, and misgiving as long as we were together. Between me and you there can only be separation. I therefore bid you farewell."

11.9 The king replied, "Know that no harm or benefit, great or small, can be done, except by preordained fate. Just as created beings do not decide the creation of what is created or the birth of what is born, so too the perishing of what perishes and the destruction of what is destroyed occur by fate, not by the decision of God's servants. Therefore, you bear no guilt for what you did to my son, nor does my son bear any guilt for the destruction of your offspring. It happened in accordance with preordained fate, and we were merely its conduits.[55] Since our offense happened first and was greater than your offense toward us, I will forgive what occurred through you."

11.10 Finzah then said, "The role of what is destined and preordained is as you have said, but that should not prevent a prudent person from taking precautions and protecting himself against what he fears. No wise person should excuse the sins he commits, when God has provided us with warnings, commandments, and prohibitions. We believe in destiny; nevertheless, we continue to act prudently and ask for God's help in protecting us from what we fear. My soul tells me that you aren't speaking the truth; the words on your tongue don't reflect what is in your heart. The matter between us is no small thing. Your son killed my son, and I scratched out your son's eyes, so now you want to avenge yourself by killing me. You're looking for a way to trick me out of my life, but my soul rejects death. Poverty, they say, is an affliction; so too are sorrow, the proximity of enemies, separation from loved ones, sickness, and old age; but death is

the greatest affliction. No one knows what is in the heart of one who is in pain and distress better than someone who has tasted the same thing. I know how you feel about me in your heart because my heart shares the same feeling. No good can come to me through associating with you. The memory of what I did to your son, or of what your son did to mine, will cause our hearts to change."

"There is no goodness in a man who cannot turn aside from something in his heart and consign it to oblivion, so that he remembers nothing of it," said the king. 11.11

Finzah replied, "If we try to walk quickly with a blister on the sole of our foot, we're sure to burst it; if we face the wind with sore eyes, we will exacerbate the inflammation. Similarly, a person who has inflicted an injury that demands retaliation runs the risk of reopening the wound if he approaches the injured party. A wise man must be wary of dangers, assess the situation, place little reliance on strength and craftiness, and avoid being deceived by those he doesn't trust. Relying on your own strength can lead you to follow a dangerous path and speed you to your own destruction. He who bites off more than he can chew often chokes to death. The fool who abandons caution is his own worst enemy. No one should scrutinize Fate, for no one knows what it will bring or avert; we should act resolutely, proceed decisively in our affairs, and keep account of ourselves.

"A wise man, as much as he is able, strikes fear into no one, and, when he can find some other place to go, doesn't stay where there is fear. I have many places to go, and hope to prosper wherever I turn. There are five things, if you equip yourself with them, that will assist you to your destination, will keep you company in foreign lands, and will gain you a livelihood and friends. They are: avoidance of injury, good manners, keeping clear of sin, generosity of character, and high-minded acts. When a wise man fears for his life, he willingly forgoes wealth, family, children, and homeland, as these can all be replaced, but he cannot expect to replace his life. The worst wealth is wealth spent badly, the worst wife is ungracious to her 11.12

husband, the worst child is a rebellious one, the worst brother abandons his brother in distress, the worst king is feared by the innocent and does not devote himself to the good of his people, and the worst country is one where there is neither safety nor prosperity. I can have no prosperity and no peace of mind near you." So saying, he bade the king farewell and flew away.

The Lion and the Jackal[56]

A parable about relations between kings and their courtiers; about restoring one of them to favor after a punishment or an estrangement due to an offense.

The king said, "Now that I've heard you speak about an aggrieved enemy who is not to be trusted, tell me a parable about kings and their assistants." 12.1

The philosopher said, "Were a king never to restore to favor any assistant who, for some offense, suffered estrangement or punishment, both he and his affairs would be harmed. A king should consider the potential usefulness of the individual who has endured such treatment; the king should be eager to restore him to favor if he is someone he can look to for assistance and rely on for his trustworthiness and sound judgment. A kingdom can be ruled only by means of ministers and assistants; ministers and assistants are useful only on account of their love and loyalty; and love and loyalty are useless without sound judgment and moderation. Kings require many assistants and officials to oversee their numerous affairs, but few men combine the necessary qualities of loyalty, soundness of judgment, and moderation. 12.2

"Things will not go well for a king unless he truly knows those he calls on for assistance—knows each man's usefulness and judgment, as well as his shortcomings. When he finds this out directly or through others in his retinue, he will assign to every task someone he knows to possess the necessary judgment, energy, and trustworthiness, and whose shortcomings, if any, will not spoil it. 12.3

Furthermore, a king must monitor his officials, so that no official's good deeds and no official's misdeeds remain hidden. No good official should be left unrewarded and no incompetent official or one guilty of misconduct should be allowed to persist in his misconduct and incompetence; otherwise, the good official will become negligent, the bad official will be emboldened, the people will become demoralized, and everything will go awry. The parable of the jackal and the lion illustrates this."

"How does it go?" asked the king.

12.4 The philosopher told the following tale: They say that in the land of India there once lived a jackal. He was God-fearing and pious, and although he lived among jackals, wolves, and foxes, he didn't behave like them by acting treacherously, wronging others, or eating meat. The other animals argued with him: "We don't approve of your way of life or your views. Your pious devotions won't do you a bit of good. You may engage in acts of devotion, but you're no different from us, because you still associate with us and run with us."

12.5 The jackal said, "I associate with you out of necessity, and it doesn't make me a sinner if I don't make myself a sinner. Sins don't derive from locations or companions, but from hearts and actions. If being in a holy place rendered our actions there righteous, or being in an evil place rendered our actions there evil, it would be no sin to commit wanton murder in a mosque, while it would be a sin to perform charitable deeds in a fire temple. I associate with you only through my body, not through my heart and actions, for I know the fruit of actions."

12.6 The jackal persevered, and became renowned for piety, asceticism, and devotion, surpassing all his contemporaries in abstemiousness, honesty, and humility. Word of him reached a lion who was king of the beasts in that region. The lion sent for him, examined him extensively, and, impressed with his mind and eloquence, invited him a few days later to become his companion. "My kingdom is vast, my works many, and I need assistants. I've received reports of your devoutness and abstemiousness. I'm even more

pleased now that I've met you in person and have talked with you and heard your excellent replies. I will appoint you to high office, raise you to the ranks of the nobility, and make you a member of my inner circle."

The jackal replied, "Kings indeed should choose assistants for their works and affairs, but they shouldn't force anyone to serve, because a reluctant assistant will not devote his best efforts to the office. I don't want the job, Your Majesty. I have no experience or skill in statecraft. As king of the beasts, you have animals of every kind at your disposal, ones with nobility and strength, skillful and eager to serve. If you employ them, they will count themselves lucky and bring you benefit." 12.7

"Enough said!" replied the lion. "I will not excuse you from the job."

"Only two sorts of people can associate with rulers and do their bidding," replied the jackal, "and I'm neither. The two sorts are an unscrupulous flatterer who gets what he wants through scheming and ensures his own safety through flattery, and a pitiful fool whom no one envies. Rarely do things turn out well for the person who would associate with a ruler on terms of truthfulness, sincerity, and modesty, untinged by flattery, for the ruler's foes and friends will join forces against him in envy, enmity, and deceit. The ruler's friends will compete with him for rank and envy him for it; the ruler's enemies will hate him for his good advice and service to the ruler. When both groups join forces against him, he is likely to perish, God forbid." 12.8

"Don't worry about the malice and envy of my companions," replied the lion. "I will protect you and raise you to the honor and rank you deserve."

"If the king wishes to show me kindness," said the jackal, "let him allow me to dwell in this wilderness, safe from envy. I have few worries and live contentedly on water and plants. A ruler's companion, I know, experiences more fear and annoyance in one hour than others experience in a lifetime: a little sustenance enjoyed in peace 12.9

and tranquility is better than a great deal of it accompanied by fear and distress."

"I hear what you're saying," said the lion, "but set aside your fears. I must have your assistance."

12.10 "If the king insists," replied the jackal, "let him promise that should any of his companions try to harm me, be it a superior who fears for his station or a subordinate who wishes to wrest my station from me, and should one of them, be it with his own lips or through someone else, mention to the king something intended to turn the king against me, the king will not act hastily against me, but will investigate and examine what has been brought to his attention and then do what God shows him to be best. If the king guarantees this, I will assist him with my life, and work for him in whatever he delegates to me with honest advice and diligent effort, striving not to expose myself to blame."

"You have my promise," said the lion.

12.11 The lion put the jackal in charge of his storeroom and preferred him over his other companions for his advice and judgment. With every passing day, he became more pleased with the jackal and increased his honors, much to the annoyance of the lion's companions and officials. Hostile and envious, they plotted to turn the lion against the jackal and do away with him. With this treacherous plan in mind, one day they sneaked into the king's larder and stole some meat that the lion, finding it especially tasty, had commanded to be stored there for later enjoyment. Then they had it hidden out of sight in the jackal's house. The next morning, the meat was missing and nowhere to be found when the lion called for his breakfast. The jackal was absent, but the artful conspirators were in attendance. The lion asked about the meat again and again and became angry. They looked at one another, and, in the tone of a well-meaning informant, one of them said, "When we know something that will harm the king or benefit him, it is our duty to inform him, whomever else it may distress. The jackal, I have been told, took the meat home with him."

Another said, "I think it unlikely that he would do this, but you must look into it. Character, after all, is very difficult to know." 12.12

Another said, "Yes, by my life, secret thoughts are hard to know. If you do look into this and find the meat in the jackal's house, everything we've been told about his faults and treachery is true, and we should believe everything that has been said against him."

Another said, "No one should fool himself about the deceit he knows to be in his own soul, let alone in the souls of others, for the deceiver is never safe, and his deceptions won't stay hidden."

Another said, "How can someone get away with deceiving the ruler? How can it be hidden from him, when deceit among friends can scarcely be hidden?" 12.13

Another said, "I was told something terrible about the jackal, but it made no impression on me until I heard your words."

Another said, "His true nature and dishonesty were obvious as soon as I laid eyes on him. As I've said many times—and I have a witness—this imposter who pretends to be so religious would turn out to be guilty of foul treachery and a great crime."

Another said, "What a great surprise if this pious fraud who protests to us that his office is nothing but toil and affliction has committed this treachery!"

Another said, "If it turns out to be true, not only is it treachery, but also ingratitude and criminal effrontery." 12.14

Another said, "You are honest, upstanding people and I can't accuse you of lying, but if the king sends someone to search the jackal's house the facts will become clear."

Another said, "If it must be, let his house be searched quickly, for he has spies and informers everywhere."

Another said, "If the jackal's house is searched and his treachery becomes known, I know he'll resort to deceit and trickery to raise doubts in the king's mind, so that he pardons him."

They sowed suspicion in the lion's mind with comments like these and more. He summoned the jackal. "What did you do with the meat I ordered you to keep?" 12.15

"I gave it to the chef to serve to the king."

The king therefore summoned the chef—he was on the side of the jackal's enemies—and questioned him.

"He gave me nothing," said the chef.

The lion then sent his agents to search the jackal's house, where they found the meat and brought it to the lion.

12.16 A wolf had said nothing about the case, and had made a pretense of being the kind of reliable witness who would speak only about what he knew for certain to be true. He approached the lion and said, "Now that the king has discovered this treachery, he mustn't pardon the jackal; if he does, no one will ever inform the king about any treachery or crime."

The lion commanded that the jackal be taken away and kept under guard.

Thereupon one of the lion's companions said, "Given the king's judgment and experience, I'm amazed at how this traitor's deceitfulness and guile escaped his notice."

Another said, "Even more amazing: I think, despite the evidence against the jackal, he'll forgive him."

The lion sent one of his companions to ask the jackal to provide some justification of his deed. When the fellow brought back a false account, the lion became so angry that he ordered the jackal to be killed.

12.17 Word of these events reached the lion's mother. Realizing that the lion had acted hastily, she sent word to those who had been ordered to kill the jackal to grant him a delay. Then she visited her son. "For what crime," she asked, "did you order the jackal to be killed?"

The lion told her what had happened.

"My son," she said, "you've acted in haste. Only by deliberateness, by avoidance of haste, and by ascertaining the facts can a wise man protect himself from regret. A hasty man will always taste regret as the fruit of bad judgment and shortsightedness. A king more than anyone needs calmness and deliberateness: a woman is

kept safe by her husband; a child by its parents; a student by his teacher; an army by its general; an ascetic by religious scholars; the common folk by kings; and kings by piety, intelligence, and careful establishment of the facts. For a king, sound judgment begins with knowing his companions, appointing them to the right positions, and being aware of their intrigues. There are people who, if they can find a way, will not hesitate to destroy others, disparage the bravery of the brave and the good deeds of the righteous, and cover up the deeds of wrongdoers.

"You tested the jackal and examined his behavior and charac- 12.18 ter before you made him your aide and placed your trust in him. You were always pleased with him; your approval, friendship, and desire for his company only increased with each passing day. You often praised him and commended him in front of your soldiers; he doesn't deserve to be put to death because a bit of meat has gone missing. Perhaps out of envy, and in collusion, his companions have falsely accused him of a crime. You can be sure that kings bring ruin on themselves when they entrust to others what they should carry out themselves or take on themselves what they should entrust to others.

"Kings need to consider an affair from many angles. If they con- 12.19 sider only one aspect, they risk misunderstanding or misjudgment. It's like someone buying wine: he needs to test it for color, taste, and fragrance. If he tests for only one of these attributes, he risks being cheated and stands to lose. Or it's like the man who, because he has an eye disease, thinks he sees what appears to be a hair before his eyes: if he gave it some thought, he'd realize that if it really were a hair, others would see it too. Or it's like a firefly that at night looks like a fire: the ignorant man judges it only from its appearance, but when he touches it he realizes his mistake.

"Your Majesty should examine the jackal's case carefully and 12.20 realize that he would not act treacherously. You've often put him in charge of large amounts of meat, and he has served it to you and your soldiers without fail. Is it likely, then, that he'd steal a small amount

you ordered him to keep? Investigate the case. Worthless men will always envy men of worth and character, and try to destroy them. The jackal is brave and worthy. His enemies among your companions may have smuggled the meat into his house without his knowing. Many birds will jostle a kite when she finds a chunk of meat; many dogs will join forces against a dog with a bone in his mouth. If the jackal's enemies among your companions haven't considered your welfare, consider it yourself and don't succumb to their allegations. Indeed, it will cause you harm. For the two most harmful things, especially to rulers, are, first, the want of good helpers, assistants, and friends, and, second, assistants and friends who aren't of good character. The jackal has always been very useful to you. He sets your interests above his desires; he procures your comfort at the cost of his own welfare, and your contentment at the cost of angering his colleagues; he conceals nothing and hides no secrets from you; and he considers no burden or exertion too great for your sake. A companion of such character should be as precious as one's parents, brothers, and children."

12.21 During the lion's mother's speech, one of the plotters came and informed the lion of the jackal's innocence.

Once the lion's mother knew that the lion had learned of the jackal's innocence and of the conspiracy, she said to him, "Don't tolerate your companions' behavior. Break up their scheming, and put an end to their foolishness. Don't let them use deception as a vehicle. Don't let them regroup to bring you harm and disgrace. Don't let your own power tempt you to underestimate them and make light of them; for weak straw, gathered and braided, becomes a strong rope that can hold a full-grown elephant. Restore the jackal to his office and to your favor. Don't despair of receiving good advice from him on account of your rash mistreatment of him. One needn't fear treachery and enmity, nor despair of receiving good advice and affection from those who have suffered mistreatment. People should be treated according to the differences in their character. In some cases, when relations are severed, the breach should

be final and irrevocable; in other cases, the person shouldn't be abandoned or cut off. The best policy is to sever relations and avoid contact with people known for wickedness and villainy; disloyalty and ingratitude; lack of piety and mercy; disbelief in the rewards and punishments of the hereafter; malice, envy, and excessive greed and ambition; swiftness to foster suspicions and break off relations; and slowness to reconsider and resume relations. However, we should eagerly seek the companionship of, and avoid any break with, people known for righteousness, honesty, gratitude, loyalty, and benevolence; people free from envy, malice, and offense; and people who bear unpleasantness from their companions and help them even when it is burdensome."

The lion summoned the jackal and apologized. "I restore you to office and entrust my affairs to you as in the past." 12.22

The jackal responded, "Your Majesty, a loyal friend who gives his friend advice he knows will be beneficial, though burdensome, and who patiently bears harsh words from his friend—such a friend is rare indeed. Therefore, Your Majesty, do not be offended if I tell you that I cannot trust you or be your companion. The ruler should neither befriend nor trust an individual who has suffered great affliction he doesn't deserve; or who has been stripped of rank and office; or whose property has been wrongly confiscated; or who once was a favorite and was then banished without cause; or who, along with his colleagues, deserved a reward, but saw them rewarded and promoted in his place; or who deserved to be punished alongside them, but they, rather than he, were pardoned; or who was mistreated, while they were not; or who has a reputation for excessive ambition and greed; or who sees harm in benefiting the ruler or fears harm to himself from it.

"Even today, I have been mentioned as still being an enemy of the king. The fact that I remain, as always, the king's friend and loyal adviser will not prevent the king from harboring evil thoughts and suspicions. He will inevitably fear that my attitude has changed because of his action. He may fear that the affection and advice I give 12.23

him are insincere. Also, I am afraid that my enemies will incite the king against me again by means of lies and falsehoods, fearing that I might requite them, eager that the lies they employed to turn the king against me not come to light. If they do try this, they will need no assistance greater than the suspicion that has already entered the king's mind. Even if the king restores his former trust and confidence in me, it would be impossible for me to know. Remembering his former haste, I would need to fear his suspicion of my advice, his evil opinion of me, and his readiness to believe my enemies' attacks on me. If I have correctly described how the king regards placing trust in me, let him consider how he thinks I feel about being his companion."

12.24 The lion replied, "I've tested your nature and character. In my mind you are among the noble and the good. One good deed makes a noble man forget a thousand bad ones, while one bad deed makes an ignoble man forget a thousand good ones. I trust that my former benevolence will make you forget what I so rashly did to you. My trust in you has been restored; now resume your trust in me. Doing this will bring you joy and happiness."

So the jackal resumed his management of the lion's affairs as before, and his devotion and happiness deepened right up to the time of his death.

Here ends the Chapter of the Lion and the Abstinent Jackal[57]

King Haylār and His Minister Baylār

Dabshalim said to Baydabā the Philosopher, "Now that I've under- 13.1
stood this parable, please tell me which quality a king must use in
order to enjoy the respect of his officials and subjects, bolster his
reign, and protect his land: judiciousness, virtue, boldness, or
generosity?"[58]

The philosopher said, "Judiciousness and intelligence are the best 13.2
means to these ends; along with consulting an intelligent, skillful,
and learned adviser, they provide the cornerstone and foundation.
In particular, a king's judiciousness is the quality most beneficial for
the people. Nothing is more helpful, and nothing more conducive
to a life well-lived, than a righteous, virtuous, well-disposed wife. If
a man is a brave leader but lacks judiciousness, and if his adviser is
unintelligent, his own ignorance and the mistakes of those he con-
sults will cause the simplest affair to overwhelm him, and he will
be regarded as disgraced and weak. Even if by some turn of fortune
he wins victory or finds the right path, he will eventually come to
grief. On the other hand, a king will achieve success over his rivals,
victory over his opponents, and joy over those who grieve him if he
and his minister possess these virtues and if he is favored by fortune.
This is what happened, we have been told, in the case of King Haylār
of India, his wife Īrākht, and his confidant and adviser Baylār."

"How did it happen?" asked the king.

The philosopher told the following tale: Baylār, they say, was a 13.3
diligent, virtuous, gentle, judicious, learned, and respected holy
man. One night the king, asleep in his bedroom, dreamt eight

dreams, waking after each. In the morning he summoned the Brahmins—the holy men, that is—told them his dreams, and commanded them to interpret. "Your Majesty has dreamt something horrible and astounding," they said, "like nothing we've ever heard. With your permission, we will go and ponder the matter for six days and report back on the seventh. Hopefully we can do something to ward off what you fear."

"Very well," said the king. "Go and determine what is my best course of action."

"Very well, Your Majesty."

13.4 They convened once they had left. "We haven't met," they said, "since he killed twelve thousand of us. But now that he has revealed his secret and his anxiety about his dreams to us, we have him in our power and may be able to exact revenge. If we speak to him bluntly, fear may drive him to agree to what we want. We will command him to hand over his dearest family members and ministers. We will say to him, 'We have searched our books and found that the only way to avert what you have dreamt is to kill those we name.' If he asks who, we will say, 'Your wife Īrākht, her son Jawbar, your nephew, your resourceful and learned minister Baylār, and your secretary and spokesman Kāl; we also need your sword, your white battle elephant, both your mighty elephants, the horse you ride, the camel of noble breed on which you journey, and the jurist Kamānzūn. We will put their blood into a basin and sit you in it. When you are about to get out, we Brahmins will assemble from all four corners of the land, recite incantations over you, wipe off the blood, and wash you with water and fragrant oil. Then we will escort you to your throne room, and, of the things you have dreamt, God will avert whatever He wishes. If you bear this patiently and willingly, you will be saved and escape imminent disaster, and you will be able to replace what you have lost. If you do not, we fear that your glory will be stripped away and your kingdom wrested from you; you will perish and your posterity will be eradicated.'"

Having agreed on the plan as devised, the Brahmins went to the 13.5
king and said, "We have examined our books thoroughly, pondered
your dreams, and put our minds to work, but we can't tell you what
we think unless you allow us to speak without fear of punishment."

He did so, and they told him what they had devised.

"Death is better than what I am hearing!" replied the king. 13.6
"Never will I slay these souls who are my very life or take such a
burden of distress and sin on myself. Death, in any case, is inevi-
table; my reign won't last forever. Separation from everybody I love
is tantamount to death."

The Brahmins said, "Don't be angry if we tell you that you're
wrong to value others' lives above your own. Don't you know that
your life is irreplaceable and that nothing, great or small, can equal
it? Better to ransom your life by sacrificing those we've named and
retain your throne. Look to your own life. Nothing can equal it."

When the king saw how harshly and boldly they had spoken to 13.7
him, he entered his chamber and fell to the ground, tossing and
turning in grief and despair, considering which course to follow:
risk imminent death, or give them what they asked. He remained
thus for some days, and news of it spread throughout the land.
People said, "Something terrible must have happened to cause the
king such grief."

Baylār became pensive when he saw the king's condition. Being 13.8
perceptive, wise, and experienced, he told himself, "It isn't my place
to confront the king about anything without being summoned, but
I'll go to the king's wife Īrākht and ask her about it."

So he went to her and said, "I've never known the king to do any- 13.9
thing, be it small or great, without first consulting me. I've always
been his confidant; he's never kept anything secret from me. He
would console himself when distressed and bear it patiently; then
he would mention it to me, and I would comfort him as gently as I
could. But now I see that for the past seven days he has sequestered
himself with the Brahmins and no one else can see him. I fear he's

made them privy to something momentous, and I don't trust them with it. Go to him; ask how he is, what he has heard, and what they have told him. Then let me know, as I can't go before him. I think they've presented an evil action in a good light and have incited him to do something disgraceful, or have angered him with their dark pronouncements. I know that when angry, the king isn't in the habit of consulting anyone, be the matter small or great. His anger, combined with the words of those evildoers, could induce him to shed blood."

13.10 Īrākht replied, "The king and I have had a falling out. I won't go before him under the present circumstances."

Baylār said, "At a time like this, when trouble is near, pay no heed to your disagreement. Banish it from your mind. No one but you can go before him. I've often heard him say, 'My deepest sadness vanishes when I look on Īrākht's face.' Go to the king, good lady. Dispel his grief and despair. Speak the words that you know will restore him to his proper state. Do us this favor, and keep us informed of what happens, for it will bring enormous relief to us and all of his kingdom."

13.11 Īrākht rose and went to the king. She sat down before him and lifted his head from the ground. "What is wrong, noble king? What have you learned from the Brahmins that troubles and saddens you? If it is something that must cause sadness, tell me and I will be sad with you, just as I rejoice when you are joyful. For when the king rejoices, I rejoice with him, and when he is sad, I ought to be sad too."

"Lady," replied the king, "do not make me sadder still. Do not ask about it."

13.12 "Have I sunk so low in your eyes," replied Īrākht, "that you answer me in this way? Don't you know what wise men have said: The person whose judgment most deserves praise is the one who is never at a loss, who bears misfortune patiently, is undismayed, and listens to his devoted advisers, so that by stratagem and acumen he escapes misfortune, doing his utmost for himself and his kingdom?

Someone who yields to a great sin can, through judiciousness and intelligence, remedy and repair his sin, and return to goodness and righteous action in order that joy and happiness may return. Therefore, Your Majesty must not grieve and be dismayed, casting aside judgment and resolve as well as abandoning determination and patience. Don't bring heartache to those who love you while giving joy and comfort to your enemies. If you do, you will not be considered a man of intelligence or judiciousness."

"Loyal and kind lady," said the king, "how compassionate you are! But nothing good for either of us will come from my telling you about an affair that means death and destruction to me, you, your son, and everyone else I love. The Brahmins have commanded me to kill you, your son, my other courtiers, and the people I love. How can I rejoice if I can no longer set eyes on you? How can I be happy if I kill everyone the Brahmins have commanded me to? Is it possible to hear this without being overwhelmed with sadness?" 13.13

When Īrākht heard this, her intelligence and judiciousness prevented her from displaying any fear of death or concern for her own life. "Do not be sad, blessed king. May God lengthen your life and grant you lasting joy. I will sacrifice my life to save yours. You have other wives to delight you—your estate is home to sixteen thousand other women, all with fine palaces and lodgings. But I beg Your Majesty, grant me one thing that my love and loyalty lead me to request. When I am dead, make certain tenfold before you trust the Brahmins, seek their advice, or put anyone to death, lest you regret it, for you cannot revive someone you've killed. As they say, don't discard a stone you deem worthless before you consult an expert on gems. 13.14

"Your Majesty, you don't recognize your enemies. You can be certain that the Brahmins will never love you, given that you've killed nearly twelve thousand of them. You shouldn't have told them your dreams or accepted their advice. They want to vent the hatred in their hearts by killing your beloved wife, the son who is your second self, the wise officials who loyally administer your kingdom, the 13.15

horse you ride, your camel of noble breed, and the two elephants on which you battle your foes and defend your kingdom. When you kill them, losing everything that delights your eyes and weakening your kingdom, they'll have you in their grip and will dare to exact vengeance. Driven by the hatred in their hearts, they'll wrest your kingdom from you, and it will revert to them as once it was.

13.16 "Send word, Your Majesty, to the sage Kamānzūn, who is learned in all things and has insight into all matters. Inform him of this, and ask his advice. He is an honest scholar of religion; though a Brahmin by descent, he excels them in understanding, learning, piety, and devout pursuit of the hereafter. Ask him about your dreams. If his words agree with theirs, do as they have commanded; but if he disagrees with them, Your Majesty has power over everything in your lands to do whatever you wish."

13.17 The king was pleased by her words. He ordered his horse to be saddled, and set out at once to see Kamānzūn. When he arrived, he dismounted, prostrated himself, greeted him, bowed his head, and stood before him.

"Your Majesty," asked Kamānzūn, "why do I see you so pale, filled with sadness and grief, wearing neither the crown nor the royal diadem?"

The king replied, "One day as I was sleeping in my chamber, I heard eight voices coming from the earth. I woke up, but then went back to sleep and dreamt eight dreams. I told them to the Brahmins. I am sad because I fear some disaster: either my death in battle or the conquest of my kingdom."

13.18 Kamānzūn said, "Rest assured, Your Majesty. Don't be sad or frightened. You aren't going to die, your kingdom won't be lost, and none of the sins and evils you fear will occur. I will tell you the meaning of the eight dreams. The two red fish you saw standing on their tails signify that a messenger will arrive from the king of Haymūn and stand before you bearing two pearl-and-ruby-encrusted crowns worth four thousand pounds of gold. The two geese you saw fly from behind you and land in front of you signify

that you will receive from the king of Balkh two horses unmatched in all the world. The snake you saw crawl up your left leg signifies that someone sent by the king of Ṣanjīn will stand before you with a peerless sword of pure steel. The blood you saw staining your body signifies that someone sent by the king of Kāsrūn will stand before you with a wondrous garment: the Crimson Cloak, which glows in the dark. The dream of washing your body with water signifies that someone sent by the king of Razīn will stand before you with linen garments fit for a king. Your dream of being atop a white mountain signifies that someone sent from the king of Kadfūr will stand before you with a white elephant that no horse can outrun. Your dream of having something like fire on your head signifies that someone sent by King Dār will stand before you with a tiara of gold encrusted with pearls and rubies. I won't interpret for you today the bird you saw above your head and that pecked your head with its beak. Don't be frightened; it won't harm you, but it involves some anger and estrangement from someone you love. All these messengers and couriers will stand before you seven days from now."

When the king heard this, he bowed before Kamānzūn and returned to his palace overjoyed. "Kamānzūn is a very wise man. I'll wait and see, as he said."

Seven days later, the king donned his robes and regalia, seated himself on the throne in the main hall, and gave audience to the most distinguished men of the kingdom. It wasn't long before the gifts foretold by Kamānzūn arrived and were set before him.

13.19

The king rejoiced at the sight of the couriers and the gifts. "I made a mistake when I told my dreams to the Brahmins and they gave me their commands. If God in His mercy hadn't restrained me through the advice of Īrākht, the best and most blessed of women, I should have perished, caused death, and lost all I have in this world and the next. Everyone should heed the opinion and accept the advice of loving and loyal friends. Īrākht gave me good advice, and to my great joy I accepted it. Through the judgment of friends and sincere advisers, God has firmly established my kingdom.

Kamānzūn's knowledge and the truth of his words have become clear to me."

13.20 The king then summoned Jawbar, Baylār, and his secretary Kāl. "It isn't right for us to put these gifts into our treasuries. I will distribute them to you, because you were prepared to die for my sake, and to Īrākht, who gave me the advice that enabled me to preserve my kingdom and that has led to our present joy and gladness."

Baylār responded, "Servants have no right to pride themselves on what they have done. What servant wouldn't die to save the master who has honored and dignified him? Any servant unwilling to die to save his master and loved ones lacks understanding. Don't marvel, Your Majesty, that a servant should die in place of the master who has honored and dignified him, and in whose survival rests his continued welfare. It isn't fitting for us servants to touch these magnificent gifts, but your beloved son Jawbar and Īrākht, the best of women, are worthy of them. Let them have what you give them."

13.21 The king said, "Because of these events, our praise and renown have already spread far and wide. So don't be shy, Baylār! Take your share. Enjoy it!"

"As the king wishes," replied Baylār. "But, if it please the king, let him first take what he desires."

The king took the white elephant. He gave Jawbar one of the horses, Baylār the sword of pure steel, and his secretary Kāl the second horse; he sent the regal linen garments to Kamānzūn, and gave the two crowns to his beloved nephew. When it came to the tiara and other garments suitable for women, he said to Baylār, "Take the tiara and the robe, and follow me to the women's quarters."

13.22 The king summoned Īrākht and Gūlpanāh,[59] and the women sat before him. The king told Baylār, "Set the robe and tiara before Īrākht, and let her pick which one she wishes."

When Īrākht saw that both were breathtaking, she looked at Baylār out of the corner of her eye, to have him show her which was superior. Baylār directed her to the robe and signaled that she

should pick that. It so happened that the king was watching and saw Baylār wink. Īrākht saw that the king had noticed, so she didn't touch what Baylār had indicated but instead took the tiara, fearing for her life and for Baylār's, lest the king suspect something was going on between them. Baylār lived another forty years and would always avert his glance in the king's presence, lest the king suspect him of having signaled to Īrākht that day. Had Īrākht and Baylār not been so astute, neither would have escaped death.

The king used to spend one night with Īrākht and one night with 13.23
Gūlpanāh. The custom was that each wife would prepare a dish of sweetened rice on her night and serve it to the king. The king came to Īrākht on her night; she had the rice ready for him and stood before the king, wearing the tiara. She held out a platter and served him. When Gūlpanāh saw this, she became jealous, and she put on the robe and came before the king. The brilliant sheen of the robe was like the radiance of the sun, and the room lit up; Gūlpanāh herself was as dazzling as the sun. When the king saw this, he was filled with desire for her and said to Īrākht, "You were a fool to take the tiara and pass up such a peerless robe, unlike anything in our treasuries."

When Īrākht heard the king belittle her judgment and praise 13.24
Gūlpanāh, she was overcome with indignation and anger; she struck the king's head with the platter she held and the rice spilled over his head: this was the fulfillment of the eighth dream, part of which Kamānzūn had begun to tell the king, without explaining it further.

The king summoned Baylār. "Do you see what this woman has done and how she has insulted the king of the world! Take her away and cut off her head. Show her no mercy."

As Baylār was taking Īrākht away, he said to himself, "I won't put 13.25
her to death until the king's anger subsides. I think the king won't be able to bear her loss; she is so intelligent and well-favored, a woman of such judiciousness and intelligence. Thanks to her, God has rescued many people from death and destruction. She has done good deeds, and our hopes for her are great. I fear that the king will say,

'Couldn't you have delayed putting her to death until I reconsidered?' I won't kill her until I see how the king's view of her develops. If he regrets her death and misses her, I'll bring her to him alive, thereby accomplishing three good things: saving his beloved Īrākht, dispelling his sadness, and earning everyone's gratitude, as she is a woman of exceptional righteousness and piety. If he doesn't mention her or yearn for her, I'll carry out his command."

13.26 Baylār took her home secretly and placed her in the safekeeping of two of the king's chamberlains who were in charge of his wives and household. He ordered them to care for her and show her every courtesy, until he'd seen how things progressed. With his sword stained with blood, a downcast Baylār then came before the king, and said, "I have carried out your command concerning Īrākht."

13.27 The king's anger soon subsided. He remembered Īrākht's beauty, the place she held in his heart, and everything she had meant to him, and he became very sad. He tried to console himself and show strength. He was ashamed to ask Baylār whether he had really carried out the order, but he began to hope that he hadn't killed her, acquainted as he was with Baylār's intelligence, judiciousness, skillful management of affairs, and thoughtfulness. Baylār, by virtue of his intelligence, perceived this. "Don't be sad or grieve, Your Majesty," he said. "Grief and sorrow will only weaken your body and damage your mind and sadden your close friends. Be patient, Your Majesty, and do not grieve for something you will never behold. If Your Majesty wishes, I will tell you a story that resembles this case."

"Tell it to me!"

13.28 And Baylār told the following tale: Two doves—a male and a
The Doves female—filled their nest with wheat and barley. The male said to his
Who Filled mate, "We shouldn't eat anything we've laid away as long as we can
Their Nest find enough in the fields to live on. We can eat what we've gath-
with Wheat ered when winter comes and we can find nothing in the fields." The
and Barley female agreed. "What a good idea! That's what we'll do, God willing."
The wheat and barley were moist when they put them into the nest.

The male flew off and was away for a time. The grain dried up and shrank when summer came. When he returned and saw the grain so diminished, he said, "We agreed to eat nothing we had laid away. Why did you eat some of it?"

The female swore she hadn't eaten a single grain, but he didn't believe her and pecked her to death. When the winter rains arrived, the grain became moist again and the nest filled up as before. When the male saw the nest full, he knew he had acted unjustly and had been too quick to accuse and pass judgment. He lay down beside her in remorse and said, "What good to me is life if I seek but cannot find you, and realize how I mistreated you whenever I think of you?" And he took neither food nor drink till he died by her side. 13.29

"Thus," said Baylār, "a judicious, intelligent man knows he shouldn't be quick to punish, especially someone he may regret losing, as the male dove did.

"I've heard, too, that a man carrying a sack of lentils entered a wood to rest in the shade. Setting down his load, he went to sleep. A monkey came down from a tree above his head, took a handful of the lentils, and climbed back into the tree. A single lentil fell from the monkey's hand; as he searched for it fruitlessly, all the lentils scattered from his hand. 13.30

The Monkey and the Lentils

"Your Majesty, you have twelve thousand women, yet instead of diverting yourself with them, you seek what you'll never find. "

When the king heard these words, he feared that Baylār had indeed killed Īrākht, and said to Baylār, "As a result of a single moment of anger on my part, did you execute my command immediately, fastening on one word, without further consideration?" 13.31

"I know of only one whose word is unvarying for me," replied Baylār.

"And who is that?" asked the king.

"God," replied Baylār, "whose word never changes. What He says is true and what He does is just."

The king said, "I am so very saddened by the death of Īrākht." 13.32

And Baylār responded, "Two kinds should feel sadness: those who sin every day and those who never do good—their joy and pleasure in this world are brief, and their regret, when they face the consequences, will be long and incalculable."

The king then said, "If Īrākht is alive, I will never be sad again."

And Baylār responded, "Two kinds should never feel sadness: those who never sin and those who strive for the sake of God every day."

13.33 The king then said, "I will never again look on anyone."

And Baylār responded, "Two kinds never see: the blind man and the fool. Just as the blind man can't see the world, the sky, the stars, and the earth, and cannot tell near from far, and before from behind, the fool cannot tell the wise from the ignorant, the beautiful from the ugly, or someone who wishes him well from someone who would do him harm."

13.34 The king said, "What a joy it would be if I could see Īrākht!"

And Baylār responded, "Two kinds truly see: those blessed with sight and those who are wise. Just as someone who can see perceives the light of the world and all that waxes and wanes in it, both near and far, the wise man perceives righteousness and sinfulness; he sees clearly the works that are rewarded in the hereafter, which saves him and guides him to a straight path."

The king added, "I could never get enough of seeing Īrākht."

And Baylār responded, "Two kinds never get enough: those concerned only with amassing wealth and those who consume everything they find and seek what they will never find."

13.35 "We should keep clear of you, Baylār," said the king. "People like you are to be feared and guarded against."

And Baylār responded, "There are two types one should keep clear of: those who say righteousness and sin, reward and punishment, exist in this world alone; and those who can't avert their eyes from what isn't theirs, stop their ears from listening to evil, keep their members away from other men's wives, or curb their hearts

from the promptings of sin and greed. Both their remorse and their everlasting punishment in the fire of Hell will be great indeed."

"I am empty without Īrākht," said the king. 13.36

And Baylār responded, "Three things are truly empty: a river without water, a land without a king, and a woman without a husband."

"You are quick to respond, Baylār," said the king.

And Baylār responded, "Three are quick to respond: a king disbursing gifts from his treasury, a woman betrothed to a kinsman she loves, and a scholar able to do good deeds and teach God's religion."

The king said, "Your consolation is making me sad." 13.37

And Baylār responded, "There are three who should be sad: the owner of a fine horse that lacks spirit; the man who spends lavishly on food that pleases neither him nor his guests; and the husband of a beautiful wife of noble family whom he cannot maintain in proper style, so that he suffers from her constant slander."

"Īrākht has perished wrongfully and pointlessly," said the king. 13.38

And Baylār responded, "Three suffer pointless loss: the blacksmith who wears white when he sits by the bellows, the laundryman who puts on new shoes when his feet are in the water, and the merchant who marries a beautiful young wife and then is never home."

The king said, "You deserve to be punished severely." 13.39

And Baylār responded, "Three types deserve to be punished: the shameless evildoer who seduces other men's wives; the guest who attends a banquet uninvited; and the man who asks his friends for what they don't have, and, when they tell him they don't have it, accepts no excuses and blackens their reputation."

"You should be considered a fool," said the king. 13.40

And Baylār responded, "Three types should be considered fools: the carpenter who cuts timber until he fills his house with so much wood that he, his wife, and his children are left with no room; the doctor who wields his razor without cauterizing the wound and is so incompetent that he slices off people's flesh; and the stranger who

lives among his foes but doesn't want to return home and regrets it in the end."

13.41 "You should have kept calm until my anger subsided," said the king.

And Baylār responded, "Three kinds should keep calm: those climbing a high mountain, those angling for fish, and those embarking on a dangerous enterprise."

13.42 "I wish I could see Īrākht," said the king. "I miss her."

And Baylār responded, "Three types wish for what they will never obtain: the godless sinner who would be numbered with the saints when he dies and receive their reward, the miser who wants his soul to dwell among the generous in the hereafter, and the man who sheds innocent blood and wants his soul to dwell with the souls of the God-fearing."

13.43 "I am someone who has brought pain on himself," said the king.

And Baylār responded, "Three types bring pain on themselves: those who go into battle without a shield and get killed; a rich man who is without children and brothers, who lives by usury and profiteering, and who in the end is killed by an envier; and an old man married to a beautiful but brazen woman who constantly hopes for his death in order to marry a younger man, and who perishes at her hands."

13.44 "I must be contemptible in your eyes," said the king, "when you dare to say such things in my presence."

And Baylār responded, "Three types show contempt for their masters: the jabberer who babbles on regardless of whether he has been asked or not, prattling about what he knows and doesn't know, thus dishonoring his owner; the rich servant of a poor master, who gives his master none of his wealth; and the servant who speaks rudely, quarrels, and argues arrogantly with his master."

13.45 "You seem to be mocking me for my sadness," said the king.

And Baylār responded, "Three kinds deserve to be mocked: those who say they have seen many campaigns, killed many foes, and captured many prisoners, though they have no battle scars on

their bodies; those who claim to be scholars of religion and zealous ascetics, but who, obese and thick-necked, are fatter than a profligate sinner—they should be mocked, and their pretentions doubted, because all who exhaust themselves obeying God are emaciated and sparing in diet; and the virgin who derides a married woman, while she herself comes to a sorrowful end."

"You are out of your mind," said the king.

And Baylār responded, "Three types seem to be out of their minds, acting like persons raving with demons: the intelligent man who educates a fool—the fool is unteachable and in his ignorance argues with the teacher, who earns nothing but regret for his effort; a person who provokes a fool, who in exasperation takes to insulting him and spreading lies about him, and thereby injures himself; and a person who reveals his secret to a friend he hasn't tested, brings him in on an important affair, and trusts him as he would trust himself."

"I've brought trouble on myself," said the king.

And Baylār responded, "Three kinds bring trouble on themselves: those who fight an opponent they know to be stronger and more aggressive, and are either killed or run away and retreat, walking backward, likely to stumble into a well or fall into a pit and break a limb; those who go on a long voyage for no purpose and gain nothing but trouble; and those who say they have no fear of battle—they may deceive others, but when war comes, they look right and left to find a way to escape."

"Our friendship is at an end," said the king.

And Baylār responded, "There are three kinds whose affection is soon severed: the friend who doesn't visit, write, or send messengers to his friend; the woman whose abusive husband has died and seeks another; and those whose friendship, based on profligacy, doesn't last, but is severed at the least mishap."

"By killing Īrākht you've shown your lack of intelligence and good sense," said the king.

And Baylār responded, "Three types by their rashness show their lack of intelligence and good sense: those who deposit money for

safekeeping with someone untrustworthy and make a person of untested honesty a witness between themselves and an opponent; those devoid of intelligence and modesty who claim to be military men and to be intelligent, skilled at acquiring friends and serving rulers, designing buildings, and every difficult task, lying with every word; and those who claim to have renounced the things of this world and to be intent on the hereafter, but do so as part of a hypocritical search for celebrity—they profit neither in this world nor the next."

13.50 "You aren't being intelligent," said the king.

And Baylār responded, "Three types shouldn't be considered intelligent: the shoemaker who sits on a seat so high that if his knife or other tool falls, he is distracted from his work looking for it; the tailor who uses such a long thread that he is distracted from his work untangling its knots; and the barber who spoils a haircut by looking right and left, and thus earns a painful beating."

13.51 "You want to teach everybody, myself included, to be adept," said the king.

And Baylār responded, "Three types prematurely claim to be adept, but have more to learn: someone who can play the harp and drums, but cannot keep time with the voices or the tunes; the painter who claims to be an adept draftsman, but cannot mix colors; and those who claim that they know better than anyone else but fail to speak clearly or know how much they ought to say."[60]

13.52 "You did not act correctly when you killed Īrākht," said the king.

And Baylār responded, "Four types do not act correctly: those whose tongues never speak the truth and whose actions do not match their words; those swift to eat, but slow to work, plow, or serve their superiors; those who become angry at no offense; and the king who rushes to carry out a grave injustice."

13.53 "Had you given the matter due consideration, you wouldn't have killed Īrākht," said the king.

And Baylār responded, "Four types give matters due consideration: those who prepare food and serve it to their masters on time;

those who are content with their own wives and seek no other; the king who embarks on an important affair only upon the advice of his scholars; and those who subdue their anger and suppress their wrath."

"I fear for you, Baylār," said the king.[61]

And Baylār responded, "Four fear needlessly: the little bird who dwells in the trees yet raises its wings for fear that the sky might fall on him, saying, 'If it falls, I'll hold it up with my wings'; the stork who stands on one leg, fearing that if he puts the other down, the earth will collapse under him; the earthworm who eats and fasts on alternate days for fear of starving to death; and the bat who won't fly by day because, fancying himself the world's most beautiful bird, he fears people will trap him and keep him for his beauty."

"Did you vow to put Īrākht to death?" said the king.

And Baylār responded, "One should vow to cling to four things: the prize steed that is its owner's mount; the ox with which you plow; the wise wife who loves her husband; and the industrious servant who is loyal, truthful, and respectful toward his master."

"I will never take pleasure in your company now that you've killed Īrākht," said the king.

And Baylār responded, "Four take no pleasure in the company of four others: the scholar takes no pleasure in the company of the ignoramus, the glutton takes no pleasure in the company of the ascetic, the man of refinement takes no pleasure in the company of a resentful foe, and the proud man who tolerates no slight takes no pleasure in the company of an arrogant, disrespectful man."

"I shall never find another woman like Īrākht," said the king.

And Baylār responded, "Four things are nearly impossible to find: a woman of much experience who becomes satisfied with one man; a habitual liar who ceases to lie; a bad-tempered, conceited man whose company one can enjoy; and a proud, insolent man who manages to change his nature."

"I wish this knowledge had come earlier, for now it is useless and has come too late," said the king.

And Baylār responded, "Four things should be ascertained and acted on in advance: soldiers going into battle should obtain intelligence and prepare their gear before the fighting begins; a man of means, before contending with his opponents, should find an honest judge who doesn't swerve from the truth, act unjustly, or accept bribes; a man of wealth who intends to acquire slaves and estates should first find trustworthy agents and assistants before acquiring the estates; and a man who intends to invite kings and nobles to dinner should prepare what he needs in advance, lest, after they arrive, he run into difficulties or fall short."

13.59 "You know neither piety nor sin, Baylār," said the king.

And Baylār responded, "Four types pay piety and sin no heed: the gravely ill, those afraid of their master or ruler, bold men badly treated who contend with their enemy, and an assailant terrorizing someone better than he."

13.60 "You are imparting discipline, Baylār," said the king.

And Baylār responded, "Four types tolerate no discipline: the man addicted to wrongdoing and licentiousness; the insolent, conceited man; the habitual thief; and those quick to anger, slow to be pleased."

13.61 "We shouldn't trust you, Baylār," said the king.

And Baylār responded, "Four things shouldn't be trusted: untamed snakes and predators; profligate sinners; wealth, which can never be trusted not to pass out of its owner's hands; and the body, whose survival and health one can never count on, condemned as it is to death."

13.62 The king said, "A wise man shouldn't jest with his servants or with colleagues he has doubts about, let alone with his master."

And Baylār responded, "There are four sorts one shouldn't jest with or speak to without reserve: an awe-inspiring, valiant, powerful ruler; a skillful, intelligent, dignified man; an insolent drunkard; and those from whom you hope to gain favor and benefit."

13.63 The king said, "We should no longer mingle with you, Baylār, after your killing of Īrākht."

And Baylār responded, "Five things do not mingle with each other: night and day, the pious and the dissolute, light and dark, good and evil, hot and cold."

"No one should share your companionship, Baylār," said the king. 13.64

And Baylār responded, "There are five sorts with whom one shouldn't share companionship: the dissolute thief, the lying cheat, the man quick to revile, the proud envier, and the wanton tyrant."

"I am very sad, Baylār," said the king, "when I see sixteen thousand women, without Īrākht among them." 13.65

And Baylār responded, "There are five women for whom no one should feel sad: a clumsy and audacious one; an impudent, foulmouthed scold; a stupid, ugly woman; a frivolous and indiscrete one; and a disobedient woman who insults her husband."

"Never before," said the king, "have I felt such sadness as I now feel recalling Īrākht's superiority and judgment." 13.66

And Baylār responded, "There are five women for whose loss one should feel sad: a noble woman of distinguished lineage; a woman chaste, fortunate, and prudent; a woman beautiful and attractive to behold; a woman content with her husband; and a woman who is ready to assist her husband."

"Whoever guides me to the living Īrākht," said the king, "shall have all the money he desires." 13.67

And Baylār responded, "Five sorts love money more than life: the mercenary who fights for pay; the man who earns his wage by digging canals and tunnels; the merchant who sails the seas; the snake charmer who, for a price, sets a snake loose on himself; and the man who risks his life by drinking poison for a wager."

"I see that my hopes for Īrākht will have no welcome outcome," said the king. 13.68

And Baylār responded, "There are seven types whose actions have no welcome outcome: those who act without commendable intention or sound judgment, those who bestow favors on a person devoid of gratitude and loyalty, the crude boor who knows

no mercy, the adulterous woman who gives birth to a bastard and raises it, those who trust an ungrateful deceiver, those quick to weary their brothers, and those who recognize neither God nor His saints."

13.69 "By killing Īrākht," said the king, "you have planted in my heart implacable hatred for you."

And Baylār responded, "Eight there are between whom implacable hatred is fixed: the wolf and the lamb, the cat and the mouse, the goshawk and the francolin, the owl and the crow, the snake and the mongoose, the saint and the sinner, the valorous and the coward, the rich and the poor."

13.70 "Have you no sympathy for me, Baylār?" said the king.

And Baylār responded, "Eight types deserve no sympathy: the malicious king who acts on his malice; the babbler whose prattling does him no good and harms others; the thief who waits for nightfall so that he can steal; the pallbearer idle for lack of work; the foul, licentious woman; the traveler who leaves the highway to take a shortcut and perishes; the soldier who wreaks havoc in the land; and someone who drinks poison as an experiment."

13.71 "Sorrow for Īrākht keeps me from sleeping, Baylār," said the king.

And Baylār responded, "Nine types do not sleep: a sick man with no physician, an anxious rich man who trusts no one with his wealth, a man who intends to shed blood, a man who wishes people ill and devises ways to harm them, a soldier who fears a night attack, a debtor who has no money, a man with no access to the woman he loves, a man who knows his wife is unfaithful but doesn't repudiate her, and someone slandered and wrongly accused of something he never did."

13.72 "Īrākht's departure was loathsome to me, Baylār," said the king.

And Baylār responded, "Nine things are loathsome: the onset of old age and the departure of youth; illness that brings with it sleepless nights and unquiet days; fear and greed that occupy the heart; anger that harms the body and degrades the mind; cares and

sadness that emaciate and destroy the body; death, which spares no one; heat and cold that damage crops; hunger and thirst that bring perdition; and the ill-fated rebel at whose hands many perish."

"Did you slay Īrākht by your own hand?" said the king. 13.73

And Baylār responded, "There are ten types whose claims remain uncertain until they are tried and tested: the soldier by combat and action; the contented man by need; the gentleman by anger; the merchant by buying and selling; the friend by adversity; the scholar by his judgment, advice, and management of affairs; the pious ascetic by persistence in worship; the generous man by his gifts; and the trustee by keeping whatever is entrusted to his care."

"Baylār," said the king, "you are addressing me with harsh words." 13.74

And Baylār responded, "Ten types are addressed with harsh words: an insolent king; an excited old man; an uncultured fool; those who offer advice to bumblers; those who undertake works for which they have no skill; those who judge with ignorance, to their detriment; the judge whose unjust judgments are motivated by greed; the miser who loses his temper when pressed for alms; and the giver who gives in order to increase his recipient's obligation."

"You've wearied me," said the king, "and wearied yourself, 13.75 Baylār."

And Baylār responded. "Ten types weary themselves and others, too. Those with little learning who lay claim to more than they know: they receive many inquiries and provide many responses; the inquiries weary them, and they weary their respondents by their meager guidance. Those charged with many tasks. Those who importune a friend for the impossible, weary him by their insistence, and exhaust themselves by their persistence. The opinionated fool who would convert everybody to his opinion, which they do not agree with, and wearies himself and everybody else by his unsuccessful persuasion. Those devoid of understanding and knowledge who serve the ruler are wearied by the ruler's rebukes and weary the ruler by their lack of understanding. Those who contract to complete a job they're

unskilled at and weary themselves with their labor and weary their employer, who must oblige them to redo the bungled job. Those charged with teaching a dunce weary both themselves and their pupils. Those who entrust their secret to a woman too weak to hide it, and who rebuke her vainly when she reveals it—each will be wearied by the other. The owner of a stupid horse, who beats it whenever it does something stupid, only increasing its stupidity, so that each is wearied by the other. The unfortunate subject who serves a mendacious ruler who breaks his promises wearies the ruler by his insistent requests, while the ruler keeps fanning his hopes, repeating his promises and disappointing them, so that each grows weary of the other."

13.76 "You've drawn the matter out at great length," said the king. "Now tell me clearly, Baylār, whether it has turned out against me or for me."

Baylār fell silent. Realizing how sad the king was and how he longed to see Īrākht, he said to himself, "I ought to bring the king the woman he loves so deeply and yearns so much to see. He has patiently endured my lengthy exchanges with him and my blunt words without punishing me."

So he said, "May God grant Your Majesty long life, preserve you in health, and increase your judiciousness and nobility. I speak now in my own words. No king on earth is your equal or like you: there never has been and never will be. Anger has not overcome you; for despite my insignificance and unimportance, you remained calm and dignified while I spoke, abundant in your knowledge, judiciousness, and mildness—in the midst of your authority. Whether angry or pleased, you never say or command what should not be said or commanded; you remain gentle and peace-loving. If, with time's vicissitudes, you suffer loss of some of the benefits that God has bestowed on you, or a calamity forces you to suffer adversity, you bear it patiently. You do not become dismayed or paralyzed by grief, but console yourself and show contentment and acceptance of what has happened. You restrain and humble him who,

not of your lineage, conducts himself with arrogance and pride in his domain. You dismiss and banish from your presence even those closest to you, those whom you regard with affection, if they manifest haughtiness and pride regarding your affairs. Severed from your favor, they grieve and become dismayed; their grief does not benefit them, but their sadness and concern grow, and thus their misfortune increases. Your Majesty has been restrained by noble lineage and great forbearance, and, for all my insignificance and unimportance, you have listened patiently to me. I am therefore grateful to Your Majesty for not commanding my death. I stand here before you, having done what I did out of devotion and love of Your Majesty. If this has involved disobedience, you have sufficient evidence and the power to punish me and to put me to death."

When the king heard Baylār's words, he knew that Īrākht, the 13.77
mother of Jawbar, was alive and that Baylār had not dared execute her. Overjoyed, he said to him, "I was kept from anger by what I knew of your sincerity and truthfulness. Knowing your wisdom, I hoped that you had not killed Īrākht; for even if she offended and behaved rudely, she acted out of jealousy, not hostility or malice. I should have overlooked it and accepted it. Also, I didn't become angry with you, for I knew the fault was mine. I was sure you would realize that my order to kill her was not my real intention and that I regretted it. But you wanted to test my mind and cause it to doubt. You feared I would punish you because of the command to kill her. But God forbid that I should think in that way or do that to you! Rather, I am grateful. You have done me a favor that deserves the greatest thanks. Go now, and bring Īrākht to me."

Baylār left the king, filled with joy and gladness. He commanded 13.78
that Īrākht be made ready in all her finery, and escorted her to the king along with both of the retainers to whose care he had entrusted her. The king was overjoyed to see her. "Do whatever you please," he said. "Never again will I refuse you anything."

And Īrākht said, "May your reign last forever! How, but for your mercy and keen intellect, would you have felt such regret over my death? Had you forgotten me forever, I would have deserved it because of the offense for which the king ordered my death. In your mercy you have thanked Baylār for not killing me. Were it not for Baylār's trust in your great moderation, and for his mercy, justness, and calmness, he would have carried out the command and killed me."

13.79 "You have done me a favor that deserves gratitude," the king said to Baylār, "something that no king has ever seen from his servants. Not killing Īrākht, Jawbar's mother, is the greatest favor you have ever done for me. I took her life and you brought her back to life, and now you have given her back to me. I have never been more pleased with you than I am today. I give you authority over my kingdom and all my subjects. I hereby make you my deputy, to rule over everything beyond the gate of my palace. Do as you please."

13.80 "I am Your Majesty's servant," replied Baylār. "All I ask today is that you not act hastily in any matter of such importance—the consequences of which you might regret and which might bring grief and sorrow in their wake, particularly regarding this queen who has no equal on earth—and that first you investigate and ascertain the facts."

"You are right, Baylār," said the king. "I accept your advice. From now on I will do nothing, great or small, let alone something as momentous as this, without consultation and careful consideration."

13.81 The king gave Īrākht the robe, bestowed many estates on her, gave her authority over his entire kingdom, and made Gūlpanāh and all his other wives her servants. He gave many gifts to Baylār, then went into his harem happy and joyful.

13.82 Later, the king consulted Baylār about executing the enemies who had sought to destroy him, his entourage, and his kingdom. With the help of the great men of the kingdom, they were all put to

death. The king praised God and thanked Kamānzūn for what he had done; for God, by His blessing and favor, had saved the king, his wife, his children, and his righteous minister through Kamānzūn's wisdom.

Here ends the Chapter of Haylār, Baylār,
and Īrākht, the Mother of Jawbar.

The Mendicant and the Goldsmith

A chapter about rendering favors to the undeserving and about trusting true friends and assistants.

14.1 Dabshalim said to Baydabā the Philosopher, "I understand what you've told me about a king's choosing to restore certain people to favor. Now tell me a parable about those to whom he should show favor, those who should be trusted and on whose help he can rely."

14.2 The philosopher said, "Kings and others should treat well those who deserve it and establish close ties with those who will return gratitude and praise. They shouldn't look only to their relatives and entourage or to the noble and wealthy who enjoy power and influence, nor should they refrain from showing favor to the weak, the distressed, and the humble. They should test and examine individuals great and small, to assess their gratitude and loyalty, or their ingratitude and disloyalty, and act according to what they discover. A skilled physician doesn't treat his patients merely by looking at them; he examines their urine, feels their pulse, and treats each patient according to what he knows about them. When a wise man finds people—and animals, too—endowed with dignity, loyalty, and gratitude, he should treat them well, for he may need them some day and they will repay his kindness. Sometimes an intelligent man is so cautious with people that he feels safe with no one, but he still puts a mongoose up his sleeve and keeps a bird on his hand. A man of intelligence, they say, should despise no one, great or small,

human or animal; he should test them and show them favor according to what he sees in them. There is a parable about this told by one of the sages."

"How does it go?" asked the king.

The philosopher related the following tale: Some men, they say, 14.3
once went to a cave and dug a pit to catch wild animals. Into it fell a goldsmith, along with a tiger, a snake, and a monkey. None of them could get out. A mendicant[62] passed by and looked into the pit. When he saw them, he thought to himself, "I can think of no deed that will earn me more merit in the hereafter than rescuing this man from his enemies." So he took a rope and lowered it to the man. The monkey, being nimble, grabbed hold of it, so he pulled him out. Then he lowered it again; the tiger clung to it, and he pulled him out. He did it a third time; the snake wrapped herself around the rope, and he rescued her. They thanked him for his good deed, but said, "Don't help this man to get out, for he knows nothing about gratitude, praise, or loyalty." He disregarded their warning, lowered the rope, and pulled the man out.

The monkey said, "I live on a hill near a city called Barjawān." 14.4

The tiger said, "I live there too, in a forest near the city."

The snake said, "I live in the city wall. If you ever come to the city or pass by and happen to need us, let us know, so that we can come and reward you for your deed."

"I too live in that city," said the goldsmith. He thanked the mendicant, praised him, and added, "You've done me a great favor, which I must remember. If you ever happen to come to the city, inquire after me, for I have my home there. Hopefully, I can repay you somehow for your good deed."

Each then went his way. Sometime later, the mendicant needed 14.5
to go to that city. The monkey met him, bowed to him, kissed his hands and feet, and said apologetically, "I own nothing, but rest here for a moment until I bring you some of my food." The monkey went off and brought back a ripe fruit and placed it before the mendicant, who ate it.

As the mendicant continued on his way to the city, the tiger came out to meet him. Bowing before him in greeting, he said, "You did me an enormous favor. Don't leave until I return." The tiger went off immediately, killed the king's daughter, and took her jewelry. He gave it to the mendicant, telling him nothing about where it came from.

The mendicant said to himself, "Seeing that these animals have done me these favors, shouldn't I try to find the goldsmith? Even if he is poor and penniless, he can sell this jewelry for me, and we can share the proceeds."

14.6 The mendicant entered the city and came to the goldsmith's house, who welcomed him and invited him in. The goldsmith recognized the jewelry the moment he saw it. "Make yourself at home," he said, "while I go and get you something to eat. I don't think what I have in the house is good enough for you."

The goldsmith then went to the palace and sent the king a message: "The man who killed your daughter and took her jewelry— I've got him. He's being held in my house."

The king sent someone to arrest the mendicant. When he saw the jewelry in the mendicant's possession, he commanded that he be tortured, paraded through the city, and beheaded. At this, the mendicant began to weep, imploring assistance, and crying aloud, "Had I obeyed the snake, the monkey, and the tiger, this misfortune would never have befallen me."

14.7 The snake heard these words and came out of her nest. When she saw him, she was distressed by his plight and pondered how she might help effect his escape. She went to the king's son and bit him. The king summoned the learned men. They recited spells to heal him, to no avail. Then they consulted the stars and drew up various schemes. Finally the boy spoke up, saying, "I will not recover until this mendicant comes and strokes me with his hand, for Your Majesty has wrongly and unjustly commanded his death."[63]

When the king heard these words, he sent for the mendicant and commanded him to recite spells over his son.

The mendicant replied, "I'm unable to do what you've commanded."

The king said, "I require only that you tell me about yourself and why you came to this city."

So the mendicant told the king his story: the favor he had done for the goldsmith, the monkey, the tiger, and the snake; what they had told him about the goldsmith; and why he had come to the city. Then he prayed: "O God, if You know that I have spoken the truth, hasten to cure the king's son and restore his health."

So God delivered the boy from his malady and he recovered. The king rewarded the mendicant with gifts, and ordered that the goldsmith be punished.

Here ends the Chapter of the Mendicant and the Goldsmith.

The King's Son and His Companions

15.1 Dabshalim said to Baydabā the Philosopher, "I understand what you have said about a king's bestowing favor only on those who know how to show gratitude and loyalty, wherever they may be, near or far. Now tell me why a simple fellow sometimes attains eminence and honor, and a wise and intelligent man suffers hardship, toil, and loss."

15.2 The philosopher said, "Just as sight requires eyes and hearing ears, knowledge, for its perfection, requires judiciousness, intelligence, and resolute conduct. But Destiny and Fortune overpower everything; they need only the slightest cause to enrich a person or destroy him. The Parable of the King's Son exemplifies this. He was seen sitting at the gate of the city of Qaṭūn, but after the turn in his fortunes, he inscribed on its gate: 'Intelligence, beauty, hard work, strength, and all else operate only in accordance with Destiny and Fortune.'"

"And what was his story?" asked the king.

15.3 The philosopher told the following tale: Four people, they say, became traveling companions: a king's son, a merchant's son, a nobleman's son, and a farmer's son. All had suffered hardship and distress, and owned only the clothes on their backs. As they walked, the king's son said, "All the affairs of this world are determined by Destiny."

The merchant's son said, "Intelligence is better than everything."

The nobleman's son said, "Beauty is better still."

The farmer's son said, "Hard work is best of all."

They traveled to a city called Qaṭūn. There they halted and said 15.4
to the farmer's son, "Go, and through your hard work earn the food
we need for today."

So he set out and asked what sort of labor, carried out from
morning till night, would earn enough to feed four people. He was
told, "Nothing is more valuable than firewood." So he went about
a league from the city, where there was some firewood, gathered
a bundle, sold it for half a dirham, and with the money bought
enough to satisfy his companions. He wrote on the city gate: "One
day's hard work is worth half a dirham." His companions ate the
provisions he returned with.

The next morning they said to the nobleman's son, "Go, and use 15.5
your beauty to earn something of benefit to us."

So he left, thinking to himself, "I'm no good at any kind of work,
but I'm ashamed to return to my friends without any food." As he
was about to abandon them in despair, he leaned against a tree in
the city, and just then a dignitary's wife passed by and was struck
by his beauty. She sent her slavegirl to bring him to her house and
ordered that he be bathed, and he spent a day of pleasure and feast-
ing with her. In the evening, she rewarded him with five hundred
dinars. So he went back to his companions and wrote on the city
gate: "One day's beauty is worth five hundred dinars."

The next morning, they said to the merchant's son, "Go, and earn 15.6
something using your business acumen."

Off he went. Soon he saw a great ship anchored by the shore, not
far from the city. Some merchants had gone out to buy its cargo.
They had bargained with the owners, but after a while, they had told
each another, "Let's leave for the rest of the day; we'll get them to
sell their merchandise bit by bit and they'll lower the price for us."
In their absence, the merchant's son bought the cargo. When the
city merchants got word of this, they came to him and upped the
price by one hundred thousand dinars. He returned to his friends
and wrote on the city gate: "One day's intelligence is worth one

hundred thousand dinars." He and his friends enjoyed their new prosperity.

15.7　　　On the morning of the fourth day, they said to the king's son, "Go, and earn something for us in accordance with your rank and destiny."[64]

At the city gate, he sat on a high bench. As fate would have it, the king of the city had died that very day, without issue, brothers, or kin. As the king's bier passed by, someone asked him, "Who are you, and why are sitting here unmoved by the king's death?" He made no answer, so the man chased him away with a curse. When they had gone, he returned to his place. On their return, the man who had treated him so brusquely saw him and said, "Didn't I forbid you to sit here?" And he ordered that he be arrested and imprisoned.

15.8　　　When the people assembled to choose a new king, the man who had sent the young man to prison told them about him and said, "I'm afraid he's an enemy spy."

So they sent for him and asked him who he was, what he was up to, and what had brought him to their country. He replied, "I am the son of King Iṣṭahr of Qurūnā. When my father died, my brother seized the kingdom from me, though I am older than he. Fearing for my life, I fled and came to you."

At these words, the people who had visited that country recognized him and praised him. They made him their king and put him in charge of their affairs. As it was their custom to process through the city with whomever they made ruler, they mounted him on an elephant and processed around the city. When he passed by the city gate and saw what his friends had inscribed, he ordered the following inscription: "Hard work, intelligence, beauty, and the good and evil a man attains come by Destiny and Fortune. Learn this lesson from the prosperity and happiness God has brought me."

15.9　　　Then, as king, he went to his council chamber, seated himself on his throne, and sent for his companions. He gave them gifts and made them wealthy. He gathered his officials and the wise men of the kingdom and said, "My companions now know for certain

that what prosperity God bestowed on them came only by Destiny and that the other things they referred to were merely ancillary. Whatever God granted and prepared for me did not come from beauty, intelligence, or hard work; it came by God's Decree and Destiny. I never imagined that I would attain this position when my brother forced me to flee in fear. I saw people in this country who surpassed me in beauty and grace, and I knew that it had people better in judgment and more diligent in their labors. Destiny and Fortune drove me into exile; then, by God's command and by His knowledge, decree, and predestation, I was made king, although I would have been content to live a life of hardship and austerity."

A mendicant stood up in the assembly and said, "Your Majesty 15.10
has spoken with judiciousness, intelligence, and discernment. We think well of you and have great hopes for you. We recognize what you have said and acknowledge its truth. We know that you were worthy of what God sent you through the favor He apportioned to you and His continued grace toward you. The most fortunate people in this world and the next, those likeliest to enjoy happiness, are those whom God has sustained as He has sustained you and to whom He has granted what He has granted you. God has favored us by making you our king. We praise God for the gift He has given us in you."

Then another mendicant stood up. Having praised, extolled, and 15.11
glorified God and recounted His bounties, he said, "Your Majesty, when I was young, I served a rich nobleman before becoming a mendicant. When I decided to abandon the world and left him, he gave me two dinars as my wage. I decided to give one away in charity and keep the other to spend. 'Nothing,' I said, 'will bring a greater reward than to buy a living soul with one dinar and set it free for the love of God.' So I went to the market and found a hunter who had two doves. Despite my haggling, he refused to sell them for less than two dinars. I tried as hard as I could to have him give me the two for one dinar, but he refused. I told myself, 'Perhaps they are mates or siblings. I fear that if I free one and separate them, the other will die

of grief.' So I bought both at the price he had set. Then I worried that if I set them free in town, they might not be able to fly away because they were weak with exhaustion. I took them to a meadow, where I released them, and they flew off and perched in a nearby tree. As I turned to leave, one said to the other, 'This mendicant has rescued us from our distress; we should reward him for his deed.' Then they said to me, 'We must thank you and reward you for the favor you have done us. At the foot of this tree you will find a jar full of dinars. Take it.' I went to the tree, dubious about what they had said, but I didn't have to dig deep before I reached the jar. I pulled it out and called on God to grant them prosperity. Then I said to them, 'I see that your knowledge is such that while flying through the air you know enough to tell me what is under the earth. How then did you get into the predicament from which I rescued you?' They said, 'Wise man, don't you know that the sight is dimmed when Fortune descends? Fortune overcomes everything; no one can go beyond it or fall short of it.'"

15.12　　The philosopher said to the king, "Let the learned men who speculate about matters acknowledge that all things come to pass through Destiny and Fortune, without which no one can attain any success or ward off any evil. All these things are from God, who does what He wishes and decrees what He likes. Let all souls trust and rest content in this, for this doctrine brings comfort and peace of mind to those whom God inspires and directs aright."

Here ends the Chapter of the King's
Son and His Companions.

THE HORSEMAN, THE LIONESS, AND THE JACKAL

About those who stop injuring others because of an injury they themselves have suffered, and, having learned a lesson from their own misfortune, turn away from injuring people.

The king said, "Now that I have heard this parable, please tell me one about someone who stops injuring others because he has been injured himself." 16.1

Baydabā the Philosopher said, "Only the ignorant, blind to the consequences in this world and the next, viciously assault other people. Little do they know the immeasurable repercussions in store for them as a result of their actions. Even if all goes well at first, the terrible requital for their deeds is inevitable. But sometimes an ignorant fellow learns a lesson from suffering an injury. Deterred by the realization that others have been similarly affected by the injuries he has inflicted on them, he desists from doing wrong; thus he benefits in the end from his misfortune. The Parable of the Lioness and the Jackal illustrates Your Majesty's inquiry." 16.2

"How does it go?" asked Dabshalim.

Baydabā the Philosopher related the following tale: Once, they say, a lioness lived in a thicket with her two cubs. One day she left her cubs behind and went in search of prey. Her cubs were killed by a horseman, who skinned them and made off with their pelts. 16.3

When the lioness returned, she was aghast at the sight of the skinned bodies of her cubs lying in the field. Weeping and raging

and overcome by grief, she trembled and roared uncontrollably. Her neighbor, a jackal, heard her voice and came to her. "What's wrong?" he asked. "What is making you cry? Why such grief? What has happened?"

"My cubs! A horseman found them. He killed them and stripped their pelts."

16.4 "Don't be so sad," said the jackal, "and don't grieve so excessively. Judge your situation fairly. The distress this horseman has inflicted on you by killing your cubs was no more than what you have inflicted on many. They felt the same grief for their loved ones as you feel for your cubs. So bear patiently your suffering at others' hands, just as others have borne what they've suffered at yours. As the saying goes: As you do, so shall it be done to you. Every deed has an outcome. The outcome of a deed is a reward or punishment proportional to the deed's magnitude, great or small: when a farmer sows seed, it yields a harvest in proportion to what he has sown."

16.5 "Explain yourself," said the lioness.

"How old are you?" asked the jackal.

"One hundred."

"What has nourished and sustained you?"

"The flesh of wild animals."

"And who fed you that meat?" asked the jackal.

"I hunted the animals myself, and killed them and ate them."

"Tell me: did the animals you ate have fathers and mothers?"

"Of course they did."

And the jackal said, "Why don't these parents display the distress, fear, sadness, and clamor we hear from you? Your misfortune is the result of how little thought you gave to the consequences and how ignorant you were of the harm that would redound to you from the harm you inflicted on them."

16.6 The jackal's words made the lioness realize that what had happened was payment for the wrongdoing and injustice she had heaped upon herself. She understood that anyone who acts wrongly

and unjustly will be repaid; so she gave up hunting, turned from meat to fruit, and began to live a life of asceticism and devotion.

The jackal, who lived on fruit, took note. When he saw the lion- 16.7 ess eating fruit, he said, "Because fruit is in such short supply this year, I thought the trees hadn't produced enough. But then I saw you, a meat eater, eating fruit, abandoning the sustenance allotted to you by God and turning to the sustenance allotted to others, interfering with it and reducing it, and I realized that the trees had produced fruit as usual and that the shortage was your fault. Alas for the trees and their fruit! Alas for those who lived on them! How swiftly they will perish when their sustenance is wrested from them by one who has no right to a share of it!"

And when she heard the jackal's words, the lioness stopped eating fruit too.

Baydabā continued, "I have told you this parable to teach you 16.8 that sometimes an ignorant fellow stops harming people because of a misfortune that has befallen him—like the lioness who, because she suffered for her cubs, abandoned meat; then, because of the jackal's words, abandoned fruit; and in the end ate grass in a life of devotion and asceticism. People should consider carefully how they deal with others. As has been said: Do not approve for others or inflict on them what you do not approve for yourself.[65] This is justice, and justice is pleasing to God and to men."

Here ends the Chapter of the Lioness and the Jackal.

The Ascetic and His Guest

17.1 King Dabshalim said to Baydabā the Philosopher, "Now that I've listened to what you've said, would you tell me about a person who abandons the trade that suits him and is appropriate for him, then turns to another trade, but fails to master it, and, having forgotten his original trade, falls into confusion?"

17.2 And Baydabā related: A certain ascetic, they say, lived in the land of Karkh. One day a guest arrived, and the ascetic called for some dates to serve as a treat. "How sweet and delicious!" exclaimed the guest. "There aren't any palm trees where we live, but we have plenty of other kinds of fruit to enjoy. You don't need dates if you have figs and other fruits—and, incidentally, dates are hard to digest and unhealthy."

17.3 "Yes," replied the ascetic. "Someone can hardly be counted happy if he seeks what he can't get and can't bear to do without it. He will only hurt himself by becoming heavyhearted and sorrowful. You, on the other hand, are fortunate to be content with what you can obtain and to have renounced what you cannot, to have curbed your appetite for what you can't reach and to be satisfied with what you can."

17.4 The ascetic knew Hebrew, which the guest found beautiful. So he set out to learn it, applying himself to the task for days, but to no avail.

The ascetic said to the guest, "If you abandon your own language and burden yourself with learning Hebrew, you'll likely suffer the same fate as the raven."

"How so?" asked the guest.

And the ascetic told the following tale: A raven, so they say, once
saw a partridge walking along with delicate steps. He liked its gait
and wanted to learn it, so he practiced, but, unable to master it,
went back to his old gait; however, he couldn't remember it, so he
became confused and hesitant: he hadn't obtained what he sought,
and in the process hadn't retained what he once had.

"I've told you this parable to demonstrate that if you abandon
your own language and set out to learn Hebrew, which doesn't suit
you, you're likely to fail and in the process forget the language you
already know. It has been said: The person who seeks what doesn't
suit him and is not appropriate for him, what his fathers and forefa-
thers never attained and for which they had no reputation, must be
judged ignorant."

Then the philosopher said to the king, "Today's rulers deserve
to be reprimanded even more for mismanagement, given their
lack of care for their subjects in this and similar matters. For kings
suffer harm when people move from one position to another and
abandon the position they occupied and that provided them with
a livelihood. When people in the lower ranks seek to rise into the
upper ranks, then comes loss of sound management, disorder in the
state, degeneration of manners, and competition between people of
low character and those of noble character. Events then take their
course until, in the end, there is grave danger of harm to the king."

Here ends the Chapter of the Ascetic and the Guest.

* * *

When the conversation between the king and the philosopher
reached the end of the Chapter of the Ascetic and the Guest, the
king fell silent, and the philosopher said, "May Your Majesty live a
thousand years and rule over the Seven Climes. May you be granted
the means to succeed in all your endeavors, amid happiness on your
part in your subjects and contentment on their part with you—with
the help of the divine Decree and Providence. Your discretion and

knowledge are complete, your intelligence and memory keen, and your courage and generosity perfect. Your intelligence, your words, and your intentions are in harmony. There is no deficiency in your judgment, no error in your speech, and nothing blameworthy in your actions. You combine strength and gentleness; you are never timid in battle or discouraged by sudden adversity.

17.9 "I have explained matters to you and answered your questions in the best possible way. To fulfill my duty to you, I have summoned my judgment, insight, and ingenuity; repay me now by a sincere intention to apply your mind and intelligence to what I have described. The person who obeys a wise command is no less fortunate than the person who gives it; the person who accepts good advice is no less fortunate than the person who imparts it;[66] and the person who learns is no less fortunate in his knowledge than the person who teaches. Whoever ponders this book with his intelligence, and acts on it according to his right judgment, and reflects on it with his sound judgment deserves an exalted position and, with the help of Providence, will be fit to deal with weighty matters when the time comes. No one can dispense with reflecting on this book and learning its lessons.

17.10 "May God grant Your Majesty success. May He correct whatever in you is amiss, calming any sharpness in your temperament and bestowing the fullness of His mercy upon you and upon your forefathers, a house renowned for intellect, cultivation, and merit."

17.11 The king then commanded that the doors of his treasuries be opened and that the philosopher Baydabā be allowed to take anything he wanted: pearls, jewels, gold, silver—nothing was to be denied him. The king bestowed many estates on him, and raised his rank and station above those aspired to by his peers.

17.12 This, then, is what took place between King Dabshalim and the chief sage and philosopher Baydabā.

Here ends *The Book of Kalīlah and Dimnah.*

Notes

1 The reading and vocalization of the name are conjectural (see Justi, *Iranisches Namenbuch*, 74a). ʿAzzām's text conjectures Ādharhirbad.

2 Later in the chapter (§1.14 and §1.17) it is implied that Barzawayh brought back more than one book.

3 The Arabic has *mithqāl*s (standard weights), a synonym for the gold dinar.

4 From here until "Buzurgmihr, you know Barzawayh's devotion to us" (§1.23), several pages in MS London Or. 4044 are lost. The translation is based on the text in MS London Or. 8751.

5 The gap in MS London Or. 4044 ends here.

6 One manuscript family (e.g., Paris 3466 and de Sacy's edition) adds, significantly, "and his journey to India in search of drugs and medicines, and how he learned their scripts and language."

7 This chapter is Ibn al-Muqaffaʿ's preface.

8 Literally "byways into which they could turn"—that is, ways to hint at doctrines whose explicit statement might imperil the speaker.

9 Correcting the manuscript's "six."

10 Another instance of an unelaborated list.

11 From information here and in the previous chapter, one can deduce that Barzawayh lived in the time of the Sasanian ruler Khosrow I Anūsharwān (r. AD 531–79).

12 In other versions, Barzawayh divides his education into two phases, the first beginning with his parents' sending him to learn to read and write, the second when he searched for a vocation and settled on medicine, based on his appreciation of its merits.

13 That is, for stringing into necklaces.

14 Wind is one of the elements or humors that constitute the body, according to some versions of the Indian tradition. See Nöldeke, *Burzoēs Einleitung zu dem Buche Kalīla wa-Dimna*, 22, 23n4.

15 Or. 4044 reads "two branches," but the copyist has added in the margin "the correct reading is a branch," although he has left the rest of the paragraph in the dual. The Indian sources of the parable point to a single branch or, at best, two branches or roots dangling from a single tree. See Ernst Kuhn, "Der Mann im Brunnen, Geschichte eines indischen Gleichnisses."

16 Or "correcting what I could of my action."

17 Or "guidance to lead me aright, power over my soul, and aides to help me in my affairs."

18 The carpenter has apparently laid the second wedge aside, to be driven in upon his return, leaving only one wedge in the log.

19 That is, many people can seek the same place or rank, which are not the exclusive property of anyone.

20 The go-between's husband is a *ḥajjām*, a cupper or phlebotomist, but since these tasks were part of the barber's trade, we translate it as "barber."

21 The Arabic has *aswad*, a large black snake, and *ghurāb*, either crow or raven. The identifications "cobra" and "crow" are taken from the *Panchatantra*.

22 The Arabic has *makkāʾ*, usually a "lark," which does not fit the context. We translate "heron," following the *Panchatantra*.

23 The lion appears to expect a party of animals escorting his "lunch."

24 The comparison can be traced to the Sanskrit, although it has been distorted in transmission. See Schulthess, *Kalīla und Dimna*, 185n139. Edgerton's reconstruction of the *Panchatantra* (2:311) reads: "Better [a king who is like] a vulture, attended by *swans* that live contentedly in the water, than [a king who is like] a *swan*, attended by savage carrion-birds that eat flesh. A mean retinue destroys even a man of fine qualities, while even one lacking in virtue becomes virtuous if his followers are above meanness."

25 "Sea's Custodian" corresponds to Arabic *wakīl al-baḥr*, an agent, administrator, or custodian of someone else's affairs or property. The Old Syriac (ed. Schulthess, 36) reads *gnīzā d-yammā*, the genius or spirit of the sea, and this seems to be the meaning here. The bird's name (Arabic *ṭīṭawā*) reproduces Sanskrit *ṭiṭṭibha*, the jacana, a tropical bird that breeds on ponds. Indian folklore makes it proverbial for conceit and therefore likely to challenge the water spirit. See Wilson, *Essays Analytical, Critical and Philological on Subjects Connected with Sanskrit Literature*, 2:18–19.

26 Phoenix (*al-ʿAnqāʾ*): The Sanskrit identifies the chief of the birds as Garuḍa, the mount of the god Vishnu. The Syriac, presumably echoing the Persian, identified Garuḍa with the legendary Iranian bird Simorg. Arabic *al-ʿanqāʾ* can be grammatically masculine or feminine. Although Or. 4044 refers to it in the masculine, we translate it as feminine in order to distinguish the Phoenix from the "king" (originally the god Vishnu) who flies through the air mounted on her and exacts vengeance from the Sea's Custodian.

27 The heart was considered to be the seat of thought.

28 Or glowworm, as the Arabic *yarāʿah* can mean either.

29 That is, someone who would guarantee the plaintiff's future appearance in court, since an unsubstantiated accusation would render the plaintiff himself subject to punishment.

30 The implication is that the judge will rule that the simpleton must pay the swindler the hundred thousand dinars he is presumed to have taken.

31 The Arabic *ʿuljūm* has been translated "heron," as in the *Panchatantra*. (François de Blois, *Burzōy's Voyage to India*, 12n3, has argued that *ʿuljūm* derives ultimately from Greek ἀλκυών, "kingfisher.")

32 The Arabic has *ibn ʿirs*, weasel, but in the *Panchatantra* the animal is a mongoose, not a weasel, and the story hinges on the well-known ability of the mongoose to kill snakes because of its immunity to venom.

33 Either a rod used for breaking up clods (*mirzabbah*) or a blacksmith's hammer or mallet (*mirzabah*). One hundred *mann* is approximately two hundred pounds.

34 The Arabic is simply *ahl al-saʿādah* (people of prosperity, fortunateness, felicity), but the religious overtone needs to be preserved.

35 The colophons at the end of each chapter have been preserved as in the manuscript. Although they may have been inserted by the copyist, they sometimes do not agree exactly with the title of the chapter and sometimes add information.

36 The text of London Or. 4044 varies between calling Baydabā "philosopher" (*faylasūf*) and "scholar" (*ʿālim*). For convenience, we use "philosopher" throughout.

37 The unidentified speaker turns against Dimnah the very arguments from physiognomy that Dimnah had used to turn the lion against Shanzabah.

38 The text is corrupt; accordingly, the translation is conjectural.

39 The lion's request depends on the legal point that anonymous testimony cannot be admitted as evidence.

40 That is, loyalty to his dove friends in their distress.

41 That is, no dependents. The point is that he lived alone.

42 The saying could be interpreted as meaning that the best intelligence is the one that foresees the outcome of affairs, or it could be interpreted as meaning that the best intelligence is the kind that is applied to managing one's affairs properly.

43 This clause, unique to this redaction, is another example of the redactor's piety. Cf. Q Yā Sīn 36:38: «And the sun—it runs to a fixed resting-place; that is the ordaining of the All-mighty, the All-knowing.»

44 Another pious insertion unique to this redaction. The phrase echoes Q Ḥijr 15:38 and Ṣād 38:82, referring in each case to the Day of Judgment, at which time the stars will cease their regular rising and setting.

45 The Arabic *dawḥ* is any tree with spreading branches. The translation as "banyan" follows the *Panchatantra*.

46 Arabic *ṣifrid*, a bird of uncertain identity. We translate it as "partridge," following the *Panchatantra*.

47 This refers to a father's obligation to arrange a suitable marriage for his daughter, preferably even before she has reached puberty.

48 There is a lacuna one or two words in length due to damage of the manuscript.

49 Likely a female horse, donkey, or mule.

50 See Q Luqmān 31:34.

51 The episode hinges on the fact that the woman must perform certain ritual ablutions after childbirth before she can lie with her husband.

52 This chapter draws its story from the twelfth book of the *Mahābhārata*.

53 Again, this reference to things ordained to happen, presumably by God's decree, is characteristic of this redaction. The clause does not occur in the Old Syriac, and appears to be unique to this manuscript.

54 The story goes back to the twelfth book of the *Mahābhārata* (trans. Benfey, *Pantschatantra*, 1:561–73). The copyists of the London and Rabat manuscripts wrote the bird's name as *Fatrah*. The copyist of the Istanbul manuscript, the basis of ʿAzzām's edition, turned it into *qubbarah* (lark) by rearranging the diacritical dots. This edition and translation follow the most likely transcription, *Finzah*, as in the editions of de Sacy and Cheikho. This agrees with the Old Syriac *Panzōh*, which apparently goes back to Sanskrit *Pūjanī* (venerating).

55 Arabic *ʿilal* (plural of *ʿillah*), literally "occasions" or "causes."

56 This story goes back to the twelfth book of the *Mahābhārata*.

57 Unlike the heading, this closing remark characterizes the jackal as abstinent (*ṣawwām*).

58 Of judiciousness (*ḥilm*), Thomas Hefter writes that it is "the virtue of self-mastery and patient, rational behaviour, and . . . may also refer to the faculty of reason (*al-ʿaql*) itself. It is used most frequently to describe an individual's forbearance and control of anger when in a position of power, and this is often the context presumed in ethical discussions or praise." Hefter, "Ḥilm" in *EI3*.

59 Gūlpanāh is a conjectural reconstruction of the name of Īrākht's rival wife. It appears in the manuscript as Jūrfanah. See Schulthess, *Kalīla und Dimna*, 226, n. 508.

60 The text of the end of the sentence is problematic. The Old Syriac is quite different: "and doesn't know an unskilled man [*hedyōtā*, literally 'an idiot'] from a reasonable/eloquent one [*mlīlā*] and even how to talk [*da-nmallel*]."

61 A variant reads: "I am afraid *of* you, Baylār."

62 Literally "traveler" (*sayyāḥ*). The term had an extended meaning of pilgrim or mendicant.

63 MS London Or. 4044 omits any explanation of how the king's son knew that only the mendicant could cure him. In some other versions, the snake's sister, a jinni, out of compassion appears to the king's son in a dream and gives him this information.

64 The Arabic involves a pun. *Qadr* means both "rank" and "destiny."

65 This echoes a well-known hadith in both Muslim and al-Bukhārī: "None of you truly believes until he loves for his brother what he loves for himself."

66 One or more final folios of MS London Or. 4044 are missing. We base our translation of the remainder of the chapter on MS London Or. 8751.

Glossary

Anūsharwān the Sasanian monarch Khusraw I, surnamed Anūsharwān (or in Middle Persian Anōshagruwān, "of immortal soul"), reigned AD 531–79.

Balkh a major city of central Asia, located in present-day Afghanistan. The language of the inhabitants was Bactrian, an eastern Iranian language.

Barzawayh the physician sent by King Anūsharwān to India to obtain and translate Indian books. Barzawayh is an Arabicized form probably corresponding to Middle Persian Burzōē.

Baydabā (or Baydanā) the fictional chief philosopher whose conversations with King Dabshalim generate the parables of Kalīlah and Dimnah. The Old Syriac form can be read Bēdawāg or Bīdwāg. In the West, the name has often been given as Bidpai.

Burdjird an unidentified city.

Buzurgmihr the minister of Anūsharwān credited with composing Barzawayh's biography, and in some manuscripts the introductory chapter.

Dabshalim (or Dabshalīm) the fictional Indian king whose conversations with the chief philosopher Baydabā generate the parables of the book *Kalīlah and Dimnah*. The Old Syriac *d-b-sh-r-m*, possibly read Debsharām, might correspond to Sanskrit Dēvaśarman ("Beloved of the gods").

Deccan a plateau in south-central India.

Dimnah the name of one of the two jackals who are the protagonists of the first story. The Old Syriac transcription Damnag apparently derived from Sanskrit Damanaka ("Victor").

dinar (dīnār) a gold coin weighing about 4.25 grams. One dinar was worth about twenty dirhams.

dirham a silver coin usually equivalent to one twentieth of a dinar.

Kalīlah the name of one of the two jackals who are the protagonists of the first story. The Old Syriac transcription Kalīlag apparently derived through Middle Persian from the Sanskrit Karaṭaka—the meaning is unclear.

Kamānzūn a jurist who appears in Chapter 13 as a member of the court of King Haylār.

kohl (kuḥl) a dark cosmetic powder used as eye shadow or mascara. Traditionally, it is prepared by grinding the mineral stibnite (antimony trisulfide).

mann a measure of weight equivalent to two *raṭl*s, approximately two pounds.

Marw a major city on the Silk Road in Central Asia. Its ruins are located near the present city of Mary in Turkmenistan.

Mārūzūd this corresponds to Sanskrit Mihilārōpya or Mahilārōpya, a city in the Deccan, in south-central India.

Qūhistān Persian for "mountain country," designating various mountainous areas of the Iranian plateau. The province was noted for *qūhiyyah*, a fine linen weave.

Sind the region of the Indian subcontinent around the lower course of the Indus River. The area was conquered by the Arabs in 93/711, during the caliphate of al-Walīd ibn ʿAbd al-Malik.

Zoroastrianism the official religion of Sasanian Iran, based on the teachings of the prophet Zoroaster (Zarathustra).

BIBLIOGRAPHY

Allen, Clifford G., ed. *L'ancienne version espagnole de Kalila et Digna.*
Mâcon, France: Protat frères, 1906.

AnonymClassic. "Kalīla and Dimna: AnonymClassic." http://www.
geschkult.fu-berlin.de/en/e/kalila-wa-dimna/index.html.

Arjomand, Said Amir. "'Abd Allah Ibn al-Muqaffa' and the 'Abbasid
Revolution." *Iranian Studies* 27 (1994): 9–36.

Audebert, Claude. "La condition humaine d'après *Kalīla wa Dimna.*"
Arabica 46 (1999): 287–312.

Audebert, Claude. "La violence dans Kalîla wa-Dimna d'Ibn al-Muqaffa'."
Alif: Journal of Comparative Poetics 13 (1993): 24–45.

Beeston, A. F. L. "The 'Alī ibn Shāh Preface to Kalīlah wa Dimnah." *Oriens*
7, no. 1 (1954): 81–84.

Benfey, Theodor. *Pantschatantra: Fünf Bücher indischer Fabeln, Märchen
und Erzählungen.* 2 vols. Leipzig: F. A. Brockhaus, 1859.

Bickell, Gustav. *Kalilag und Damnag, alte syrische Übersetzung des
indischen Fürstenspiegels.* Leipzig: F. A. Brockhaus, 1876.

Bosworth, C. E. "Ebn al-Moqaffa', Abū Moḥammad 'Abd-Allāh Rōzbeh."
In *Encyclopaedia Iranica.* http://iranicaonline.org/articles/
ebn-al-moqaffa.

Brockelmann, Carl. "Kalīla wa-Dimna." In *Encyclopaedia of Islam, Second
Edition.* Brill Online.

Brunschvig, Robert. "'Abd." In *Encyclopaedia of Islam, Second Edition.*
Brill Online.

Bürgel, Johann Christoph. "Language on Trial, Religion at Stake:
Trial Scenes in Some Classical Arabic Texts and the Hermeneutic

Problems Involved." In *Myths, Historical Archetypes and Symbolic Figures in Arabic Literature: Towards a New Hermeneutic Approach; Proceedings of the International Symposium in Beirut, June 25th – June 30th, 1996*, edited by Angelika Neuwirth, Birgit Embaló, Sebastian Günther, and Maher Jarrar, 189–204. Stuttgart: Franz Steiner Verlag, 1999. http://menadoc.bibliothek.uni-halle.de/inhouse/content/pageview/2073796.

De Blois, François. *Burzōy's Voyage to India and the Origin of the Book of Kalīlah wa Dimnah*. London: Royal Asiatic Society, 1990.

———. "Zindīk." In *Encyclopaedia of Islam, Second Edition*. Brill Online.

Dozy, R. P. A. *Supplément aux dictionnaires arabes*. 2 vols. Leiden, Netherlands: Brill, 1881. Reprinted Beirut, 1968.

Edgerton, Franklin. *The Panchatantra Reconstructed: An Attempt to Establish the Lost Original Sanskrit Text of the Most Famous of Indian Story-Collections on the Basis of the Principal Extant Versions*. 3 vols. New Haven, CT: American Oriental Society, 1924.

Enderwitz, Suzanne. "Al-Shuʿūbiyya." In *Encyclopaedia of Islam, Second Edition*. Brill Online.

Fahd, Toufic, and A. Rippin. "Shayṭān." In *Encyclopaedia of Islam, Second Edition*. Brill Online.

Gabrieli, Francesco. "Ibn al-Muḳaffaʿ." In *Encyclopaedia of Islam, Second Edition*. Brill Online.

Gimaret, Daniel. "Muʿtazila." In *Encyclopaedia of Islam, Second Edition*. Brill Online.

Gruendler, Beatrice. "Les versions de *Kalīla wa-Dimna*: Une transmission et une circulation mouvantes." In *Énoncés sapientiels et littérature exemplaire: Une intertextualité complexe*. Edited by Marie-Sol Ortola, 385–416. Nancy, France: Éditions Universitaires de Lorraine, 2013.

Gruendler, Beatrice, Jan J. van Ginkel, Rima Redwan, Khouloud Khalfallah, Isabel Toral, Johannes Stephan, Matthew L. Keegan, et al. "An Interim Report on the Editorial and Analytical Work of the AnonymClassic Project." *Medieval Worlds* 11 (2020): 241–79.

Guidi, Ignazio. *Studii sul testo arabo del Libro di Calila e Dimna*. Rome: Libreria Spithöver, 1873.

Hämeen-Anttila, Jaakko. "Adab (a) Arabic, Early Developments." In
 Encyclopaedia of Islam, Three. Brill Online.

———. *Khwadāynāmag: The Middle Persian Book of Kings.* Studies in
 Persian Cultural History 14. Leiden, Netherlands: Brill, 2018.

Hefter, Thomas. "Ḥilm." In *Encyclopaedia of Islam, Three.* Brill Online.

Hertel, Johannes. *Tantrākhyāyika: Die älteste Fassung des Pañcatantra.* 2
 vols. Leipzig: B. G. Teubner, 1909.

Ibn Khallikān, Abū l-ʿAbbās Shams al-Dīn Aḥmad ibn Muḥammad.
 Wafayāt al-aʿyān. Edited by Iḥsān ʿAbbās. 8 vols. Beirut: Dār
 al-Thaqāfah, 1968–72.

Ibn al-Muqaffaʿ, ʿAbdallāh. *Calila et Dimna: Ou fables de Bidpai en Arabe.*
 Edited by Sylvestre de Sacy. Paris: Imprimerie Royale, 1816.

———. *Le livre de Kalila et Dimna.* Translated by André Miquel. Paris:
 C. Klincksieck, 1957.

———. *Kalila and Dimna, or, The Fables of Bidpai.* Translated by
 Wyndham Knatchbull. Oxford: W. Baxter for J. Parker, 1819.

———. *Kalilah and Dimnah: An English Version of Bidpai's Fables Based
 upon Ancient Arabic and Spanish Manuscripts.* Translated by Thomas
 Ballantine Irving. Newark, DE: Juan de la Cuesta, 1980.

———. *Kalīlah wa-Dimnah.* Edited by ʿAbd al-Wahhāb ʿAzzām. Cairo:
 Matbaʿat al-Maʿārif, 1941.

———. *La version arabe de Kalîlah et Dimnah.* Edited by Louis Cheikho.
 Beirut: Imprimerie Catholique, 1905.

Ibn al-Nadīm, Abū l-Faraj Muḥammad ibn Abī Yaʿqūb. *Kitāb al-Fihrist.*
 Translated by Bayard Dodge as *The Fihrist of al-Nadīm.* 2 vols. New
 York, NY: Columbia University Press, 1970.

Ibn Qutaybah. *The Excellence of the Arabs.* Edited by James E.
 Montgomery and Peter Webb, translated by Sarah Bowen Savant and
 Peter Webb. New York, NY: New York University Press, 2017.

Justi, Ferdinand. *Iranisches Namenbuch.* Marburg, Germany: N. G. Elwert, 1895.

Keegan, Matthew L. "'Elsewhere Lies Its Meaning': The Vagaries of *Kalīla
 and Dimna*'s Reception." *Poetica* 52 (2021): 13–40.

Keith-Falconer, I. G. N. *Kalīlah and Dimnah, or The Fables of Bidpai:
 An English Translation of the Later Syriac Version.* Cambridge, UK:

Cambridge University Press, 1885. Reprinted Amsterdam: Philo Press, 1970.

Khalfallah, Khouloud. "Digital Reconstruction." http://www.geschkult. fu-berlin.de/en/e/kalila-wa-dimna/topics/Digital-Reconstruction. html.

Kristó-Nagy, István. *La pensée d'Ibn al-Muqaffaʿ: Un "agent double" dans le monde persan et arabe.* Studia Arabica 19. Versailles: Éditions de Paris, 2013.

———. "Wild Lions and Wise Jackals: Killing Kings and Clever Counsellors in Kalīla wa-Dimna." In *Prophets, Viziers and Philosophers: Wisdom and Authority in Early Arabic Literature*, edited by Emily J. Cottrell, 147–209. Groningen: Barkhuis & Groningen University Library, 2020.

Kuhn, Ernst. "Der Mann im Brunnen, Geschichte eines indischen Gleichnisses." In *Festgruss an Otto von Böhtlingk*, 68–76. Stuttgart: W. Kohlhammer, 1888.

Lane, Edward. *An Arabic-English Lexicon.* London: Williams and Norgate, 1863–93. Reprinted Beirut, 1968.

Latham, J. D. "Ibn al-Muqaffaʿ and Early ʿAbbasid Prose." In *ʿAbbasid Belles-Lettres*, edited by Julia Ashtiany, T. M. Johnstone, J. D. Latham, and R. B. Serjeant, 48–77. Cambridge, UK: Cambridge University Press, 1990.

Lowry, Joseph E. "The First Islamic Legal Theory: Ibn al-Muqaffaʿ on Interpretation, Authority, and the Structure of the Law." *The Journal of the American Oriental Society* 128, no. 1 (2008): 25–40.

Marlow, Louise. "Adab al-Mulūk: The Mirrors for Princes of Classical Islam." In *Encyclopedia of Mediterranean Humanism*, edited by Houari Touati. http://www.encyclopedie-humanisme.com/?Adab-al-Mulūk.

Marsham, Andrew, and Chase F. Robinson. "The Safe-Conduct for the Abbasid ʿAbd Allāh b. ʿAlī (d. 764)." *Bulletin of the School of Oriental and African Studies* 70, no. 2 (2007): 247–81.

Miskawayh, Abū ʿAlī Aḥmad ibn Muḥammad. *Al-Ḥikmah al-khālidah: Jāvīdān khirad.* Edited by ʿAbd al-Raḥmān Badawī. Cairo: Maktabat al-Nahḍah, 1952.

Nöldeke, Theodor. *Burzoēs Einleitung zu dem Buche Kalīla waDimna.* Strassbourg: Trübner, 1912.

———. "Zu Kalīla waDimna." *Zeitschrift der Deutschen Morgenländischen Gesellschaft* 59 (1905): 794–806.

Nöldeke, Theodor, ed. and trans. *Die Erzählung vom Mäusekönig und seinen Ministern.* Abhandlungen der Königlichen Gesellschaft der Wissenschaften zu Göttingen 25. Göttingen, Germany: Dieterich, 1879.

Al-Qāḍī, Wadād. "ʿAbd al-Ḥamīd al-Kātib." In *Encyclopaedia of Islam, Three.* Brill Online.

Riedel, Dagmar. "Kalila wa Demna i. Redactions and Circulation." In *Encyclopedia Iranica.* http://iranicaonline.org/articles/kalila-demna-i.

Rieu, Charles. *Supplement of the Catalogue of the Arabic Manuscripts in the British Museum.* London: Longmans, 1894.

Schiefner, Anton. *Mahâkâtjâjana und König Tshaṇḍa-Pradjota: Ein Cyclus buddhistischer Erzählungen.* Mémoires de l'Académie impériale des sciences de St.-Pétersbourg (series 7, vol. 22, no. 7). St. Petersburg: Académie des sciences, 1875.

Schulthess, Friedrich, ed. *Kalīla und Dimna: Syrisch und Deutsch.* Berlin: G. Reimer, 1911.

Shamma, Tarek. "Translating into the Empire: The Arabic Version of Kalila wa Dimna." *The Translator* 15 (2009): 65–86.

Sourdel, Dominique. "La biographie d'Ibn al-Muqaffaʿ d'après les sources anciennes." *Arabica* 1 (1954): 307–23.

Sprengling, Martin. "Kalîla Studies. I." *The American Journal of Semitic Languages and Literatures* 40, no. 2 (1924): 81–97.

Van Ruymbeke, Christine. "Kalila and Dimna as a Case Study: Ibn al-Muqaffaʿ's and Nasrullah Munshi's Translations." In *The Routledge Handbook of Arabic Translation.* Edited by Sameh Hanna, H. El-Farahaty, and A.-W. Khalifa. Abingdon, UK: Routledge, 2020.

Vishnusharman. *Five Discourses on Worldly Wisdom.* Translated by Patrick Olivelle. New York, NY: New York University Press, 2006.

Wensinck, A. J. "Bidpai." In *Encyclopaedia of Islam.* 1st ed. Brill Online.

Wilson, Horace Hayman. *Essays Analytical, Critical and Philological on Subjects Connected with Sanskrit Literature.* 3 vols. London: Trübner, 1864.

Wood, Ramsay. *Kalila and Dimna: Selected Fables of Bidpai, Retold.* London: Granada Books, 1982.

Wright, William, ed. *The Book of Kalīlah and Dimnah, Translated from Arabic into Syriac.* Oxford, UK: Clarendon Press, 1884.

Al-Yamanī, Abū ʿAbdallāh Muḥammad ibn Ḥusayn. *Kitāb Muḍāhāt amthāl kitāb Kalīlah wa-Dimnah bi-mā ashbahahā min ashʿār al-ʿArab.* Edited by Muḥammad Yūsuf Najm. Beirut: Dār al-Thaqāfah, 1961.

Al-Yaʿqūbī, Aḥmad ibn Abī Yaʿqūb. *Ibn-Wādhih Qui Dicitur Al-Jaʿqubī Historiae.* Edited by M. Th. Houtsma. 2 vols. Leiden, Netherlands: Brill, 1883. Translated as *The Works of Ibn Wāḍiḥ al-Yaʿqūbī.* Edited by Matthew S. Gordon, Chase F. Robinson, Everett K. Rowson, and Michael Fishbein. 3 vols. Leiden, Netherlands: Brill, 2018.

Yousefi, Najm al-Din. "Islam without Fuqahāʾ: Ibn al-Muqaffaʿ and His Perso-Islamic Solution to the Caliphate's Crisis of Legitimacy (70–142 AH/690–760 CE)." *Iranian Studies* 50:1 (2017): 9–44.

Zilio Grandi, Ida. "Ḥilm or 'Judiciousness': A Contribution to the Study of Islamic Ethics Based on the Traditional Sources." *Studia Islamica* 110 (2015): 81–100.

FURTHER READING

On the life and works of Ibn al-Muqaffaʿ, F. Gabrieli's article "Ibn al-Muḳaffaʿ" in the second edition of the *Encyclopaedia of Islam* is a good starting point. The latest work in Gabrieli's bibliography dates from 1966. C. E. Bosworth's 1997 article "Ebn al-Moqaffaʿ" in the *Encyclopedia Iranica* is a more recent general treatment. Dominique Sourdel's 1954 article "La biographie d'Ibn al-Muqaffaʿ d'après les sources anciennes" examines the sources for the author's biography. István Kristó-Nagy's *La pensée d'Ibn al-Muqaffaʿ* (2013) is a recent examination of Ibn al-Muqaffaʿ's oeuvre as a whole. Ibn al-Muqaffaʿ's treatment of Persian historical sources is discussed by Jaakko Hämeen-Anttila in Khwadāynāmag: *The Middle Persian Book of Kings* (2018).

The article "Kalīla wa-Dimna" by C. Brockelmann in the second edition of the *Encyclopaedia of Islam* deals specifically with *Kalīlah and Dimnah*; its bibliography ends in 1964. Brockelmann provides an introduction to the Arabic work and also traces in detail the work's subsequent adaptations into Arabic verse, later Syriac prose, Persian prose and verse, and into Western languages: Hebrew, Latin, medieval Spanish, and medieval Greek. Dagmar Riedel's 2010 article in the *Encyclopedia Iranica*, "Kalila wa Demna i. Redactions and Circulation," focuses in greater detail on the many New Persian adaptations of the work.

Readers interested in comparing the present translation, based on a single manuscript, with translations based on other versions of the text will find little in English at present. This deficiency is being remedied by AnonymClassic, a remarkable project underway in Germany. Professor Beatrice Gruendler and her team of scholars have identified about 140 manuscripts and have obtained copies of 95 to date. They are creating a

digital library that will make it possible to employ sophisticated computer tools to make detailed comparisons of the versions. AnonymClassic intends to publish representative chapters of the text in parallel-text editions, with translations into English, to illustrate the changes the text underwent in the course of its transmission. The reader can form an idea of its scope by visiting the project's website: http://www.geschkult.fu-berlin.de/en/e/kalila-wa-dimna. Especially valuable as an introduction to the project is the article by Beatrice Gruendler et al.: "An Interim Report on the Editorial and Analytical Work of the AnonymClassic Project" (2020).

A very different work, intended as a reworking made from several earlier translations (the author admits to knowing no Arabic), is *Kalila and Dimna: Selected Fables of Bidpai, Retold* by Ramsay Wood. It is a thoroughly enjoyable free retelling, much to be recommended for its liveliness.

The text of 'Azzām's edition, based on manuscript Aya Sofya 4095, was translated into French as *Le livre de Kalila et Dimna* (1957) by André Miquel and includes valuable notes. Cheikho's text formed the basis of T. B. Irving's *Kalilah and Dimnah: An English Version of Bidpai's Fables* (1980).

Readers interested in the Indian sources of *Kalīlah and Dimnah* can consult Franklin Edgerton's *The Panchatantra Reconstructed* (1927), whose second volume provides an English translation of the reconstructed Sanskrit text, or Patrick Olivelle's *Five Discourses on Worldly Wisdom* (2006). Although the Middle Persian text from which Ibn al-Muqaffaʻ produced his Arabic translation does not survive, a single manuscript of the older Syriac translation, which predates Ibn al-Muqaffaʻ's translation, did survive, and was carefully reedited and provided with a German translation and notes by Friedrich Schulthess, *Kalīla und Dimna: Syrisch und Deutsch* (1911). Schulthess's version is invaluable, as its notes frequently compare the Syriac text with the Arabic versions and with the early translations of the Arabic. It supersedes the earlier edition by G. Bickell (1876), which, however, contains a useful introduction by Theodor Benfey.

For most readers, the later Syriac version will be something of a curiosity: evidence of how *Kalīlah and Dimnah* was adapted by redactors for specific purposes—in this case, the interest of a writer intent on giving the work Christian resonances. It is available in the translation made by

I. G. N. Keith-Falconer, *Kalīlah and Dimnah, or The Fables of Bidpai* (1885, reprinted 1970). Readers of Spanish will enjoy the medieval version (dated to 1251) in the edition published in 1906 by Clifford G. Allen as *L'ancienne version espagnole de Kalila et Digna* or in later editions published in Spain.

The additional preface to *Kalīla wa-Dimnah* by ʿAlī ibn al-Shāh al-Fārisī (also known as Bahnūd ibn Saḥwān) was later added to many manuscripts and formed part of many editions of the Arabic text. A. J. Wensinck's article "Bidpai" in the first edition of the *Encyclopaedia of Islam* summarizes its content. A more recent discussion is A. F. L. Beeston's article "The ʿAlī ibn Shāh Preface to Kalīlah wa Dimnah" (1954). The preface was edited and translated into German by T. Nöldeke, *Burzōes Einleitung zu dem Buche Kalīla waDimna* (1912). In 1879, Nöldeke also edited and translated an additional chapter, "Die Erzählung vom Mäusekönig und seinen Ministern" ("The Story of the King of the Mice and His Ministers").

In addition to the works mentioned above, the following articles on various aspects of Kalīlah and Dimnah are of interest:

- Said Amir Arjomand, "'Abd Allah Ibn al-Muqaffaʿ and the ʿAbbasid Revolution" (1994), places the author in his historical context, noting the connection between the discussion of human dignity in *Kalīlah and Dimnah* (see, for example, §3.25 of the present translation) and the invocation of "Abdalla the Saracen" (apparently Ibn al-Muqaffaʿ) on the same subject at the beginning of the *Oration on the Dignity of Man* by the Renaissance humanist Pico della Mirandola.

- Najm al-Din Yousefi, "Islam without Fuqahāʾ: Ibn al-Muqaffaʿ and His Perso-Islamic Solution to the Caliphate's Crisis of Legitimacy (70–142 AH/690–760 CE)," explores the intersection of Persian and Islamic ideas about legitimate rule in Ibn al-Muqaffaʿ's *Risālah fī l-ṣaḥābah* (*Epistle on the Caliph's Entourage*).

- Tarek Shamma, "Translating into the Empire: The Arabic Version of Kalila wa Dimna" (2009), explores the ways in which Ibn al-Muqaffaʿ "domesticated" the text in an Islamic context.

- Christine van Ruymbeke, "Kalila and Dimna as a Case Study: Ibn al-Muqaffaʿ's and Nasrullah Munshi's Translations," explores the

ways in which Kalīlah and Dimnah "transcended the boundaries of time and culture and was able to adapt to new contexts, languages and cultures."

- Claude Audebert, "La violence dans Kalîla wa-Dimna d'Ibn al-Muqaffa'" (1993) and "La condition humaine d'après Kalīla wa Dimna" (1999), considers the ethical universe of the work.

- Johann Christoph Bürgel, in "Language on Trial, Religion at Stake: Trial Scenes in Some Classical Arabic Texts and the Hermeneutic Problems Involved" (1999), places the trial of Dimnah in the context of another trial scene in early Arabic literature, "Man and Animal before the King of Demons," in the collection of essays attributed to the Brethren of Purity (Ikhwān al-Ṣafā').

- István Kristó-Nagy, "Wild Lions and Wise Jackals: Killing Kings and Clever Counsellors in Kalīla wa-Dimna" (2020) explores the image of rulers and their advisers in the book, especially in "The Lion and the Ox" and "The Owls and the Crows," but with some discussion of the theme as it appears in other chapters, with attention to how certain themes were expanded and adapted as the work traveled from its Indian sources.

- Matthew L. Keegan, "'Elsewhere Lies Its Meaning': The Vagaries of Kalīla and Dimna's Reception" (2021), explores how interpreters reconfigured the book's generic affiliation, making it by turns "a Quranic competitor, a repository of proverbs, an allegory for the soul, a source of law, and a model for storytelling that imparts practical wisdom."

Index of Proper Names

About the NYU Abu Dhabi Institute

The Library of Arabic Literature is supported by a grant from the NYU Abu Dhabi Institute, a major hub of intellectual and creative activity and advanced research. The Institute hosts academic conferences, workshops, lectures, film series, performances, and other public programs directed both to audiences within the UAE and to the worldwide academic and research community. It is a center of the scholarly community for Abu Dhabi, bringing together faculty and researchers from institutions of higher learning throughout the region.

NYU Abu Dhabi, through the NYU Abu Dhabi Institute, is a world-class center of cutting-edge research, scholarship, and cultural activity. The Institute creates singular opportunities for leading researchers from across the arts, humanities, social sciences, sciences, engineering, and the professions to carry out creative scholarship and conduct research on issues of major disciplinary, multidisciplinary, and global significance.

About the Translators

Michael Fishbein studied English literature at Columbia and at Yale University, and Arabic as a CASA fellow at the American University in Cairo. He obtained a Ph.D. in Arabic from the University of California at Los Angeles in 1988, and taught Arabic language and literature at that university until his retirement in 2007. Interested primarily in Arabic historical writings and narrative, he contributed to the 1994 translation of the works of the Egyptian historian al-Jabartī, translated Volumes VIII, XXI, and XXXI of the SUNY *History of al-Ṭabarī*, and contributed several sections to the Brill *Works of Ibn Wāḍiḥ al-Yaʿqūbī*. He lives in Los Angeles.

James E. Montgomery is Sir Thomas Adams's Professor of Arabic, Fellow of Trinity Hall at the University of Cambridge, and an Executive Editor of the Library of Arabic Literature.

The Library of Arabic Literature

For more details on individual titles, visit www.libraryofarabicliterature.org

Classical Arabic Literature: A Library of Arabic Literature Anthology
Selected and translated by Geert Jan van Gelder (2012)

A Treasury of Virtues: Sayings, Sermons, and Teachings of ʿAlī, by al-Qāḍī
al-Quḍāʿī, with the *One Hundred Proverbs* attributed to al-Jāḥiẓ
Edited and translated by Tahera Qutbuddin (2013)

The Epistle on Legal Theory, by al-Shāfiʿī
Edited and translated by Joseph E. Lowry (2013)

Leg over Leg, by Aḥmad Fāris al-Shidyāq
Edited and translated by Humphrey Davies (4 volumes; 2013–14)

Virtues of the Imām Aḥmad ibn Ḥanbal, by Ibn al-Jawzī
Edited and translated by Michael Cooperson (2 volumes; 2013–15)

The Epistle of Forgiveness, by Abū l-ʿAlāʾ al-Maʿarrī
Edited and translated by Geert Jan van Gelder and Gregor Schoeler
(2 volumes; 2013–14)

The Principles of Sufism, by ʿĀʾishah al-Bāʿūniyyah
Edited and translated by Th. Emil Homerin (2014)

The Expeditions: An Early Biography of Muḥammad, by Maʿmar ibn Rāshid
Edited and translated by Sean W. Anthony (2014)

Two Arabic Travel Books
 Accounts of China and India, by Abū Zayd al-Sīrāfī
 Edited and translated by Tim Mackintosh-Smith (2014)
 Mission to the Volga, by Aḥmad ibn Faḍlān
 Edited and translated by James Montgomery (2014)

Disagreements of the Jurists: A Manual of Islamic Legal Theory, by
al-Qāḍī al-Nuʿmān
 Edited and translated by Devin J. Stewart (2015)

Consorts of the Caliphs: Women and the Court of Baghdad, by Ibn al-Sāʿī
 Edited by Shawkat M. Toorawa and translated by the Editors of the
 Library of Arabic Literature (2015)

What ʿĪsā ibn Hishām Told Us, by Muḥammad al-Muwayliḥī
 Edited and translated by Roger Allen (2 volumes; 2015)

The Life and Times of Abū Tammām, by Abū Bakr Muḥammad ibn
Yaḥyā al-Ṣūlī
 Edited and translated by Beatrice Gruendler (2015)

The Sword of Ambition: Bureaucratic Rivalry in Medieval Egypt, by
ʿUthmān ibn Ibrāhīm al-Nābulusī
 Edited and translated by Luke Yarbrough (2016)

Brains Confounded by the Ode of Abū Shādūf Expounded, by
Yūsuf al-Shirbīnī
 Edited and translated by Humphrey Davies (2 volumes; 2016)

Light in the Heavens: Sayings of the Prophet Muḥammad, by
al-Qāḍī al-Quḍāʿī
 Edited and translated by Tahera Qutbuddin (2016)

Risible Rhymes, by Muḥammad ibn Maḥfūẓ al-Sanhūrī
 Edited and translated by Humphrey Davies (2016)

A Hundred and One Nights
 Edited and translated by Bruce Fudge (2016)

The Excellence of the Arabs, by Ibn Qutaybah
 Edited by James E. Montgomery and Peter Webb
 Translated by Sarah Bowen Savant and Peter Webb (2017)

Scents and Flavors: A Syrian Cookbook
 Edited and translated by Charles Perry (2017)

Arabian Satire: Poetry from 18th-Century Najd, by Ḥmēdān al-Shwēʿir
 Edited and translated by Marcel Kurpershoek (2017)

In Darfur: An Account of the Sultanate and Its People, by Muḥammad
 ibn ʿUmar al-Tūnisī
 Edited and translated by Humphrey Davies (2 volumes; 2018)

War Songs, by ʿAntarah ibn Shaddād
 Edited by James E. Montgomery
 Translated by James E. Montgomery with Richard Sieburth (2018)

Arabian Romantic: Poems on Bedouin Life and Love, by ʿAbdallah
 ibn Sbayyil
 Edited and translated by Marcel Kurpershoek (2018)

Dīwān ʿAntarah ibn Shaddād: A Literary-Historical Study,
 by James E. Montgomery (2018)

Stories of Piety and Prayer: Deliverance Follows Adversity, by al-Muḥassin
 ibn ʿAlī al-Tanūkhī
 Edited and translated by Julia Bray (2019)

*Tajrīd sayf al-himmah li-stikhrāj mā fī dhimmat al-dhimmah: A Scholarly
 Edition of ʿUthmān ibn Ibrāhīm al-Nābulusī's Text*, by Luke Yarbrough
 (2019)

*The Philosopher Responds: An Intellectual Correspondence from the Tenth
 Century*, by Abū Ḥayyān al-Tawḥīdī and Abū ʿAlī Miskawayh
 Edited by Bilal Orfali and Maurice A. Pomerantz
 Translated by Sophia Vasalou and James E. Montgomery
 (2 volumes; 2019)

The Discourses: Reflections on History, Sufism, Theology, and Literature—Volume One, by al-Ḥasan al-Yūsī
Edited and translated by Justin Stearns (2020)

Impostures, by al-Ḥarīrī
Translated by Michael Cooperson (2020)

Maqāmāt Abī Zayd al-Sarūjī, by al-Ḥarīrī
Edited by Michael Cooperson (2020)

The Yoga Sutras of Patañjali, by Abū Rayḥān al-Bīrūnī
Edited and translated by Mario Kozah (2020)

The Book of Charlatans, by Jamāl al-Dīn ʿAbd al-Raḥīm al-Jawbarī
Edited by Manuela Dengler
Translated by Humphrey Davies (2020)

A Physician on the Nile: A Description of Egypt and Journal of the Famine Years, by ʿAbd al-Laṭīf al-Baghdādī
Edited and translated by Tim Mackintosh-Smith (2021)

The Book of Travels, by Ḥannā Diyāb
Edited by Johannes Stephan
Translated by Elias Muhanna (2 volumes; 2021)

Kalīlah and Dimnah: Fables of Virtue and Vice, by Ibn al-Muqaffaʿ
Edited by Michael Fishbein
Translated by Michael Fishbein and James E. Montgomery (2021)

Love, Death, Fame: Poetry and Lore from the Emirati Oral Tradition, by al-Māyidī ibn Ẓāhir
Edited and translated by Marcel Kurpershoek (2022)

The Essence of Reality: A Defense of Philosophical Sufism, by ʿAyn al-Quḍāt
Edited and translated by Mohammed Rustom (2022)

The Requirements of the Sufi Path: A Defense of the Mystical Tradition, by Ibn Khaldūn
Edited and translated by Carolyn Baugh (2022)

The Doctors' Dinner Party, by Ibn Buṭlān
 Edited and translated by Philip F. Kennedy and Jeremy Farrell (2023)

Fate the Hunter: Early Arabic Hunting Poems
 Edited and translated by James E. Montgomery (2023)

The Book of Monasteries, by al-Shābushtī
 Edited and translated by Hilary Kilpatrick (2023)

War Songs, by ʿAntarah ibn Shaddād (2018)

The Life and Times of Abū Tammām, by Abū Bakr Muḥammad ibn Yaḥyā al-Ṣūlī (2018)

The Sword of Ambition, by ʿUthmān ibn Ibrāhīm al-Nābulusī (2019)

Brains Confounded by the Ode of Abū Shādūf Expounded: Volume One, by Yūsuf al-Shirbīnī (2019)

Brains Confounded by the Ode of Abū Shādūf Expounded: Volume Two, by Yūsuf al-Shirbīnī and *Risible Rhymes*, by Muḥammad ibn Maḥfūẓ al-Sanhūrī (2019)

The Excellence of the Arabs, by Ibn Qutaybah (2019)

Light in the Heavens: Sayings of the Prophet Muḥammad, by al-Qāḍī al-Quḍāʿī (2019)

Scents and Flavors: A Syrian Cookbook (2020)

Arabian Satire: Poetry from 18th-Century Najd, by Ḥmēdān al-Shwēʿir (2020)

In Darfur: An Account of the Sultanate and Its People, by Muḥammad al-Tūnisī (2020)

Arabian Romantic: Poems on Bedouin Life and Love, by Ibn Sbayyil (2020)

The Philosopher Responds: An Intellectual Correspondence from the Tenth Century, by Abū Ḥayyān al-Tawḥīdī and Abū ʿAlī Miskawayh (2021)

Impostures, by al-Ḥarīrī (2021)

The Discourses: Reflections on History, Sufism, Theology, and Literature— Volume One, by al-Ḥasan al-Yūsī (2021)

The Yoga Sutras of Patañjali, by Abū Rayḥān al-Bīrūnī (2022)

The Book of Charlatans, by Jamāl al-Dīn ʿAbd al-Raḥīm al-Jawbarī (2022)

The Book of Travels, by Ḥannā Diyāb (2022)

*A Physician on the Nile: A Description of Egypt and Journal of the Famine
Years*, by 'Abd al-Laṭīf al-Baghdādī (2022)

Kalīlah and Dimnah: Fables of Virtue and Vice, by Ibn al-Muqaffaʿ (2023)

Love, Death, Fame: Poetry and Lore from the Emirati Oral Tradition, by
al-Māyidī ibn Ẓāhir (2023)